Anti-Abortion Activism in the UK

Anti-Abortion Activism in the UK is a must read for any scholar, student or person interested in understanding the intractability of the contemporary conflict over abortion. Although modern activists package their opposition to abortion in secular paper to gain political traction with a public that largely views religion as a private matter, Lowe and Page's meticulously researched, five-year ethnographic study reveals that the heart of the conflict is profoundly religious. *Anti-Abortion Activism in the UK* illuminates the degree to which anti-abortion activism is moored to a distinct worldview where the relationship between activists' lived religion and opposition to abortion is inseparable. Drawing on multiple sources of data, Lowe and Page brilliantly demonstrate that an ultra-sacrificial construction of motherhood is centered as both sacred and profane in this worldview, which gives abortion opponents meaning and an indefatigable edge in their activism over both time and space.

–Alesha E. Doan, Professor, Women, Gender & Sexuality Studies, School of Public Affairs & Administration University of Kansas

Although this book is primarily UK focused; I implore US readers not to let this deter you as there is a great deal to be learned. Lowe and Page provide a brilliantly original and sharply-focused articulation of this activism as an invocation of 'lived religion', which is ritualized in the public zone outside of reproductive health clinics. The authors also stress the importance of recognizing national contexts. This contextualization offers potentially new and productive ways of seeing and conceptualizing that which is familiar. I also want to commend Lowe and Page for their clear and highly comprehensible writing style. No terse overly-academic language here. This makes the book an invaluable and appealing read for multiple audiences, including academics, students, activists, policy-makers, and the interested public.

–Shoshanna Ehrlich, JD Professor Women's, Gender, and Sexuality Studies, University of Massachusetts Boston

Emerald Studies in Reproduction, Culture and Society

Series Editors: Petra Nordqvist, Manchester University, UK and Nicky Hudson, De Montfort University, UK

This book series brings together scholars from across the social sciences and humanities who are working in the broad field of human reproduction. Reproduction is a growing field of interest in the UK and internationally, and this series publishes work from across the lifecycle of reproduction addressing issues such as conception, contraception, abortion, pregnancy, birth, infertility, pre and post-natal care, pre-natal screen and testing, IVF, prenatal genetic diagnosis, mitochondrial donation, surrogacy, adoption, reproductive donation, family-making and more. Books in this series will focus on the social, cultural, material, legal, historical and political aspects of human reproduction, encouraging work from early career researchers as well as established scholars. The series includes monographs, edited collections and shortform books (between 20 and 50,000 words). Contributors use the latest conceptual, methodological and theoretical developments to enhance and develop current thinking about human reproduction and its significance for understanding wider social practices and processes.

Published Titles in This Series

Egg Freezing, Fertility and Reproductive Choice
Authored by *Kylie Baldwin*

The Cryopolitics of Reproduction on Ice: A New Scandinavian Ice Age
Authored by *Charlotte Krołøkke, Thomas Søbirk Petersen, Janne Rothmar Herrmann, Anna Sofie Bach, Stine Willum Adrian, Rune Klingenberg and Michael Nebeling Petersen*

Voluntary and Involuntary Childlessness
Edited by *Natalie Sappleton*

When Reproduction meets Ageing: The Science and Medicine of the Fertility Decline
Authored by *Nolwenn Bühler*

Lived Realities of Solo Motherhood, Donor Conception and Medically Assisted Reproduction
Authored by *Tine Ravn*

Surrogacy in Russia: An Ethnography of Reproductive Labour, Stratification and Migration
Authored by *Christina Weis*

Forthcoming

Reproductive Governance and Bodily Materiality: Flesh, Technologies, and Knowledge
Edited by *Corinna Sabrina Guerzoni and Claudia Mattalucci*

(In)Fertile Male Bodies: Masculinities and Lifestyle Management in Neoliberal Times
Authored by *Esmee Hanna and Brendan Gough*

The Personal Lives of Egg and Sperm Donors: Curious Connections
Authored by *Petra Nordqvist and Leah Gilman*

Integrating Reproductive Technologies: Propositions for a Life Course Approach in Social Studies of Reproduction
Edited by *Katharine Dow and Victoria Boydell*

Contingencies, Complexities and Normativities in Uterus Transplantation: A Gift for Life?
Authored by *Lisa Guntram*

Anti-Abortion Activism in the UK: Ultra-sacrificial Motherhood, Religion and Reproductive Rights in the Public Sphere

BY

PAM LOWE
Aston University, UK

And

SARAH-JANE PAGE
Aston University, UK

United Kingdom – North America – Japan – India – Malaysia – China

Emerald Publishing Limited
Howard House, Wagon Lane, Bingley BD16 1WA, UK

First edition 2022

Reprints and permissions service
Contact: permissions@emeraldinsight.com

British Library Cataloguing in Publication Data
A catalogue record for this book is available from the British Library

ISBN: 978-1-83909-399-9 (Print)
ISBN: 978-1-83909-398-2 (Online)
ISBN: 978-1-83909-400-2 (Epub)

Printed and bound by CPI Group (UK) Ltd, Croydon, CR0 4YY

ISOQAR certified
Management System,
awarded to Emerald
for adherence to
Environmental
standard
ISO 14001:2004.

ISOQAR
REGISTERED
Certificate Number 1985
ISO 14001

INVESTOR IN PEOPLE

Table of Contents

List of Figures

Abbreviations

40DFL	40 Days for Life
ALRA	Abortion Law Reform Association
ARCH	Abortion Recovery Care and Helpline
BMA	British Medical Association
BPAS	British Pregnancy Advisory Service
CBR	Centre for Bioethical Reform UK
CEDAW	Committee on the Elimination of Discrimination against Women
CofE	Church of England
CPC	Crisis Pregnancy Centre
DUP	Democratic Unionist Party
GCN	Good Counsel Network
HOGPI	Helpers of God's Precious Infants
MFL	March for Life
NHS	National Health Service
NI	Northern Ireland
NILT	Northern Ireland Life and Times
OAPA	1861 Offences against the Person Act
PAS	Post-abortion Syndrome
PASE	Post Abortion Support for Everyone
PSPO	Public Spaces Protection Order
SPUC	Society for the Protection of Unborn Children
UK	United Kingdom
US	United States
UPAA	Ulster Pregnancy Advisory Association

About the Authors

Pam Lowe is a Senior Lecturer in Sociology and Policy at Aston University. She has researched and written extensively in the area of women's reproductive and sexual health, with a particular interest in pregnancy, abortion and early parenting. This includes her work published in her monograph *Reproductive health and maternal sacrifice: women, choice and responsibility* (Palgrave). Recently she has worked on a number of projects including the sexual health of online sex workers and understandings of risk surrounding mental health in the perinatal period. This book emerges from a longitudinal ethnographic study of abortion debates in public spaces.

Sarah-Jane Page is a Senior Lecturer in Sociology at Aston University. Her research focuses on religion and its interaction with sexuality and gender issues. She has specifically worked on projects examining religion, youth and sexuality and women priests in the Church of England. She has published three monographs, *Religious and sexual identities* (Ashgate; with A.K.T Yip); *Understanding young Buddhists* (Brill; with A.K.T. Yip) and *Religion and sexualities* (Routledge; with H. Shipley). She has worked closely with Pam Lowe over a number of years, undertaking the research for this book.

Chapter 1

Introduction

> ...we must offer support and protection to those who are visiting
> the [abortion] clinic and are vulnerable. If that means that as
> churches we need to adapt our activities to enable that
> protection and to prevent others using 'prayer' improperly and
> unethically to apply pressure or coercion then we must do so.
> –Methodist Minister

This book stems from a five-year ethnographic study on abortion debates in
public spaces within the United Kingdom (UK), drawing on extensive documentary analysis, interviews with anti-abortion activists, observations at clinic
vigils and public demonstrations, to present a comprehensive understanding of
anti-abortion activism and its implications for abortion service provision and
service users (a methodological account can be located in Appendix 1).[1] It focuses
predominantly on individual activists, although we also consider the organisations that some of them are affiliated with. Opposition to abortion has declined
significantly since the 1970s, and is largely unsupported nationally, yet in the last
decade, there has been evidence of increased activism outside abortion clinics,
with more faith-based groups beginning to organise 'vigils' which seek to deter
women from entering abortion clinics. In response, new pro-choice activities and
groups have emerged to campaign for bufferzones – a designated space outside
clinics where no one can protest or approach those seeking services. At the time of
writing, three legally enforced bufferzones have been established in England. In
Wales, one has been informally agreed between anti-abortion groups and the
police. There is growing political support for national bufferzone legislation. The
opening quotation is taken from a public consultation on the first legally enforced
bufferzone in Ealing, London. This quote highlights the role religion plays in
public debates over abortion. As we will show, anti-abortion activists are motivated primarily by their highly conservative faith position – a stance largely
unsupported by the majority of the public, whether or not they are religious. The
book thus sets out the motivations, beliefs and practices of the anti-abortion
activists in the specific context of a country which overwhelmingly supports

---

[1]We are grateful to the British Academy for funding parts of this project (Award number
SRG/170721). We are also grateful to all who participated in the study.

Anti-Abortion Activism in the UK, 1–17
Copyright © 2022 Pam Lowe and Sarah-Jane Page
Published under exclusive licence by Emerald Publishing Limited
doi:10.1108/978-1-83909-398-220221001

abortion and is largely uncomfortable with ostentatious public displays of religion.

As we will show, our encounters with anti-abortion activists over the last five years revealed the complexity of their position. During one encounter where activists were praying outside a clinic in the Midlands, Sarah-Jane said she was a sociologist of religion, but she was told that their campaign was not necessarily about religion. Rather, it was about 'life' – the fact they were religious was incidental. Yet during the conversation, the activist agreed that their campaign was underpinned by prayer, and this was a religious act. Despite these prayers to God, the woman stated that it was her 'passion for life' that had brought her to the clinic, rather than her faith.[2] Whilst on the surface this could be read as a contradiction, or even a form of religious denial, our book will reveal that this would misconstrue their position. When these statements are positioned within the broader worldview of anti-abortion activism, the underplaying of their religious motives makes far more sense.

In order to understand the context of the book, it is important to set out the cultural, political and religious landscape of abortion in the UK. First, we are using specific UK geographic conventions. UK means we are talking about the whole country, whereas Britain refers to England, Scotland and Wales but does not include Northern Ireland (NI). Also, whilst we acknowledge that not all pregnant people identify as women, as will be explained in more depth later, the cultural understandings of abortion that we are examining in the book are entwined with specific biologically essentialised understandings of women, their bodies and behaviour. Such worldviews need to be understood in relation to the broader policy context around abortion, which has arisen through specific constructions of women, gender, pregnancy and motherhood.

Abortion Acceptance

Despite a history of opposition, abortion is a settled issue in Britain and as a whole, the UK is overwhelmingly a pro-choice country. The British Social Attitudes survey reveals that over 90% of people think that abortion should be available in at least some circumstances and over 70% think it should be an individual choice (Swales & Taylor, 2017). In NI, which is recognised as the most conservative nation in the UK, there is very strong support for abortion in a range of circumstances, such as a serious risk to life, physical or mental health and sexual crime, although fewer people support individual choice (Gray, 2017). Moreover, the National Health Service (*NHS*) provides abortion free to all those who qualify for treatment, which was, in 2019, 99% of all abortions in Britain (Dept. of Health and Social Care, 2020; Public Health Scotland, 2020). However, despite the widespread public acceptance, negativity towards abortion persists

---

[2]We use God as a proper noun in our discussion to reflect the worldviews of the activists themselves. We acknowledge that different faiths and non-believers understand 'god' differently in a pluralistic society.

(Hoggart, 2017; Purcell, Maxwell, Bloomer, Rowlands, & Hoggart, 2020). Abortion stigma is often perpetuated in media reporting (Purcell, Hilton, & McDaid, 2014) and political debates (Amery, 2020; Pierson & Bloomer, 2018). In particular, the notion that there are 'good' and 'bad' abortions is common (Hoggart, Newton, & Bury, 2017; Weitz, 2010). Abortion stigma contributes to the silencing and constraints on the narrating of abortion experiences (Beynon-Jones, 2017; Bloomer, O'Dowd, & Macleod, 2017; Hoggart, 2017). We suggest that this also contributes to the assumption that the UK is less accepting of abortion than it actually is.

In Parliament, by convention, abortion is considered a conscience issue so political parties do not dictate how MPs vote. In most elections, abortion is rarely mentioned by politicians or in the media. Moreover, on the rare occasions when British politicians speak out publicly with a hard line against abortion, they frequently need to moderate their position. For example, in 2017, a senior Conservative politician, Jacob Rees-Mogg, who is a devout Catholic and had been touted as a future leader of the party, stated on television that because of his religious beliefs, he was 'completely opposed' to abortion, even in cases of sexual crime (Good Morning Britain, ITV 2017). However, he also stated his personal views did not matter because abortion was lawful and that would not change. Despite this caveat, his position was widely seen as extreme and his suitability to be a party leader was questioned. Even amongst the anti-abortion community, support for him was not straightforward. Although his position on abortion was lauded, his record on welfare cuts was criticised by some. As one interviewee stated, 'I'm not with those Americans who say it's an all-or-nothing issue'.

In Britain, politicians tend not to foreground their religious beliefs in general, let alone their position on abortion, and successive leaders of both Labour and Conservative parties have taken steps not to make conscience issues a matter of party politics (Halfmann, 2011). Halfmann (2011) suggests that British politicians are often wary of what has happened in the United States (US) and are keen to avoid both faith and abortion being foregrounded for either politicians or political parties. The situation in NI is completely different due to the history of the ethno-nationalist conflict which still divides the political landscape on a sectarian basis (Pierson & Bloomer, 2018). Even for those who are not religious, or support a non-sectarian party, it is difficult to escape from this. As Pierson and Bloomer (2018) have shown, opposition to abortion in NI has tended to be positioned as the only issue that unites the different faiths and political allegiances, and this has blocked attempts to allow access to abortion within NI for decades. When debates occur, opposition to abortion is rooted in faith-based positions, often repeating discursive positions from international faith-based lobbying (Pierson & Bloomer, 2018). Although the opposition to abortion by nationalist parties softened after the successful campaign in Ireland to introduce abortion, because of the governance structures of Stormont that allow either side to block legislation on sectarian grounds, this had little practical impact.

Abortion Law

The four nations of the UK are in different positions regarding the development and responsibility for abortion law. The *1861 Offences Against the Person Act* (OAPA) covered England, Wales and Ireland and contained a penalty of up to life imprisonment for abortion. The OAPA did not cover Scotland, although abortion is a crime under common law. The *1967 Abortion Act*, which covered England, Wales and Scotland, provided legal access to abortion if certain conditions were met. Contrary to popular belief, abortion was not decriminalised. Despite repeated attempts to change the *Abortion Act*, it has remained largely the same today as when it was written (Sheldon, Davis, O'Neill, & Parker, 2019). Yet this does not mean that its interpretation and cultural positioning have not shifted (Sheldon et al., 2019). It authorises doctors to decide in 'good faith' whether or not an abortion is justifiable under the legislation; medical paternalism is therefore central to the workings of the law. Whilst this legal necessity remains in place, the *Act* is usually interpreted permissively, not least due to broader shifts in understandings of the doctor–patient relationship in which paternalism is no longer seen as clinically appropriate (Lee, Sheldon, & Macvarish, 2018).

Although there are a number of clauses in the *Abortion Act* that can be used to legally justify an abortion, one in particular accounts for the majority of abortions (Dept. of Health and Social Care, 2020; Public Health Scotland, 2020). It states that abortions are lawful if two doctors in good faith believe:

> ...that the pregnancy has not exceeded its twenty-fourth week and that the continuance of the pregnancy would involve risk, greater than if the pregnancy were terminated, of injury to the physical or mental health of the pregnant woman or any existing children of her family (Abortion Act, 1967 section1 (1a) as amended).

As Sheldon (2016) points out, this gives doctors wide clinical discretion to approve abortions, not least because abortion is almost always statistically safer than continuing a pregnancy to term, and being forced to continue a pregnancy will have negative mental health consequences.

Despite the liberal interpretation of the *Abortion Act* and the widespread availability of abortion, there are cases where the law is still applied. Although exceedingly rare, criminal charges have been brought against women who have purchased abortion pills themselves. For example, in two cases in England (2012, 2015) women received prison sentences (3½ and 2½ years respectively) for self-managed abortion. Abortion remaining a crime also gives scope for anti-abortion activists to bring legal challenges. For example, in 2003, a Church of England (CofE) curate brought an unsuccessful judicial review against the police for not investigating the legality of performing abortions for bilateral cleft palette at 28 weeks, arguing that it did not meet the criteria in the *Act* (McGuinness, 2013). In 2013, Aisling Hubert, backed by the Christian Legal Centre, attempted to bring a private prosecution against doctors she accused of illegally carrying out sex-selection abortions (McGuinness, 2015). Whilst the case failed, it nevertheless illustrates the difficulties of the current law and loopholes that anti-abortion activists can use to try to reduce abortion access (McGuinness, 2015; Sheldon, 2016).

NI was excluded from the *1967 Abortion Act*, which has meant for most of the last 50 years, women seeking abortion often had to travel to England, adding practical difficulties to the emotions already being experienced (Bloomer & O'Dowd, 2014). Moreover, unlike the rest of the UK, abortions were not provided free on the *NHS* until 2017, compounding the inequalities experienced by Northern Irish women (Fox & Horgan, 2020). Although the development of international telemedical services for abortion enabled Northern Irish women to access abortion without travelling, they risked criminalisation (Aiken, Padron, Broussard, & Johnson, 2019; Bloomer & O'Dowd, 2014; Fox & Horgan, 2020). In 2016, a couple received a police caution for using abortion pills, and in March 2017, customs seized the pills of 15–20 women, many of whom were contacted by the police (Fox & Horgan, 2020). This was investigated in a *UN Committee on the Elimination of Discrimination against Women* (CEDAW) Inquiry. The CEDAW Report found the lack of access to abortion resulted in grave and systematic violations of human rights in relation to specific cases (Fox & Horgan, 2020). As a devolved issue, the lack of access to abortion was a criticism of the NI Assembly. However, as the UK government has overall responsibility for human rights, they were ultimately accountable for the situation. The combination of the legal judgements and CEDAW report led to the UK Parliament decriminalising abortion in NI in 2019. The effect of this legislation means that pregnant people in NI cannot be prosecuted for procuring their own abortions. Because abortion was straightforwardly decriminalised, this means that NI now has a more progressive law than the rest of the UK, though at the time of writing, accessing services is still a major impediment, especially for those who are more than 10 weeks' gestation (Bloomer, McNeilly, & Pierson, 2020). At the time of decriminalisation, the devolved NI assembly was disbanded, adding to the political tensions over the issue. As part of this research, we witnessed a candle-lit vigil at Stormont attended by approximately 3,500–4,000 people drawn from both NI and the Republic of Ireland in protest at the decision.

In recent years, the governance of abortion has become more devolved for Scotland and Wales. When the Scottish Parliament was initially established in the *Scotland Act 1998*, responsibility for abortion law was retained in Westminster, despite health being devolved to Scotland. It was only in the *Scotland Act 2016* that abortion became a fully devolved issue. In Wales, whilst health was also a devolved issue, it was not until 2018 that the Minister for Health in Wales was granted regulatory powers over abortion service provision. The Welsh Assembly cannot change the legal status of abortion. Since these devolved powers were given, both Scotland and Wales have acted before Westminster to liberalise services. For example, both nations changed the regulations to allow abortion pills to be taken at home before this provision was enacted in England (Lord, Regan, Kasliwal, Massey, & Cameron, 2018).

Motherhood and Medicine

In the debates during the passing of the *1967 Abortion Act*, there was little discussion about women's rights. Although the main campaigning group, the *Abortion Law Reform Association (ALRA)*, were committed to the right of women to make autonomous decisions, tactically, they made pragmatic decisions to gain sufficient political support for the legal change (Brookes, 1988). By focusing on the deaths and injuries caused by unsafe abortion, they framed the issue as a medical necessity rather than a moral issue (Brookes, 1988). Moreover, at the time, doctors were concerned about preserving their medical autonomy; whilst many of them supported access to abortion, they did not support abortion on request (Amery, 2020). The support of the medical organisations was considered crucial to getting the law passed (Hindell & Simms, 1971).

Motherhood was a central concern during the debates on the *Abortion Act*. Sheldon (1997) identified three particular narratives in these Parliamentary debates. First was the positioning of women as immature or selfish, a position largely taken by those who opposed liberalising abortion. The second narrative, used mainly by those who supported reform, focused on women as victims of their circumstances who risked injury or death from backstreet abortions. Examples were given of those who had large families or lacked support from husbands, as well as women judged to be unfavourable mothers, such as women who abused substances. The final narrative identified by Sheldon (1997), that motherhood was 'natural' for women, was presented by supporters and opponents of the legislation. Those who were against liberalisation saw abortion as an 'unnatural' act, one that would be harmful to women. As this book will illustrate, this viewpoint still circulates. For abortion supporters, reform could ensure 'desperate' or 'deserving' women could better perform their motherhood role to existing or future children. As Greenwood and Young (1976) argued, this was an important strategy in stressing that the *Act* was not a mechanism to introduce abortion 'on demand'. Consequently, to a large extent, the intention of those who supported the *Abortion Act* was to allow abortions when there was a risk to 'good' motherhood; the notion that motherhood was compulsory for women was left unchallenged (Sheldon, 1997).

As indicated above, the *Abortion Act* placed the issue of abortion firmly into the realm of medicine. It is doctors that were given the responsibility as to whether an abortion was covered by the legal framework. This framing clearly positions doctors, rather than politicians, as the experts; it also positions them in a paternalistic position over women (Sheldon, 1997). As Amery (2020) argues, the tactical choice of positioning women seeking abortion into patients enabled the Act to pass and has fended off all attempts to overturn it; it left the medicalisation of abortion uncriticised:

> The 1967 Abortion Act did not, and was never meant to, establish a 'right to choose' in law. Instead, it was meant as a partial fix to social problems including poverty, poor housing, and 'overlarge' families with tired mothers. (...) This was to be achieved not by

liberating women to exercise their reproductive rights, but by engaging medical professionals to work as social agents and deliver (especially working-class) women into their care and control.

(2020, p. 177)

The focus on medicine rather than politics has been largely retained, and whilst this has prevented abortion becoming a party political football, it has also largely stymied any progressive changes to the *1967 Abortion Act* (Amery, 2020; Halfmann, 2011; Sheldon, 2016).

As Amery (2020) has shown, it was after the *Abortion Act*, during the many unsuccessful attempts to restrict abortion, that feminist discourses on abortion started to be properly articulated in Parliament. Yet whilst there was an increased emphasis on abortion as a necessity to enable women's rights, it did not seriously challenge its medicalised position and often reaffirmed the idea of women's vulnerability (Amery, 2020). This created space for anti-abortion 'pro-woman' arguments to be articulated with a renewed emphasis on abortion as harmful to women, building on earlier debates (Amery, 2020; Sheldon, 1997). As calls for the decriminalisation of abortion have increased, anti-abortion MPs have been placed in a position where they feel a need to defend the *1967 Abortion Act*, a law that they fundamentally disagree with, using these 'pro-woman' arguments (Amery, 2020; Lowe, 2019). As will be detailed later, this framing of abortion is central to the anti-abortion activists arguments, frequently displayed in signs stating 'Abortion hurts women'. Included in this frame is the claim that abortion causes mental health issues, often articulated as post-abortion syndrome (PAS) (Lee, 2003). Numerous studies have shown there is no evidence that abortion has an adverse impact on mental health; it is being denied an abortion that leads to worse mental health outcomes in the short term (Foster, 2020). However, this position is not accepted by abortion opponents and they retain the view of abortion as trauma (Millar, 2017), and, as we will show, this arises from their religious beliefs.

Impact of Clinic Activism

Anti-abortion activism lacks public support and has largely been unsuccessful since 1967. However, it is important to recognise that outside abortion clinics, anti-abortion activists can have a significant detrimental impact on those seeking abortion. Whilst this book does not include detailed experiences of abortion seekers, service providers, or those who live or work close to an abortion clinic who encounter them frequently, we nevertheless feel it is important to reiterate that these experiences remain crucial within our analysis. As we have argued elsewhere, anti-abortion activism outside abortion clinics is a specific form of street harassment that is interrelated with gendered public space (Lowe & Hayes, 2019). As Goffman argues, the normative social rules of public engagement require 'civil inattention', that is, strangers only briefly act to register each other's presence but then withdraw attention so as not to show undue curiosity

(Goffman, 1963). 'Street accosting', to use Goffman's (1963) term, is when a stranger oversteps this norm and instigates an encounter that may be unwelcome or threatening. Importantly, within this framework, as Gardner (1995) pointed out, women experience public attention in a different way to men, and the failure to grant women the same level of civil inattention is a form of public harassment.

The level of street harassment faced by women in daily life means that they often utilise public space differently, seeking to minimise the risks of street harassment and having increased levels of fear and awareness within public spaces (Logan, 2015). When anti-abortion activists are present outside an abortion clinic, it becomes impossible to apply risk-avoidance techniques. They are seen as potentially dangerous strangers, as it is impossible for abortion seekers to know the exact intentions of activists standing outside the clinic (Lowe & Hayes, 2019). It also can be impossible to avoid them. Moreover, their presence outside of clinics draws public attention to the issue of abortion, inviting others in the vicinity to pay attention to those seeking to enter. This is experienced as a loss of healthcare privacy (Lowe & Hayes, 2019). Consequently, we argue, that the presence of anti-abortion activists outside clinics should always be considered as potential harassment, regardless of what actions they are performing:

> The failure by anti-abortion activists to civilly disattend directly challenges women's expectations of privacy and confidentiality, and makes their access of a specific reproductive healthcare service material and public. Moreover, the context of abortion stigma heightens the discrediting that some women feel when seeking services.
>
> (Lowe & Hayes, 2019, p. 344)

As will be detailed throughout the book, most of the actions outside UK abortion clinics are not violent or verbally aggressive to those seeking services. But the surveillance, loss of privacy and fear generated by their presence need to be recognised as having a significant detrimental impact on those forced to encounter them.

Local Contexts to Global Movements

Abortion has long been a transnational issue. For example, the *1861 OAPA*, which confirmed abortion as a criminal offence in England, Wales and Ireland, was replicated across the world as a colonial process. It was enacted in numerous countries including 18 in Africa, 12 in the Caribbean and 11 in the Asia-Pacific region and many of these nations still have the legislation today (Dutch, 2020). Other colonising European nations also exported their penal codes on abortion across the world and there is an ongoing legacy of criminalised abortion which results in detrimental care for women in many nations (Ngwena, 2014). Anti-abortion organisations regularly transmit strategies, tactics and frames across nations, with the US anti-abortion movement singled out for its global reach

(Mason, 2019). Whilst it is important not to underestimate the political significance of this, we argue that in practice, as we will demonstrate, the local context
makes a significant difference to the success, failure and interpretation of anti-
abortion activities imported from elsewhere. Moreover, we suggest that as the
North American anti-abortion movement has been researched more than those in
other places, there is often an assumption that they are the originators of
particular ways of campaigning, whereas in practice this is not necessarily the
case. For example, as we will detail later, the adoption of foetal images in anti-
abortion campaigns occurred at the same time as the original development of the
technology in Scotland in the 1960s (Davis & Davidson, 2006). This is likely to
have been some of the earliest use of that particular anti-abortion strategy.

Research on anti-abortion activism across the world provides significant
insights, although the different national context cannot always be translated
straightforwardly to the UK. There have been some important studies in North
America. Luker's (1984) and Ginsburg's (1989) research on how those who
support and oppose abortion have different beliefs and values about women and
motherhood has been useful as that divide occurs in the UK context as well.
However, the 'imposition' of abortion through the *Roe v Wade* Supreme Court
judgement in 1973 that was often important to how the anti-abortion activists felt
about abortion provision is clearly different. In Britain, abortion had been
actively debated for years before the 1967 reforms, and key organisations
including the CofE were supportive of some liberalisation (Keown, 1988).
Research by Munson (2002) and Mason (2002) drew significant attention to the
importance of specific faith positions in the lives of US anti-abortion activists, but
as we will explain shortly, the religious context of the UK is different, not least in
the distaste for 'public religion'. It has also been useful to compare the specific
discourses of the adoption of 'pro-woman' abortion narratives in North America
(Saurette & Gordon, 2015) with the earlier adoption of motherhood claims which
shaped British law reform in the 1960s (Lowe & Page, 2019a). The recent insights
by Haugeberg (2017) and Ehrlich and Doan (2019) have also been useful in
thinking through how being involved in anti-abortion activism gives women in
traditional communities spaces for personal empowerment and how they can use
narratives of abortion regret as an essential role in this. Research in Australia by
Millar (2017) and Baird (2018) on foetal-centric grief and public and private
political abortion spaces have also been illuminating.

The Religious Composition of the UK

Understanding the place of religion in the UK context is complex; here we offer
key points relevant to this particular study. In 2018, a British Social Attitudes
survey revealed that 52% of the British population said they had no religion – this
is a significant emerging category generating much research interest (Curtice,
Clery, Perry, Phillips, & Rahim, 2019; Lee, 2015). Whilst historically the CofE
has held a privileged position in the UK, given its remit as the established church

in England (Brown & Woodhead, 2016; Guest, 2007; Guest, Olson, & Wolffe, 2012; Page, 2017), it is in the CofE where religious affiliation has declined the fastest (Curtice et al., 2019). Of those who identified as Christian in the 2018 British Social Attitudes Survey, 15% identified with Protestant traditions such as Anglicanism and Methodism, 7% with Catholicism, and a further 13% identified with Christianity in general terms rather than a specific denomination. Meanwhile 9% identified with a religion other than Christianity (Curtice et al., 2019). As we will explain later, as the majority of anti-abortion activists are Catholic, the potential to increase the numbers active against abortion from within their church is small. Christians who described themselves as 'extremely' or 'very' religious were more likely to identify with Catholicism, with 23% of Catholics attending church at least weekly – more than double the religious population as a whole (Curtice et al., 2019). In short, within the British context, whilst Catholicism is a minority religious tradition, it constitutes the largest Christian tradition after the CofE, and does marginally better in terms of generating religious belonging (Bullivant, 2019).

In NI, 36% identify as Catholic, with 20% claiming no religious identification (*Northern Ireland Life and Times* [*NILT*], 2019). Presbyterian is the largest Protestant identifier at 18%, but collectively Protestant affiliation is 40% (*NILT*, 2019). Therefore within the Northern Irish context, the split between Protestants and Catholics is far more even compared with the rest of the UK. NI generates higher religious affiliation (typically Christianity), owing to how religious identity has contributed to political allegiances, in the context of ethno-nationalist conflict (Mitchell, 2004, 2006). Churches played a pivotal role in supporting their communities through extremely challenging circumstances, thereby consolidating loyalty and affinity (Mitchell, 2004). As Hayes and McKinnon argue, whether looking at identity, religious observance or belief, 'NI remains a deeply religious society' (2018, p. 356).

Overall, the religious landscape of the UK has changed considerably in recent years; far more people (especially young people) are likely to identify as having no religion, and there has been increasing religious diversity beyond Christianity (Curtice et al., 2019; Lee, 2015; Woodhead, 2012). Even in NI where religiosity rates have remained stronger, non-religious identification is growing (Hayes & McKinnon, 2018; Mitchell, 2006). Nevertheless it must be remembered that to identify as non-religious does not mean one would equally embrace the 'atheist' label, or show hostility to religion (Lee, 2015).

Understanding Institutional Religion and Abortion

When the *1967 Abortion Act* was passed in Britain, most churches were in favour, due to the persuasive arguments put forward regarding the damaging consequences of so-called backstreet abortions, and the fact that wealthy women were already able to obtain legal abortion – it was agreed that there was a pressing need for some form of reform, given the devastating consequences of existing arrangements to (especially poorer) women's health (McLeod, 2007). More recently, the CofE has decried the numbers of abortions now performed annually and its current position is that abortion should only be permissible in limited circumstances, but generally they remain rather silent on the issue (Church of England, 2017). In contrast, NI conservative religious leaders have been very vocal in their opposition to abortion. Bloomer et al. (2017) outline that all four main churches, comprising Roman Catholic, Church of Ireland, Presbyterian and Methodist churches, have all resisted the expansion of abortion provision in NI. For both Protestant and Catholic NI groups, opposition to abortion is rooted in the symbol of the mother embodying particular forms of self-sacrificial nationalism; abortion therefore comes to be understood as a rejection of motherhood, and a rejection of one's national allegiance (Bloomer et al., 2017; Pierson, 2018).

Beyond NI, there has been far less research about evangelical approaches to abortion (Clements, 2014). Evangelicalism emerged in Britain in the 1730s and spans liberal and conservative theologies (Bebbington, 1989). Evangelicalism in the UK incorporates churches from numerous Christian traditions, from independents to churches within the CofE (Bebbington, 1989). As a movement, it lacks a hierarchy, but groups do exist which coalesce around a collective interest. Influential associations like *Evangelical Alliance*, the 175-year-old conservative umbrella group connecting together numerous evangelical churches, strongly opposes abortion, homosexuality and the broader displacement of Christianity within British society, and deem same-sex partnerships 'unbiblical' (Evangelical Alliance, 2006, p. 16). It therefore appeals to evangelicals on the conservative end of the spectrum. Regarding abortion, they recently advised their members to oppose a government consultation on the use of abortion pills at home (*Evangelical Alliance*, 2021a) and they co-founded *Both Lives Matter* in NI, an anti-abortion group which seeks to align the rights of the foetus with that of women (Evangelical Alliance, 2021b).

Given the mission to evangelise and vocalise their message, and their involvement in activism to target sin (Bebbington, 1989; Cliff, 2019), it is interesting that evangelically derived anti-abortion activism in public spaces is less common in Britain than NI; although when it is encountered, it is highly conspicuous and more likely to be associated with the use of graphic images – described by Ginsburg (1989) as 'war pictures'. We do not profess to have all the answers regarding why evangelical activism is less pronounced; more research would be needed to understand this further. But taking Strhan's (2015) findings regarding conservative evangelicals, it may be the case that given their broader proselytising reluctance within the UK context, and what Strhan identifies as much doubt in their identities, there is not the will to stand outside clinics and oppose abortion – they are focused on other things, with abortion not high on the agenda. Cliff's (2019) analysis of Evangelical Alliance identifies abortion as one issue where there is not a position of consensus amongst conservatives, and abortion therefore does not generate any specific social action – it is a low-priority issue, and evangelical leaders are less likely to speak about it.

As few evangelicals are involved, particularly outside abortion clinics, this book will inevitably focus more extensively on the Catholic activists, who make up the vast majority of participants in the anti-abortion cause. The symbols and style of activism that are largely present in Britain are constructed to specifically appeal to the Catholic activist, rather than Protestant traditions.

Religious Attitudes to Abortion

The key church mobilising against the *1967 Abortion Act* was Roman Catholicism, although as will be explained later, many Catholics in Britain opposing abortion were disappointed in their efforts. The Vatican retains strong opposition to abortion to the present day (Miller, 2014). Pope Francis has been deemed a more liberal pontificate, and has suggested a softening towards issues such as same-sex identity, but on abortion, his stance has remained firmly conservative (Caruso, 2020). However, as previously outlined, overall, the UK population is overwhelmingly supportive of abortion, and this includes rank-and-file Catholics, who do not necessarily endorse Vatican policy (Page & Lowe, 2021b).

Hornsby-Smith's (1991) parish studies of English Catholics in the 1970s and 1980s indicated that even then, the idea of Catholics united in opposing abortion was a myth. Only one quarter of his sample took an absolutist view; with many arguing there were certain situations where it was acceptable – principally on the grounds of health or life of the woman, rape, and a child who would have a life-limiting disability – the so-called 'hard' reasons. Meanwhile, 10% believed it was entirely an individual decision. Clements' (2014) more recent analysis of British Social Attitudes and European Values Study data reveals liberalisation since the 1980s. Catholics are more likely to deem abortion to be wrong compared with other Christian groups, but those arguing it is 'always wrong' comprise only 14.2% of Catholics, whilst 51.6% of Catholics believed it should be a woman's decision regarding whether she wants to have a child or not.

Regarding evangelicals, the data are scarce (Cliff, 2019) but even the conservative *Evangelical Alliance*'s own survey of their membership reveals diversity of opinion. Whilst 49% agreed to some extent that abortion could never be justified – the majority – 51% – disagreed or were unsure (*Evangelical Alliance*, 2011). Clements (2014), like Woodhead (2013), highlights that the key defining factor underpinning a conservative view is the level of strictness towards one's religion (measured through things such as biblical literalism, biblical inerrancy, theological exclusivism), and how important one sees one's religion. Higher religious commitment and greater church attendance is correlated with conservatism. Woodhead (2013) calls this group the 'moral minority', identifiable across numerous conservative Christian traditions (Baptist and Roman Catholic) and Islam in Britain, and generally comprising 8.5% of the religious population. It is specifically from this minority that anti-abortion activists are found. Religiously identifying individuals who do not comprise the moral minority (i.e. the majority of the faith-based population) become their own moral arbiters on personal life issues such as abortion.

In NI, as we have argued, abortion has a different symbolism. In 2016, the *NILT* survey indicated that 75% of Catholics and 85% of Protestants agreed that abortion should 'definitely' or 'probably' be legal if a woman is likely to die if she continued with the pregnancy, whilst a serious threat to the woman's health generates 65% support for abortion from Catholics and 78% from Protestants (Pierson 2018). As elsewhere, conservative attitudes are correlated with greater religious observance.

Public and Private Religion

Sociologists of religion in the twentieth century largely assumed that religion was in decline and becoming an increasingly privatised affair in the UK. Yet this assumption has been extensively critiqued, given the greater prominence of religion in recent years (Lee, 2015; Reilly & Scriver, 2014). The reasons for this apparent resurgence in religion in the public sphere are multifaceted. As Woodhead (2012) outlines, the diversity of religiously identified migrants of the post-war period, and the alignment of certain religious traditions such as Islam with terror and extremism, is only part of the story. For example, the rolling back of the welfare state has resulted in religions stepping into the gaps left in service provision. In addition, the idea that religion ever disappeared has been questioned; the links between terrorism, extremism and religion were not so long ago associated with sectarian violence in NI.

What is clear is that the public space accorded religion causes anxiety, especially regarding whether giving voice to conservative forms of religion will erode the hard-won rights of women and queer people (Reilly & Scriver, 2014). As Reilly and Scriver (2014) explore, how religious authority and gender is reconfigured and renegotiated as the public role of religion alters matters, as there is a need to get the balance right between protecting the rights of religious individuals whilst challenging religious authority which seeks to erode the rights of women, amongst others.

Indeed, the relationship between religion and the public sphere is highly complex in the UK context. The general public remain attached to Anglican buildings, most notably aesthetically pleasing cathedrals, even if they are visited infrequently (Davie, 2007); the CofE generates nostalgic acceptance, esteemed because it becomes bound up with an imagined understanding of nation and heritage (Guest et al., 2012; Woodhead, 2012). But there is distrust of other worship spaces, particularly the religious buildings of minority religions such as Islam, where mosques become read through otherness and non-Britishness (Gale, 2009). Whilst personal religiosity, displayed through, for example, religious garments like the hijab, cross or turban, is generally tolerated and understood as a marker of one's personal beliefs, there is also suspicion of overtly religious displays or personal faith deemed to go 'too far'.[3] For example, whilst the Muslim

---

[3]We recognise that some controversies over religious garments and objects have emerged, most notably, the court case surrounding a British Airways employee who in 2006 was told she could not wear a cross to work. This was upheld in UK courts until the European Court of Human Rights deemed it an infringement of the employee's human rights (Article 9). Whilst Islamic garments have generated consternation, no explicit bans are in place, as is the case in other European countries. As Joppke argues, British liberalism favours 'private choice and non-interference' (2009, p. 83), hence to some extent, clothing choices are deemed an extension of one's personal identity rather than a public matter per se.

hijab – covering the hair but not the face – is relatively accepted, and has not provoked the same outrage as experienced in other European countries like France – the niqab – which covers the face – has prompted debate, and described by Tony Blair (a former Prime Minister) as a 'marker of separation' (Joppke, 2009, p. 104).

Equally there is disdain for explicit outspoken invocations and public proclamations of religion, such as the activities of anti-abortion activists. Such religious expression is interpreted as intrusive to the freedom of others. For example, the *Atheist Bus Campaign* was a response by a comedian to an evangelical Christian advertisement which led to a website telling unbelievers they would end up in hell (Aston, 2016; Tomlins & Bullivant, 2016). With support from both the *British Humanist Association* and Richard Dawkins, the campaign funded an advertisement on public transport with the tagline: 'There's Probably No God. Now Stop Worrying and Enjoy Your Life', and inspiring a world-wide campaign (Tomlins & Bullivant, 2016, p. 1). Whilst the campaign provoked backlash elsewhere, in Britain it progressed without incident – in fact, some Christian leaders welcomed it as an opportunity to discuss the existence of God (Aston, 2016). As noted above, the UK's religion–non-religion identifications are split, with the 'no religion' category growing, although this does not equate with negativity to religion (Aston, 2016; Lee, 2015). As Taylor describes it, 'faith, even for the staunchest believer, is one human possibility among others' (2007, p. 3). Studies of young people demonstrate a respect for a multi-religious society, and being inclusive of those who identify religiously and non-religiously, but they are critical of religions which undermine liberal values, such as any negative expression towards same-sex relationships, undermining gender equality and any tradition promoting extremism (Madge, Hemming, & Stenson, 2014). Meanwhile any attempt to force one's beliefs onto others is intensely disliked. Whilst evangelical Christians are most associated with proselytisation, they too can express discomfort with attempts at conversion (Strhan's, 2015).

Whilst avoidance is one strategy in managing anything deemed 'too religious' in the public sphere, humour and comedy is another. Not only was the *Atheist Bus Campaign* started by a comedian, but the ongoing discussion evoked humorous overtones, such as Judy Walker's cartoon depicting a bus displaying a pantomime-esque dialogue about the existence of God ('God does Exist... Oh, no he doesn't... Oh Yes he does' – Aston, 2016, p. 349). More generally, humour in relation to religion is embedded in British culture, from the gentle mocking of clergy and parishioners in sitcoms like *Dad's Army* and *The Vicar of Dibley* (Woodhead, 2012), the 'casual and dismissive' religious humour that frequents the background of British life, such as depicted on greetings cards (Lee, 2015, p. 72), to the outrageously comedic where claims of blasphemy are levelled, with *Monty Python* narrowly escaping such sanctioning in the 1970s (Almond, 2019). Blasphemy laws, which had protected Christianity from attack, were abolished in England and Wales in 2008, though blasphemy remains on the statute books in Scotland and NI. Yet humour can backfire, offence is caused, and disputes end up in the court room. In 2012, *Stonewall*, a charity for queer rights, ran an advertisement on London transport – 'SOME PEOPLE ARE GAY, GET OVER IT!'

(Aston, 2016, p. 360) to which *Core Issues Trust*, a Christian organisation advocating conversion therapy, wanted to run a rebuttal advert of 'NOT GAY! EX-GAY, POST-GAY AND PROUD. GET OVER IT!' (Aston, 2016, p. 360). *Transport for London* refused. The comments of one of the judges when it reached the High Court was that not only was *Stonewall*'s advert offensive to Christians; so too was the *Atheist Bus Campaign*'s previous advertisement – a decision roundly critiqued (Aston, 2016). As Aston argues, 'the public sphere and the urban landscape are becoming contested sites, where the boundary between freedom of religion and freedom of speech are played out' (2016, pp. 361–362).

In short, the UK can be understood as both religious *and* secular, hence the complexity in teasing out how religion is constituted in relation to public and private spheres (Woodhead, 2012). At the level of values, a key ethos is liberalism, which Joppke defines as prioritising 'private choice and non-interference' (2009, p. 83) with pluralism generated through the personal and private choices one makes, hence an emphasis on tolerance when encountering religion in the public sphere. Critique of religion is upheld as a cornerstone value in the public sphere, though this is tempered by caution when ridicule is individualised or goes too far. Respect is expected to be retained at the individual level for those who religiously identify; indeed in 2010, the *Equality Act* made religion or belief a protected characteristic. Expressions of religion that can be equated with the private realm are usually tolerated, but public displays of religion are viewed with suspicion, for 'visible expressions of religiosity still challenge widely held feelings that religion is or should be a private matter' (Aston, 2016, p. 363). This is the context in which public displays of anti-abortion activism are understood.

Plan of the Book

Chapter 2 will start by giving an overview of the history of opposition to abortion in the UK, and the legal position, also considering the religious dimensions to this history. It will illustrate the historical roots of many current anti-abortion discourses, particularly how religious concerns about women's bodies and behaviour have been a central issue. Ultimately, access to abortion was premised as a medical, rather than a moral, concern, with medical professionals given much autonomy and power.

Chapter 3 will outline the conceptual framing of the book, linking together the perspectives of the sociology of reproductive health with the sociology of religion. We explain the concept of lived religion as a means of understanding the practices of the anti-abortion activists, and how these religious engagements were rooted in particular conceptualisations of the sacred and the profane. Using Lynch's idea of sacred forms, we explain how ultra-sacrificial motherhood, rooted in particular religious beliefs, becomes a fundamental idea driving their activism. Meanwhile this chapter also considers materiality and spatial dynamics to anti-abortion activism, both of which contribute to the broader theoretical engagement with lived religion.

Chapter 4 embarks on the dataset, and outlines the worldviews of the anti-abortion activists. Despite claims that this is not a religiously-instigated campaign, we demonstrate that the activists are deeply connected to particular understandings of God, such as the idea that God opposes abortion. We examine how anti-abortion activism is linked to their perceptions of salvation and doing God's work, with disbelief shown to those belonging to their faith who did not share their activist inclinations. More broadly, activists subscribed to highly conservative notions of gender roles, and were critical of a liberalised society.

Chapter 5 explores the centrality of the mother to the anti-abortion campaign, and how the kind of motherhood being endorsed was of an ultra-sacrificial nature. As pregnancy is deemed a divine gift, any rejection of pregnancy is problematised. We will examine the various harms that anti-abortion activists claim abortion causes, including not only a threat to physical and mental well-being, but also putting a woman at risk of grave spiritual harm. This chapter also emphasises how anti-abortion activists negotiate science in their claimsmaking, but this was always rooted through their religious beliefs.

Chapter 6 focuses on the meanings generated in relation to the foetus, and where a foetal-centric understanding is endorsed, with women expected to prioritise the foetus over their own needs, at whatever cost. Building on the arguments presented in Chapter 5, this chapter articulates how anti-abortion activists come to endorse these sacrificial expectations placed on women, through emphasising the equality, independence and personhood of the foetus. Because the anti-abortion activists typically take an absolutist view on abortion, we also examine their understandings of abortion in relation to the 'hard cases', revealing that their understanding is ultimately premised on ultra-sacrificial motherhood.

Chapter 7 examines the actual practices undertaken by activists, with an explicit focus on the religious practices, iconography and material objects. This chapter therefore gives a detailed understanding of the lived practices of activists and the meanings given to particular prayers, objects like rosary beads, and Our Lady of Guadalupe as a key intercessor for prayer, and depicted on jewellery, clothing, and even shopping bags. These embodied practices contributed to a community of belonging. The anti-abortion activists did not recognise the distress they caused from being outside abortion clinics, because their actions are rooted in religious practice.

Chapter 8 offers a spatial analysis of clinic sites from the perspective of those opposing the activists – the counterdemonstrators. Here, we examine two kinds of intervention – firstly, in escorting service users to the door of clinics, and secondly, in forming a rebuttal and counter-protest to the anti-abortion activists. These activities take on their own materiality, and express a very different sacred commitment – that of reproductive justice, and also emphasise the broader harms caused by the anti-abortion activism.

Chapter 9 offers a more conceptual analysis of the anti-abortion activists and how they view themselves and the world around them. Engaging in a spiritual battle against the 'evil' of abortion involves particular investment in specific theological understandings and emotional regimes. Ultimately, ending abortion is equated with stopping a broader moral decline that they see in society more generally; hence, they only perceive of their actions in positive and godly terms.

The Conclusion outlines the key conceptual points of the project. It also shows why legislating for bufferzones outside of abortion clinics is important, drawing on the research data and recent legal cases.

Summary

As this short introduction to religion in the UK demonstrates, it is a complex business and as Woodhead (2012) argues, it is best understanding Britain as being sacred and secular concurrently. Meanwhile, abortion is something most of the UK population broadly agrees with. And it is typically those with a conservative religious mindset – of whatever religious persuasion – who oppose abortion. Woodhead emphasises that religious conservatives exist across religious traditions, and calls this group the 'moral minority'. By and large, the people we encounter engaging in anti-abortion activism constitute this moral minority, in that they are regularly religiously observant, with a strong sense of Christian belief, with highly conservative attitudes on gender and sexuality issues. In our study, it is mainly Roman Catholics who participate in anti-abortion activism, despite the saliency of evangelical support in other countries like the US. In Britain, conservative evangelicals are a far more minor contingent, with evangelicalism being more frequent in NI.

Chapter 2

Opposition to Abortion: A UK History

Introduction

This chapter begins with an outline of the history of abortion law and practice
across the United Kingdom (UK), including the role that religion and religious
actors have played in the opposition to abortion. It will use key examples to
illustrate the ways in which abortion came to be seen as a medical rather than a
moral concern, and how this was later institutionalised in the *1967 Abortion Act*.
It will outline the development of abortion opposition and how this became
cemented in the development of specific anti-abortion organisations. Throughout
the chapter, we seek to show the variations in policy and practice between the four
nations of the UK. Whilst the evidence shows that the tactics and strategies of
anti-abortion activism have a long history of crossing borders both within and
beyond the UK, it is important to recognise that they are always locally interpreted. This explains, as we will later show, the abject failure of the plan to
introduce United States (US)-style clinic blockades to the UK by those involved
in *Operation Rescue*.

Historical Opposition to Abortion

The extent to which abortion was accepted or denounced in history is complicated. As Keown (1988) has shown, abortion cases were brought to ecclesiastical
and common-law courts prior to the first criminal law in England in 1803. For
example, in 1602, Margaret Webb was prosecuted for consuming poison with the
intention of 'destroying' a foetus in her womb. The early common law cases are
likely to be built on earlier ecclesiastical courts, and thus religious beliefs were
important in the formation of ideas about abortion and the way it was treated
legally (Keown, 1988). However, as early pregnancy was not easily detectable by
others, and methods used to prevent conception, regulate menstruation, or
terminate pregnancy often overlapped, the extent to which abortion was a common historic practice is unclear (Marcotte, 2016; McLaren, 1990). Moreover, as
Cook (2004) points out, spontaneous miscarriage is frequent even today, so even
if women had taken steps to end a pregnancy, whether or not methods were
successful is largely unknowable. Yet there is evidence that abortion was used,
and not just from the records of cases that ended up in court. For example,
Francis Place (1771–1854) researched abortion, collecting working-class women's

Anti-Abortion Activism in the UK, 19–36
Copyright © 2022 Pam Lowe and Sarah-Jane Page
Published under exclusive licence by Emerald Publishing Limited
doi:10.1108/978-1-83909-398-220221004

accounts, producing the first handbill on birth control in 1820 (Cook, 2004). Cook (2004) argues that whilst abortion lacked respectability, Place's research did not specify why. So, whilst it is impossible to know the extent to which women had abortions, the earliest historic records clearly show that abortion was not necessarily a rare occurrence and there was some opposition to it, including prosecutions.

The history of abortion law is interlinked with theological debates. Gavigan (1984) highlights the importance of the moral status of the foetus when considering abortion, whilst Maguire (1988) has raised the possibility that the church was actually more concerned with sinful sex. For Gavigan (1984) the importance given to 'quickening', the first detection of foetal movement, illustrates the importance of the church's influence. Whilst there is a debate about the extent to which abortion before quickening was historically seen as an offence, it is clear that a distinction was often made (Gavigan, 1984; Keown, 1988). It is also important to remember that, as is usually the case today where abortion is unsafe and/or illegal, it is when abortions cause the death or serious risks to women's health that it becomes a matter of public concern (Gavigan, 1984; Keown, 1988). Importantly as well, for at least some of the legal profession, historic concerns about the 'unnaturalness' of abortion were based on assumptions about women's nature. Gavigan illustrates how in a trial of a midwife in 1732 comments were made about a female abortion provider being 'barbarous' and 'unnatural' and 'contrary to the female sex' (1984, p. 29). As we will show throughout the book, questions about women's 'natural' role have been of ongoing importance within abortion opposition, and a central part of opposing abortion today.

Little is known about why abortion was further criminalised in England, Wales and Ireland as part of Lord Ellenborough's *1803 Malicious Shooting* and *Stabbing Act*. Keown (1988) suggests it was a combination of concerns about the frequency of abortion, difficulties in prosecution under the existing common law, and the increasing influence of science, both in terms of understandings of conception and the development of medicine. He also argues that this was the beginning of the development of medicine as an organised profession, and doctors were keen to distinguish themselves from irregular practitioners including midwives. However, the decision to include abortion in a law dealing with violent crimes might also have stemmed from Lord Ellenborough's own faith position; he was said to be a devout Christian who was critical of moral lapses (Gavigan, 1984; Keown, 1988). The Act itself criminalised all abortions, but used quickening to differentiate the severity of the crime. The quickening distinction ended in law three decades later in the *1837 Offences Against the Persons Act*. The most significant change to abortion law following its introduction was the subsequent *1861 Offences Against the Person Act* (OAPA), which remains the basis of abortion law in England and Wales. It also applied to Northern Ireland (NI) until 2019. Scotland was never included in this legislation although abortion was a common law offence (as will be detailed later, this allowed greater flexibility in relation to abortion). The *1861 Act* sought to consolidate and simplify earlier statutes across a range of offences, including those surrounding abortion. Keown (1988) argues that whilst the changes and extension to abortion offences relate to issues and judgements in earlier legal cases, the continuing concerns raised by medical professionals were important. Between 1803 and 1861, medical journals carried articles condemning the 'criminal trade' of 'unprofessional' abortion providers which posed risks to women's health and lives (Keown, 1988, p. 43). Yet despite medical condemnation of abortion, and the introduction of criminal laws with harsh penalties, women continued to have abortions and, in at least some circumstances, medical practitioners provided them (Keown, 1988).

During the early part of the twentieth century, abortion remained an unsettled issue politically. Whist the prohibition in the law was evidence of official disapproval, women continued to seek abortions, and developments in medical practice meant that, for those who could afford to see private doctors, abortion was becoming safer. Moreover, despite there being no clear provision in the *1861 Act*, there was recognition that therapeutic abortion, when the mother's life was threatened, was a legitimate medical procedure, appearing in medical textbooks both before and after the statute was passed (Keown, 1988). Maternal mortality, of which abortion-related deaths were a key feature, was a subject of numerous reports and government inquiries (Brookes, 1988; McIntosh, 2000). Moreover, studies have shown that not only did women seek abortions regularly, in some cases, this was seen as less problematic than using birth control (McCormick, 2015; McIntosh, 2000). Often in accounts at this time, a lay understanding of quickening was used; taking steps to 'put yourself right' before quickening are recorded (McIntosh, 2000, p. 88). Fisher's oral history of working-class women in South Wales found:

> ...[they] were little concerned by the legal and 'moral' issues surrounding abortion. Most were aware that abortion was illegal, though some gave the impression that they felt self-induced abortions were within the law. (...) Fear of being caught or sent to jail is not mentioned as a reason why abortion was not attempted or decided against.
>
> (1998, p. 30)

Importantly too, there were differences in medical opinions on the issue, such as debates within the *British Medical Association* (*BMA*), with some doctors supporting therapeutic abortions whilst others viewed even a discussion of the issues as being immoral (Brookes, 1988; Hindell & Simms, 1971). Despite earlier opposition, the *BMA* set up a committee to examine the issues which concluded (in 1936) that the law needed clarification, outlining some medical grounds for abortion, including where there was a risk to the physical or mental health of the woman, rape of children, and where it was likely that the foetus would have a 'serious disease' (Hindell & Simms, 1971, p. 68). The conclusions, especially the evidence that legalised abortion would reduce maternal mortality, were not supported by all (Brookes, 1988; Hindell & Simms, 1971). Smith suggests that some of those opposed were not necessarily against abortion per se, but felt that the current law was sufficient and were worried about 'irresponsible' demands being placed on the medical profession (1979, p. 43). That fear might have been realised shortly after with the formation of the *Abortion Law Reform Association* (*ALRA*), who sought to liberalise the law and widen access to safe abortions (Brookes, 1988; Smith, 1979).

ALRA was formed in 1936 by a group of women who sought to reform the Victorian law on abortion and were already active in campaigns to make birth control more accessible (Brookes, 1988; Dee, 2020). Amongst the founding members, there was a debate as to the extent to which abortion law reform should be available on request, with others advocating a more qualified right based on circumstances, divorced from ideas about sexual liberation (Brookes, 1988; Dee, 2020). *ALRA* focused its efforts on lobbing parliament and the medical profession and was successful in attracting support from some MPs and high profile doctors, including Aleck Bourne, a well-established gynaecologist. In 1938, Bourne carried out an abortion on a 14-year-old rape victim, having first observed her in the hospital for a number of days, coming to the conclusion that she was a 'decent girl', and that her ordeal was significantly detrimental to her mental health (Brookes, 1988, p. 69). Bourne notified the police about the abortion and was arrested, tried and subsequently acquitted. The case established that doctors could lawfully carry out therapeutic abortions if, in good faith, continuing a pregnancy would leave women 'a physical or mental wreck' (Brookes, 1988). As Dee (2020) has outlined, despite the importance of the *Bourne* judgement on abortion law, his need to establish her as a 'real victim' was clearly problematic, and indicates that he was not a whole-hearted advocate for abortion. He understood women seeking abortion as either 'worthy' or 'unworthy' and positioned doctors as the arbiters who could make this distinction. His ambivalent relationship to the right of women to request abortion is also illustrated by his opposition to abortion law reform in the 1960s, including becoming a founding member of the *Society for the Protection of Unborn Children* (*SPUC*) in 1967 (Dee, 2020).

In response to the pressure from *ALRA* and others, the government established the *Interdepartmental Committee on Abortion*, often known as the *Birkett Committee* (named after the chair). The *Birkett Committee* was established the year before the *Bourne* case and reported afterwards in 1939. Evidence was taken from a range of medical, religious and secular organisations which held a range of perspectives. It confirmed that abortion law was widely disregarded, not least because most women did not consider early abortion to be a crime (Brookes, 1988). The *Birkett Committee* recommended reforming abortion law, albeit only in a limited way which was largely in line with the *Bourne* judgement (Keown, 1988). The evidence given to the *Birkett Committee* suggests a number of reasons why many opposed abortion. It was seen as against the 'natural' order of women's role, and marriage more generally. The *League of National Life* and the *Westminster Catholic Federation*, for example, were concerned about 'moral laxity' and breaking the link between sex and reproduction, which was seen as harmful for both individuals and wider society; they expressed little sympathy for 'unmarried mothers' (Brookes, 1988; Smith, 1979). Others, such as the *Mothers' Union* (affiliated to the Church of England), recognised the difficulties for many women in raising children in poverty, but called for increased welfare support (Beaumont, 2007). Concerns were also raised about the falling birth rate and women's citizenship role in bearing children for the nation (Beaumont, 2007; Brookes, 1988). It is important to note that whilst the majority of those opposed were commenting from a religious position, this was not a uniform perspective. Whilst the Church of England (CofE) and Catholic Church condemned abortion, the Chief Rabbi outlined that this was permissible to save women's lives and the *Modern Churchman's Union*, a lay Christian organisation, supported reform (Smith, 1979).

Brooke (2001) argues that central to the deliberations of the *Birkett Committee* was the issue of women's role in society. He argues that the rejection of more radical reform at this time was due to a fear that it would encourage promiscuity and women rejecting their place as mothers in the home:

> It was the uncertainty of gender identity that the committee apparently found so frightening. Legalising abortion would service to embrace rather than reject such complexity: affirming the separation of reproduction from sexuality as a choice for women would erode the importance of motherhood as a credible signifier and assertion of gender difference.
>
> (Brooke, 2001, p. 458)

The recommendations of the *Birkett Committee* to reform abortion law were never acted on. Brookes (1988) suggests that this was not necessarily just because of the start of the Second World War, but related to the status of the Report (it was not an official publication), and the decision is also likely to have reflected the fears of those opposed to change, that it was an immoral act, against religious teaching, and one which would undermine society. As we will illustrate later, these ideas are still prevalent amongst anti-abortion activists today.

Women continued to have abortions, both lawful and unlawful, and deaths, injuries and prosecutions continued to be reported during the 1940s and 1950s (Brookes, 1988). *ALRA* continued to press for reform, and in the 1950s, a couple of bills were introduced to Parliament. As Brookes (1988) indicates, these were often for very limited reform, and, as so often happens in the case of private members' bills, they were talked out.[1] At this point, it seems that whilst there was still limited support for law reform, the position that some abortions were important and necessary seems to have become established. For example, in 1951, when Pope Pius XII stated that it was not permissible to directly 'kill' a baby to save a mother's life, there was indignation in the press and questions asked in Parliament about women's right to change doctors to access abortion (Brookes, 1988). Yet this moment of interest, and support, for abortion did not seem to result in any immediate government action, presumably as the answers they received were sufficiently reassuring.

---

[1]Private Members' Bills are usually only allocated a short time to be debated, and a common tactic is for opposing MPs to talk for so long, that the bill is stopped from making progress due to lack of time to complete the passage through Parliament.

Towards the *1967 Abortion Act*

During the 1960s, there was renewed public interest in abortion law reform, culminating in the passing of the *1967 Abortion Act* and the establishment of national anti-abortion organisations. This change was part of a broader social context which saw many other social reforms around sexuality and family life, such as the introduction of the contraceptive pill, the partial decriminalization of homosexuality and the liberalisation of divorce. Opinion polls at the time indicated that there was public appetite for reform. For example, Smith (1979) reports that polls revealed that two-thirds of the population, and over 90% of women, were in favour of abortion reform in at least some circumstances. Whilst those of the Catholic faith were more likely to be opposed, this was far from universal with, by 1967, 44% of Catholics in favour of abortion for 'social reasons' (Smith, 1979). The context for this new attention on abortion was that the decade saw both an epidemic of rubella and the revelation that Thalidomide, prescribed to pregnant women for pregnancy sickness, led to babies developing congenital disabilities (Dee, 2020). As McGuinness (2013) argues, the framing of the debates on disability and abortion was closely related to the way that disability was conceptualised as a tragedy. Moreover, alongside abortions for foetal anomaly becoming a subject for wider public debate at this point, the evidence suggests that some doctors were terminating pregnancies for this reason; in 1956 the *British Medical Journal* reported a legal opinion that it was likely to be lawful if the diagnosis would have a serious negative impact on women's mental health (Brookes, 1988).

Whilst national statistics were not gathered, there is evidence that medically supervised abortion was becoming increasingly common. Francome (1986) estimated that in Britain, over 20,000 'legal' abortions took place in 1966, the majority in private practice. Indeed the disparity between rich and poor women's access to abortion was a significant theme in campaigns for liberalisation. Accounts of injury and death at the hands of 'backstreet' abortionists were contrasted to the ability of wealthier women to buy a safe, medically supervised procedure (Brookes, 1988; Dee, 2020; Sheldon, 2016). Jones's (2011) study of letters written to *ALRA* in the 1960s shows how many women wanted to access a 'legal' abortion, and an advice leaflet sent in return stressed how to present their cases to doctors. In most cases, this was the only assistance *ALRA* could legally give, other than recommending travelling to countries with more liberalised laws (Jones, 2011). Importantly though, as Jones (2011) argues, the letters demonstrate increasing desire to have a medically supervised termination.

In Scotland, the reliance on common law on abortion meant that abortion access was not as constrained by the law as in the other UK nations. Abortions performed in good faith on the grounds of women's health would always be lawful (Davis & Davidson, 2006). Moreover, to bring a prosecution, a higher standard of proof would be needed than under the *OAPA 1861* (Davis & Davidson, 2006). As Davis and Davidson (2006) have outlined, this allowed the development of a fairly unique abortion service in Aberdeen which carried out therapeutic abortions for 'social' reasons well before the *1967 Abortion Act*. This liberal position was not universal but was dependent on the work of the pioneering doctor Sir Dugald Baird. Baird's experience of the impact of repeated childbirth and high maternal mortality during the early part of his career led him to develop these services. Importantly, Aberdeen had greater religious diversity and was politically more liberal than some other areas of Scotland (Davis & Davidson, 2006). As Davis and Davidson (2006) argue, this allowed Baird to not just run the service, but to openly promote the idea for women to be able to achieve reproductive autonomy through access to contraception and abortion.

The service in Aberdeen was in sharp contrast to other places in Scotland. Professor Ian Donald, a prominent obstetrician, was a staunch opponent of abortion and used his position to restrict access in Glasgow even after the *1967 Abortion Act*. Glasgow was a more conservative city than Aberdeen and had a larger population of Roman Catholics (Davis & Davidson, 2006). Both men were active in campaigning around abortion in the 1960s with Baird aligning with those seeking to liberalise abortion and Donald becoming a council member of *SPUC* (Davis & Davidson, 2006; Hindell & Simms, 1971). Donald, a member of the Scottish Episcopal Church, argued that abortion, unless to save the mother's life, was similar to the extermination of Jewish people in the Holocaust (Davis & Davidson, 2006). It is also important to note that Donald was involved in the development of ultrasound scanning as a diagnostic technology and used the images to try to dissuade women from having abortions, as well as using pictures and heartbeat sounds in anti-abortion speeches (Davis & Davidson, 2006). As Davis and Davidson (2006) note, these actions in the 1960s were highly unusual, not least because ultrasound scanning was still in development and rarely used in clinical practice. Whilst it is not clear if Donald was the first person to use foetal imagery as an anti-abortion tactic either individually or as part of a campaign, it is likely that his prominent position in *SPUC* meant that his actions were significant in popularising this particular strategy. Also at this time, arguments were made that abortion 'hardened' women, threatening their 'natural' womanhood, and led to feelings of guilt, as well as claims that the foetus could feel pain (Hindell & Simms, 1971). These examples of Holocaust comparisons, use of foetal imaging and assertions about 'abortion hardening' illustrate the long history to many of the claims and tactics currently in use by anti-abortion groups.

There were a number of attempts to reform abortion legislation during the 1950s and 1960s. The early bills did not cover Scotland, as the focus was on reforming *OAPA 1861* which did not apply to Scotland (Davidson & Davis, 2014). As Dee (2020) argues, whilst none where successful, it ensured that the question of abortion reform remained in the political arena, against the preference of many politicians. *ALRA* played a significant role in lobbying for and supporting reform (Brookes, 1988; Dee, 2020). Abortion reform was also under serious discussion in wider society, with features in the media and discussions within other organisations (Smith, 1979). For example, the *University Humanist Association, Co-operative Women's Guilds*, and *National Union of Townswomen Guilds* all passed motions in favour of abortion reform (Smith, 1979). The CofE's *Church Assembly Board for Social Responsibility* published a report in 1965 endorsing abortion if 'the mother's health or well-being is seriously threatened' (*Church Assembly Board* in Hindell & Simms, 1971, p. 93). This report was considered within the *BMA*'s own deliberations in 1966 which also advocated for reform (Smith, 1979). As Keown (1988) has detailed, amongst the different medical organisations, there was considerable debate about reform, with particular professional interests often shaping their approach, but there was broad agreement regarding the need to clarify and extend the existing legal framework. Whilst the earlier bills did not pass, they did provide opportunities for extensive discussion, both in Parliament and beyond, about the impact of specific clauses in the bill, regarding access and medical decision-making. This later fed into the passing of the *1967 Abortion Act* (Keown, 1988). It is also important to note here that Baird's progressive abortion policy in Aberdeen was highly significant in promoting and shaping abortion law reform (Davis & Davidson, 2006). Indeed whilst the work of *ALRA* was pivotal in getting the law liberalised, the eventual law was significantly influenced by medical organisations and it entrenched medical authority over abortion decision-making (Keown, 1988; Sheldon, 1997).

The Foundations of the Anti-Abortion Movement

As outlined above, opposition to abortion has a long history, and is often rooted in particular religious beliefs. For example, the liberalising private members 'Digby Bill' in 1966 was talked out by Catholic MPs who spoke about the impact of the bill on Catholics (Dee, 2020). At this time, the only organised opposition to abortion was the Catholic Church, but despite it looking likely that abortion reform would be introduced, it remained largely silent (Dee, 2020). It was only after it was becoming more certain that the *Medical Termination of Pregnancy Bill 1966* (as the *Abortion Act* was known then), that a new organisation, *SPUC*, was founded to galvanise and organise opposition. *SPUC* claims to be the first specific anti-abortion group in the world, and it made a strategic decision to not only be nominally secular, but, at that time, to distance themselves from the Catholic Church in order to present the opposition of abortion as coming from a broader spectrum (Dee, 2020; Hindell & Simms, 1971). Despite this formal separation, it utilised the structure and resources of the Catholic Church for membership, funding and general support (Dee, 2020; Marsh & Chambers, 1981).

As Dee (2020) argues, the silence of the Catholic Church during the introduction of the *Abortion Act* was an issue of concern for those opposed to abortion. It was believed by some anti-abortion activists that the church took this stance to avoid legitimising abortion as an issue for debate, and a belief that the *Medical Termination of Pregnancy Bill* would fall, just like previous attempts (Dee, 2020). As we will explain in more detail later, at this time, the Catholic Church globally was in the midst of debating birth control, with a wide expectation that the strict prohibition would be relaxed. The uncertainty over this meant it was difficult for them to publicly comment on fertility issues. Dee (2020) outlines how some of those opposing the abortion bill felt betrayed by the lack of leadership by the Catholic Church at this time.

Many have suggested that the formation of *SPUC* came too late to have a significant impact on the passing of the *Abortion Act*. Despite their ability to use the infrastructure of the Catholic Church to mobilise support, they were unable to stop the bill becoming law (Francome, 2004; Hindell & Simms, 1971; Marsh & Chambers, 1981). The support for abortion from a wide range of organisations, including medical practitioners and the general public, meant that although there were strong debates about the scope of the law, it was generally agreed that there should be some level of liberalisation (Hindell & Simms, 1971; Marsh & Chambers, 1981). It was in the period following the implementation of the *Act* that *SPUC* became more effective, building on accounts of difficulties of establishing the service and media accounts of unethical practice and profiteering (Dee, 2020). This period also saw the beginning of numerous attempts by anti-abortion MPs to change the law to restrict access to abortion, which have to date been largely unsuccessful (Sheldon, Davis, O'Neill, & Parker, 2019).[2]

There is little doubt that there were difficulties with the development of abortion services after the *Act* was passed. A key issue was uneven provision. In many places, the National Health Service (*NHS*) was unprepared for the rapid growth in people seeking abortion, and this had a detrimental impact on women (Lane Committee, 1974). In some places, providing abortion meant delays to other gynaecological procedures, and in others, a lack of access to abortion (Lane Committee, 1974). Some senior anti-abortion consultants were able to restrict access. In Birmingham, Professor McLaren, a founding member of *SPUC*, was said to have been able to use his position of authority to prevent the development of *NHS* abortion services (Dee, 2020). Similarly in Scotland, access to abortion was extremely difficult and many women had to travel to England and pay privately (Davis & Davidson, 2006; Hay, 2020). Davis and Davidson (2006) report that this journey was so well known that the Glasgow to Liverpool train was often called 'the Abortion Express'. Indeed as Hay (2020) points out, in Westminster, many of the staunchest opponents of abortion were from Scotland, including those who led attempts to overturn the *Abortion Act*. As well as issues in Scotland, women in Wales often had to travel to England to access abortion during much of the 1970s, with an abortion service not established in Cardiff until 1977 (South Wales Echo, 1977). England also became a destination for others travelling for abortion from further afield. During the early 1970s, there were media reports of abortion services being advertised in other countries, with claims that taxi drivers at London airports were acting as abortion service agents, with private doctors profiteering (Lane Committee, 1974; Wivel, 1998). The focus on unseemly profits, and concerns for the public image of Britain overseas highlighted in these reports usually glossed over the reasons for abortion travel: a lack of proper access near home (Sethna, 2019).

---

[2]All legal attempts to restrict abortion since the *1967 Abortion Act* have failed apart from one, detailed later.

The *Lane Committee* was set up in 1971 to explore the working of the *Abortion Act* in response to both pressure from *SPUC* and anti-abortion MPs, and the adverse media stories about abortion services (Dee, 2020; Wivel, 1998). It was widely expected that they would recommend restrictions to the law, but this did not materialise. Over the course of the inquiry, some of those who were initially opposed to abortion came to support the *Act* (Wivel, 1998). It concluded, in 1974, that many of the difficulties were not due to the law, but its implementation, and that the evidence of abusive practices and profiteering were exaggerated (Lane Committee, 1974). However, as we will later show, the notion that abortion service providers are only really interested in money is an idea that has persisted amongst anti-abortion activists. Despite the depth of the *Lane Report*, accounts that the *Abortion Act* was being 'abused' continued in the media. In particular, a series of stories later published in the book *Babies for Burning* (Litchfield & Kentish, 1974) were particularly influential (Dee, 2020; Marsh & Chambers, 1981).

Numerous claims were made in *Babies for Burning* about abuses carried out by abortion service providers, many of which can still be seen in anti-abortion campaigns today. Practitioners were described as 'seedy' people and abortion referral agencies deemed dark and dirty places (Litchfield & Kentish, 1974). The book also claimed that abortion service providers were Nazi sympathisers. It is also notable that many of the descriptions were explicitly racist about providers. Much of the book argues that the law was being flouted: rather than having a 'proper' reason for abortion, the authors argue that private clinics were offering abortion on request (Litchfield & Kentish, 1974). They claimed that some clinics were lying about the results of pregnancy testing, and thus carrying out unnecessary medical procedures, for which they received payment (Litchfield & Kentish, 1974). The title of the book comes from the claims that in some cases, babies were incinerated alive. It also claimed that foetal tissue was being sold for profit, in particular, to make soap. Such anti-abortion claims continue in new forms today, particularly in the US, with a focus on protecting those 'born alive' after abortion, and accusing *Planned Parenthood* of 'selling baby parts' – claims which are unfounded (Committee on Oversight and Reform, n.d.; Grady, 2019). Although *Babies for Burning* was later completely discredited (including a court order for the publisher to destroy all remaining copies), it was influential in gaining support for restricting the *Abortion Act* (Dee, 2020; Marsh & Chambers, 1981).

Dee (2020) has shown how *Babies for Burning* was foundational to the *White Bill*, introduced in 1975, which sought to restrict abortion, despite the recommendation in the *Lane Committee Report* that law reform was unnecessary. The *White Bill* sought to introduce restrictions around grounds for abortion, make access more difficult, and tighten the regulations, for example by making it harder for abortion service providers to gain registration. It was a complex bill, which some argued was badly drafted (Dee, 2020). White argued that he was not seeking a full repeal, but sought 'necessary' reforms (Dee, 2020). As Dee argues, it was evident at the time that this was not necessarily true, and the *White Bill* could be seen as an example of the anti-abortion movement seeking to restrict access to abortion by targeting specific areas on a 'piece-by-piece' basis (2020, p. 76). As McGuinness (2015) shows, the approach of making abortion inaccessible, rather than directly ban it, has now become a dominant strategy. This can include, as the *White Bill* did, seeking to increase regulations on service providers, a strategy which in the US is often now referred to as TRAP laws – Targeted Regulation of Abortion Providers (Medoff, 2012).

The *White Bill* passed the second reading in the House of Commons with a high majority, but a low turnout of MPs (Dee, 2020; Marsh & Chambers, 1981), but it ultimately failed to become law. As its introduction was closely linked to the 'abuses' reported in the media, it was fatally undermined when the authors of *Babies for Burning* were unable to produce evidence to support their allegations (Dee, 2020). In addition, the *White Bill* was still in progress when the *General Medical Council* dismissed the cases against doctors named in the book, with libel cases then ensuing (Dee, 2020). Whilst the anti-abortion groups lobbied in favour of the Bill, and *SPUC* had grown considerably in numbers since its formation a few years previously (Marsh & Chambers, 1981), this was not sufficient to overturn medical support for abortion or the evidence in the *Lane Committee Report* (Dee, 2020; Marsh & Chambers, 1981). Importantly, whilst the stated intent was to 'reform', during the debates it was clear that its supporters were often against abortion completely, and this is also likely to have reduced support (Francome, 2004). The unsuccessful passage of the *White Bill* illustrates the difficulties that anti-abortion groups have in finding convincing evidence to support legal change, particularly in the context of a society that has widespread generalised support for abortion.

There were other notable attempts to restrict abortion after the *White Bill*. In 1979, Corrie introduced another complex bill, targeting a number of elements, but including a considerable reduction to the time limit for abortion and abolishing the 'statistical' clause. The latter, which states that abortion can be carried out if continuing the pregnancy is a greater risk, was introduced into the *1967 Act* by those opposed to abortion, without realising that as abortion is almost always safer, this effectively gave approval to all abortions (Dee, 2020). The complexity of the *Corrie Bill* caused difficulties in making it workable, despite being given a significant amount of time in Parliament, but Corrie refused to drop parts of the bill in order to help its progress (Dee, 2020). Moreover, like the *White Bill* before it, it illustrated that to be successful, anti-abortion law change would require MPs to compromise their absolutist stance of completely banning abortion in favour of introducing restrictions to limit some abortions, something that many found difficult at this time (Dee, 2020).

The debate over whether to hold an absolutist stance or not also led to divisions between anti-abortion activists. When *SPUC* was formed, some of its supporters were not wholly against abortion but felt that the legal position prior to the *Abortion Act* was sufficient to permit all 'necessary' abortions (Dee, 2020; Hindell & Simms, 1971). This position was debated in the early years and led to some former *SPUC* members forming a separate organisation, *Life*. *Life*, who claim to be one of the first anti-abortion organisations to use that term, started what we would now call a crisis pregnancy centre (CPC).[3] They developed services for women, including housing, in order to encourage them to continue with a pregnancy. *Life*, and other CPCs still operate, but the widespread availability and general public acceptance of abortion means that they have never developed to the extent that they have in other nations. As Dee (2020) argues, whilst the claim was that *SPUC* and *Life* were complementary in their aims, with one focused on lobbing and the other on support, they did split the available resources. In later years, however, *SPUC* have adopted the same absolutist stance as *Life*, and *Life* started to support parliamentary attempts to restrict, rather ban abortion completely (Dee, 2020). Neither of these changes seemed to make any significant difference to British public support for abortion.

Both the unsuccessful *White* and *Corrie* bills came during a period of intense feminist activity, encapsulated in the *Women's Liberation Movement*. Since the 1970s, support for abortion has been embedded in the trade union movement, and other forms of left-wing organising (Orr, 2017). For example, during the campaign against the *Corrie Bill*, trade union branches across the country passed motions condemning the *Bill*, and a march supported by the *Trade Union Congress* in 1979 was one of the biggest pro-choice marches ever to be held (Hoggart, 2000). Importantly, this meant that access to abortion was, and still is, routinely positioned as only one aspect of broader campaigns to improve women's lives, such as equal pay, and access to childcare. Indeed, from its inception *ALRA* had drawn attention to inequality as a central reason for abortion reform and the book published by founder member Alice Jenkins *Law for the Rich* (1960) was said to have influenced the passing of the *1967 Abortion Act*.

So whilst there were single-issue organisations focused on abortion, such as the *National Abortion Campaign* formed in 1975 and the *Scottish Abortion Campaign* in 1980, their understanding of abortion was developed in a context of feminism, and left-wing political organisations (Hay, 2020; Hoggart, 2000). In addition, the calls for reproductive rights and promoting reproductive choice was also very much embedded in an understanding of the UK welfare state, and therefore included the responsibility of governments to support the formation of families (Himmelweit, 1988; Hoggart, 2000; McBride Stetson, 2001). It is important not to underestimate the lack of proper attention to some areas of inequality, particularly racism, within pro-choice communities. Nevertheless, it does highlight the importance of remembering that discursively, terms such as abortion 'rights' or 'choice' are embedded in the cultural context, and can vary even within majority of English-speaking nations. This is also an important issue for anti-abortion framing. For example, the term 'abortion industry', implying a profit-driven enterprise, has very little traction in the UK, as abortion is now largely provided free through the *NHS* (Lowe & Page, 2019a, 2019b).

---

[3]Field notes at Life Ignite event 25/6/2016.

The *Alton Bill*, introduced in 1987, followed a similar pattern to the *White* and *Corrie* Bills in terms of its defeat. Like his predecessors, Alton was a committed Christian, and his religious beliefs underpinned his opposition to abortion. It was a much more restricted bill, focusing specifically on the time limit for abortions, and it was hoped that this would mean it would be more likely to succeed (Dee, 2020). Notably too, in all three bills (*White, Corrie, Alton*) those opposing abortion adopted feminist language, claiming to speak for women, arguing that the abortion restrictions they were advocating were in women's interests (Amery, 2015, 2020). These debates reinforced the medicalised legal framework to abortion, positioning women as potential victims (Amery, 2015; Sheldon, 1997). However, unlike the debates over the *Abortion Act*, doctors were often portrayed as 'unethical villains who prey on vulnerable women' (Amery, 2015, p. 564). This framing actually undermines the central working premise of the *Abortion Act*, in which doctors are positioned as trusted professionals who have the decision-making power (Amery, 2015, 2020; Lowe, 2019). Although there was general support for reducing the existing time limit from 28 weeks, their tactic of making the bill more restrictive led to defeat. Dee (2020) argues that the *Alton Bill* debate and defeat forced anti-abortion groups to reconsider the tactics needed for legal change. The time limit was eventually reduced in 1990 in the *Human Fertilization and Embryology Act* to 24 weeks for most abortions, but it also clarified the exceptions when this limit did not apply, such as a significant threat to women's life or severe foetal anomaly. As most abortions post-24 weeks take place for these reasons, and by then, abortion clinics were only licensed up to 24 weeks, there was little impact on services (Isaac, 1994). The anti-abortion groups had campaigned for a more substantial change to the time limit, but there was little support for this. Moreover, the sending of plastic foetuses to MPs during the passage of the bill was widely seen 'as a crass and inappropriate lobbying tactic' (Isaac, 1994, p. 178). Thus the only legal success of the anti-abortion movement since 1967 failed to have any significant impact.

Dee (2020) argues that the failure of the *Alton Bill*, and the general support for abortion during the passing of the *Human Fertilization and Embryology Act*, led to recriminations within the anti-abortion movement, with some later seeing their support for the *Alton Bill* as a mistake. As Dee argues:

> In short, 1990 was a turning point for the English anti-abortion movement, and represented to many observers the overall failure of the movement to secure even the least controversial elements of their agenda, according to one former SPUC associate, it was nothing less than a 'fiasco'.
>
> (2020, p. 147)

Whilst this was not the end of attempts in Parliament to change the law, it did lead to some in the movement to adopt different strategies.

A Brief Turn to Militancy

In the US, the lack of progress in restricting abortion through political means led to the emergence of more militant anti-abortion groups. *Operation Rescue*, formed in the late 1980s, was a militant anti-abortion movement who sought to close clinics through blockades (Youngman, 2003). Anti-abortion groups in Britain were likewise encouraged to adopt militant tactics, and whilst there were some incidences, they were nothing like the scale that took place elsewhere. A Catholic priest, Fr. James Morrow, was a key figure in the organisation of *Rescues UK* (Isaac, 1994). In 1990, Fr. Morrow and a couple of others were convicted of assaulting the pregnant manager of a clinic in Birmingham during a small demonstration (The Independent, 1990). Other places targeted over the next couple of years include Stockport, Leeds, Liverpool and London. Our analysis of newspaper coverage of the UK rescues suggests the highest numbers of people attending was around 40, with most other occasions having far fewer participating. In 1993, a small number of American anti-abortion activists arrived from the US to reinvigorate the British rescue movement, working with Fr. Morrow (Hohmeyer, 2005; Isaac, 1994). Whilst this generated a lot of interest and concern, some of the reports at the time suggest that the anti-abortion activists were outnumbered by the journalists who had come to cover their actions (Braid, 1993). Moreover, Don Treshman, the American leader, was arrested shortly after his arrival and received a deportation order, cancelling his right to remain in the UK (Isaac, 1994). Both major UK anti-abortion groups, *SPUC* and *Life*, denounced the 'rescues' (Isaac, 1994). Whilst there was considerable disruption to clinic services on the days they were present, there were only small numbers involved, and abortion clinics reported that women seeking abortion rebooked for other days (Cohen, 1993).

The greatest impact of more militant action took place in NI, despite the fact that the law was much more restrictive than the rest of the UK. As NI was excluded from the *1967 Abortion Act* due to the devolved government in power at the time, the legal framework until 2019 was the *1861 OAPA* and the *Bourne* judgement. Due to these restrictions, most women had to travel to England to access abortion. The *Ulster Pregnancy Advisory Association* (*UPAA*) was founded to offer advice, support and counselling to NI women seeking abortion. It had a small office and a number of counsellors in different parts of the province. *Precious Life*, formed in 1996 and specific to NI, began to target *UPAA*, and other referral organisations. Their actions included the picketing of the *UPAA* counsellors' homes with leaflets and graphic pictures of abortion (Birchard, 1999). In July 1999, there was an arson attack on their Belfast office, and *UPAA* decided to close (Birchard, 1999). Whilst *Precious Life* denied any involvement in the arson attack, they stated that the closure was a 'victory' for their tactics of direct action (O'Connor, 1999). *Precious Life* has continued to hold regular protests outside other organisations that support or refer for abortions. However, whilst there are still some aggressive protests across the UK, particularly in NI, the organised militant strategy had largely disappeared by the beginning of the twenty-first century.

Framing around Risks and Harms

In recent years, anti-abortion groups have framed their opposition to abortion using frames of health, risk and harm. Whilst there is no room here to document all their unsuccessful attempts to restrict abortion in the last couple of decades, we will use three examples to illustrate the issues. The first two examples, attempts to bring in mandated counselling and a ban on sex-selection abortion, both occurred at Westminster. The third example is the use of disability rights arguments in NI. All three examples show the ways in which the language of risk and harm is deployed in their claimsmaking, including constructing specific 'victims' of abortion. As we will illustrate, the adoption of claims about risk and harm has become central to moral regulation movements, thus it is unsurprising that the anti-abortion movement utilises these tactics.

As Hoggart (2015) has illustrated, there were attempts in 2006 and 2007 to amend the *1967 Abortion Act* to mandate abortion counselling, both of which failed to become law. In 2012, an amendment was put forward to the *National Health Service and Social Care Bill* to introduce 'independent' abortion counselling – removing the provision from abortion service providers and making women undergo counselling elsewhere. It is important to point out there is a significant difference between non-directive decision-support to ensure informed consent, and therapeutic counselling about abortion. Whilst the former should be available to all, there is little evidence that the latter is needed universally (Hoggart, 2015). These attempts to change the law were not the first time the issue of counselling was debated. As Hoggart (2015) points out, the Lane Committee (1974) had considered the issue, as had the *Department of Health and Social Security* in the 1980s. However, as we mentioned in the introduction, in the 1990s there were increasing claims being made by anti-abortion organisations about abortion being harmful to women's mental health (Lee, 2003), and this, led to anti-abortion campaigners arguing for more counselling before abortion (Amery, 2020; Hoggart, 2015).

As Amery (2020) points out, in Parliamentary debates over counselling, those arguing for the change often positioned themselves as both caring and progressive. They argue that the 'new' evidence about the impact of abortion meant that women needed to be informed of the harms in order to make better 'choices'. Their arguments adopted feminist language but also blamed feminists for the plight of women's suffering (Amery, 2020). In these debates, the moral argument is not made about abortion itself; instead it is constructed around the harm from both abortion service providers and the feminist movement for encouraging abortions. Moreover, women are positioned as potential 'victims' of abortion, and this problem is solved by the 'progressive' change of mandating obstacles to abortion access (Amery, 2020).

This emphasis on 'risks', 'harms' and 'victims' by anti-abortion campaigners is in line with broader shifts within moral regulation movements. A moral regulation movement is one that seeks to end an immoral issue by focusing on a moralised subject and moralised object using a moralised discourse (Hunt, 1999). In this case, abortion is deemed to be the immoral issue, and women are positioned as the moralised subject whose behaviour can be changed to 'save' the foetus, the moralised object. As Hunt (1999) argues, moral politics have undergone an important shift in terms of the way that moral issues are campaigned on. Whereas previously, ideas of 'sin' or 'vice' were often used to frame the issue, this has shifted to claims about social harms, health and risk, with a specific construction of 'victims'. Common to many moral reform movements is an imagined golden past where the 'social evil' did not occur, and thus retraditionalisation can be a central feature of the movement's aims. Retraditionalisation, Hunt (1999) suggests, involves finding new justifications to reintroduce traditional values, but the values may have been reconfigured for current society, for example, an emphasis on essentialised gender roles that accept women working outside the home. Moral regulation movements also often have an emphasis on self-help – so individuals are encouraged to reject the 'immoral' path (Hunt, 1999). As Hunt (drawing on Valverde) argues:

> Moral regulation (…) relies less on theology, but is more likely to employ the language of self-health, nutrition, medical science and proliferating forms of expertise ranging from modern quackery to high science. It remains profoundly moral in that its target is focused on the ethical subjectivity of the individual.
>
> (1999, p. 216)

In the case of abortion counselling, the discourse of harm is taken from claims about ongoing mental health issues constructed through the invention of post-abortion syndrome (PAS), which, as Lee (2003) has shown, is, in Hunt's (1999) terms, 'modern quackery'. It rests on the idea that women are 'naturally' mothers, and that it is broader unwelcome changes in society, such as feminism, that has led them away from their traditional path.

Similar processes can also be seen in the second example to attempt to outlaw sex-selection abortions, although in this case the 'experts' have shifted away from ideas about health, to a focus on those with 'knowledge' of abuse. Concerns about sex-selection abortion began in 2012, following a newspaper story that service providers were 'illegally' carrying out sex-selection abortions. As Lee (2017) points out, the medical framing of British abortion law is silent on 'reasons' for abortion, relying instead on a 'good faith' judgement by doctors about physical or mental health. In 2015, an anti-abortion MP tried to specifically outlaw sex-selection abortions through an amendment to the *Serious Crime Bill* in the name of promoting gender equality. This move was aligned with a new campaign, *Stop Gendercide*, which appeared shortly before the introduction of the amendment in Parliament. *Stop Gendercide* was positioned as an expert feminist movement, headed by South Asian women, and linked the harms of sex-selection abortion, forced marriage and Female Genital Mutilation (Amery, 2020; Lee, 2017). As Amery argues 'the claims about the threatened female foetus seem to be yet another permutation that abortion harms women' (2020, p. 167). Moreover, the arguments explicitly drew on assumptions of South Asian women as passive, repressed and in need of saving by (white) Western feminists who the anti-abortion people hoped would support the legal change (Anitha & Gill, 2018). Pivotal to defeat of this suggested amendment was the statements made by other Black and Asian women's organisations who argued that criminalising abortion-seeking would not protect women (Amery, 2020; Anitha & Gill, 2018).

Alongside claims about gender equality, the anti-abortion movement has also positioned itself as supporters of disability rights. As Amery (2020) has shown, they argue that the specific clause around abortions for foetal anomaly after 24 weeks is a form of disability discrimination. As previously mentioned, the NI Assembly failed to change the law on abortion leading to the UK Parliament legislating change in 2019. Even though it was clear that they were obliged to bring in an abortion service, to date, Stormont have neglected to do so (Bloomer, McNeilly, & Pierson, 2020; Sheldon, O'Neill, Parker, & Davis, 2020). They have, however, made time to debate restricting abortion in the province, even though they had not commissioned any services. At the time of writing, the *Severe Fetal Impairment Abortion (Amendment) Bill* is at the Committee stage in the Assembly. It proposes restricting abortions for foetal anomaly, even though the proposed changes would most likely be deemed a breach of human rights. In the speeches, people with disabilities are positioned as 'victims' of the harm caused by the discriminatory abortion laws, but they are also positioned as experts on the issue.

These examples illustrate the different framings used by anti-abortion campaigners as a moral regulation movement. Whilst the issues of counselling, sex-selection and disability discrimination are different, they all seek to frame a moral objection to abortion through ideas of harm, risk or health, and adopt specific 'expertise' to support their aim of ending the immoral behaviour of abortion. They seek to adopt 'plausible' moral discourses that are displaced from their main intention, in order to bring about retraditionalisation (Hunt, 1999). In this case, they attempted, unsuccessfully so far, to use the piece-by-piece strategy of making abortion inaccessible rather than directly challenging it (McGuiness, 2015). Moreover, the narratives were framed around 'secular' issues, despite anti-abortion activism being largely motivated by religious beliefs.

Summary

This chapter has outlined the history of opposition to abortion law in the UK, how the *1967 Abortion Act* came into being, and how it was understood in relation to reproductive rights. We have also outlined the different circumstances in NI, where there has been an absence of abortion provision until very recently. Ultimately, abortion in the UK is typically understood as a medical, rather than a moral issue, although many of the actors who continue to oppose abortion are motivated by religion. In this history, we can see a number of specific narratives about abortion, and abortion service providers, that reoccur frequently in abortion debates today, such the 'illusory' and 'avaricious' motivations of those providing abortion. The chapter also illustrates the importance of situating opposition to abortion within its specific cultural context. Whilst strategies and tactics of the anti-abortion movement cross borders, the impact will be shaped by local circumstances. Importantly too, we have shown that from the medieval period onwards, objections to abortion were often framed around gendered ideas about motherhood being 'natural' for women, in line with specific Christian beliefs. This then leads to abortion being constructed as a risk to wider society as it challenges ideas about traditional family life. These beliefs continue today and will be examined in the following chapters.

Chapter 3

Understanding Anti-Abortion Activism as Lived Religion

Introduction

This chapter will outline the conceptual framework of the book, which combines understandings from the sociology of religion and reproductive health. The activities of anti-abortion activists take place in a cultural context in which motherhood is sacralised. It is expected that women will make sacrifices for the benefit of actual or future children. As we will show, Christianity also has specific understandings about motherhood being natural for women and this shapes the worldview of anti-abortion activists. Yet anti-abortion activists configure motherhood in slightly different ways, going much further in the sacrificial demands that they place on women. Firstly, this chapter explains the lived religion approach that we have taken to explore the everyday practices of anti-abortion activism. Given that anti-abortion activists make particular distinctions between the sacred and profane, we will explain how conceptual understandings of the sacred and profane help us to explain the everyday faith practices of United Kingdom (UK) anti-abortion activism. Using Lynch's (2012a, 2012b) notion of sacred forms, we will articulate how ultra-sacrificial motherhood becomes the sacred commitment of anti-abortion activists, whilst also highlighting the contrasting sacred commitments of pro-choice counterdemonstrators. The chapter will then move on to consider materiality and spatiality as important concepts in understanding anti-abortion activism.

Conceptualising Lived Religion

The concept of lived religion foregrounds the everyday practices of religion. It focuses on how the faith lives of individuals are constructed through everyday practices, rather than relying on doctrinal understandings and/or interpretations of religious leaders (Ammerman, 2014; McGuire, 2008; Orsi, 2007). At its heart, lived religion demonstrates the ways in which faith positions are created through ongoing negotiation. Participants create their own meanings from the religious resources available to them, rather than unconsciously following the rules and guidance set out within a specific religious tradition. Importantly in this context, using a lived religion perspective allows us to understand the complexity of the

Anti-Abortion Activism in the UK, 37–51
Copyright © 2022 Pam Lowe and Sarah-Jane Page
Published under exclusive licence by Emerald Publishing Limited
doi:10.1108/978-1-83909-398-220221005

anti-abortion movement, including, for example, how ideas such as science and human rights are reinterpreted through a religious lens, and how identities are embodied through engaging in prayer practices outside abortion clinics (Lowe & Page, 2019b; Page & Lowe, 2021a).

The everyday, embodied practices of religion are important because it is through them that individuals experience and express their faith and create meaningful lives. Practices include both those which are explicitly tied with 'religious' practices such as prayer, using rosary beads or reading the Bible, but also accommodates more general practices, where 'spiritual' feelings are generated, including activities such as gardening, walking or feeling awe at the top of a mountain (Ammerman, 2014; McGuire, 2008). Lived religion therefore encompasses a wide variety of practices, including some that may be described as 'spiritual' rather than religious. Indeed, as McGuire (2008) points out, the ordinary, embodied, day-to-day practices which constitute faith explain how people 'do' religion. Lived religion challenges traditional understandings of religion as fundamentally cerebral. Whilst this approach has allowed a broader sociological understanding of religion to be explored, much of the interest to date has been on positive and affirmative practices that are meaningful for individuals. There has been less attention on the broader outcomes and consequences of lived religion practices that might cause upset and anxiety either to the individuals themselves or to others who do not share their particular understandings or practices of faith (see Ganzevoort & Sremac, 2017 as an exception). This latter element is particularly important for examining practices of anti-abortion activism. As McGuire argues:

> There are darker elements in most official religious traditions, as well as in their relatively unregulated, but parallel, popular religious traditions. History provides plenty of examples of religious beliefs and practices honing people's fears and hatreds, resulting in witch hunts, pogroms, crusades, massacres, and enslavements of peoples. Contemporary spiritualities of hatred and violence can be and have been developed – with a vast repertoire of religious and quasi-religious rituals, because historically rituals have long been associated with power and violence (...) We need to allow for the very real possibility that just as there are creative spiritualities, there may also be destructive spiritualities. Just as some people may seek spiritual practices that bring their lives into a greater sense of harmony, beauty, peace, and compassion, others may engage in practices that develop a purer hatred of the Other and that literally, as well as figuratively, embody violence and aggression.
>
> (2008, p. 117)

McGuire (2008) uses the example of *Ku Klux Klan* ceremonies to outline the way that embodied lived religion practices can include racism and hatred, ritualised through particular material objects such as clothing and burning crosses.

Meanwhile both Ammerman (2014) and Orsi (2007) in their account of lived and everyday approaches to religion, specifically reference the more militant tactics of the anti-abortion movement and how this is negatively impactful on others. Orsi (2007), for example, speaks of aggressive tactics such as thrusting rosary beads in women's faces. Indeed, at the extreme end of anti-abortion activism, emotional abuse, intimidation, murders, vandalism and firebombing have occurred. The United States (US) has seen intense forms of anti-abortion activism, with thousands of incidents reported each year including obstruction, trespassing, vandalism, online abuse, as well as extreme actions of intimidation, such as stalking, and the murders of healthcare providers (Cohen & Connon, 2016; National Abortion Federation, 2019). As outlined in Chapter 2, in the past, the UK has also experienced some extreme tactics, including an assault by a Catholic priest on a healthcare worker. Murders have also taken place elsewhere, such as the shooting of an abortion clinic security guard in Australia in 2001 (Allanson, 2006). Whilst extreme anti-abortion actions such as these are routinely condemned by faith leaders, there are clear connections between everyday anti-abortion faith practices and extreme actions. As Allanson (2006) highlights, whilst the gunman who murdered the security guard was not regularly outside the Melbourne clinic, security was deployed due to the persistent harassment and aggression by anti-abortion activists, including death threats to staff. Moreover, the day after the shooting, they returned, standing outside the gates with their anti-abortion messages.

Hence, in order to understand the complexity of the motivations, beliefs and practices of the anti-abortion activists, it is important to consider the broader cultural context and the day-to-day religious practice of those involved in anti-abortion activism in public spaces. We hope to shed new light on the sacred and profane commitments of the movement, and how this is constituted in relation to the public space outside the abortion clinic.

Sacred/Profane Commitments

Antonnen (2000) outlines how the sacred has been deployed in various ways by scholarship including sociology, anthropology and theology. As Antonnen's overview demonstrates, the sacred is a slippery concept which can be applied to all manner of social elements – the emotional, material, ideational, behavioural, the personal, the temporal and the spatial. Durkheim's (1915) theory of the sacred and profane has been highly influential in the sociology of religion, which understands the sacred as clearly distinct from, yet dependent on, the profane, with the purpose being the fostering of social bonds and boundary-marking of groups. Here, the sacred is understood as a social construct and sacred classifications are therefore subject to change. Whilst traditionally, the sacred has been exclusively associated with religious objects, ideas, persons, spaces and festivals, the association of the sacred solely with religion has been critiqued (Antonnen, 2000; Demerath III, 2007; Lynch, 2012a). Religious configurations of the sacred typically relate to a god and/or the transcendent, whereas non-religious sacred commitments can depict life principles such as love, freedom, equality and justice, whereby 'People participate in sacred-making activities and processes of signification according to paradigms given by the belief systems to which they are committed' (Antonnen, 2000, p. 281). In a society where the status of religion is changing, the notion of the sacred equally needs to be reviewed, in order to understand the various ways in which the sacred gets constructed, and how sacred meaning-making is generated (Lynch, 2012a). As Lynch argues, despite Durkheim's concerns with the demise of the sacred when traditional forms of religiosity wane, contemporary society is replete with sacred engagements, such as equality, human rights and justice. In a pluralistic society, there is clearly a need for the religious and the sacred to be decoupled in order to understand the various sacred commitments of individuals and communities.

Here we deploy Lynch's (2012a) understanding of the sacred, an encompassing definition that does not exclusively tie the sacred to the religious; indeed, Lynch's starting point is that the sacred and the religious are two different things; the religious can take sacred forms, but not always. Lynch (2012a) discusses sacred forms, which are akin to sacred commitments that are ideational – for example, nature, the care of children, church authority. In contemporary society, there is not a singular sacred form; instead, various sacred forms co-exist – some complement each other; others exist in conflict. As Lynch argues:

> Sacred forms consist of specific symbols, as well as patterns of thought, emotions, and actions grounded in the body, which recursively reproduce the sacrality of that particular sacred form, and draw together social collectivities around these shared forms of thinking, feeling and acting. Sacred forms are historically contingent, in terms of both their content and their structure. (...) the nature and operation of power in relation to other sacred forms also has a significant bearing on the extent to which the sacrality is widely recognized and it becomes a powerful motive force in social life.
>
> (2012a, pp. 133–134)

Lynch therefore takes a sacred form – such as nature or childcare – as the starting point. Underpinning a sacred form are emotional ties, material objects, influential individuals, constituted through various spaces and temporalities. This definition therefore offers precision regarding what elements comprise sacred forms, as well as recognising their socially constructed nature; it is recognised that sacred forms change over time.

The relevance of the sacred to this particular book relates to how the sacred is operationalised by anti-abortion groups and activists, and the role the sacred plays in the boundary-marking between themselves and others. In the enactment of living out their religion, the sacred is deployed as a means of heightening and framing their activities, to give them godly significance. As we shall go on to examine, anti-abortion activists adopt a strictly religious worldview. For them, God endorses a rigid moral code, refracted through church teaching. This is a highly traditional and conservative understanding of Christianity, typically Roman Catholic in nature, and places exacting controls on sexuality. Sex should take place only within heterosexual marriage, and that marriage should be open to the potential of conception, without using artificial contraceptive means (Geiringer, 2019; Miller, 2014). Evangelical anti-abortion activists are less focused on contraception but they abide by the same strict controls on sexual behaviour. Whether evangelical or Catholic, the anti-abortion activists constitute Woodhead's (2013) 'moral minority' – individuals within a faith tradition who are the most conservative. It has been clearly demonstrated that Christians in general tend not to endorse these very strict moral codes. For example, many Catholics who have access to it will use contraception (Geiringer, 2019; Harris, 2013). However, because of their particular conservative stance, Catholic anti-abortion activists are more likely to follow Catholic teaching very strictly. As Jordan argues,

> Catholic sexual morality is founded upon the 'nature' of the 'human person', (…) upon the 'norms' or 'precepts of the natural law', upon principles contained in the 'divine, eternal objective and universal law' of God.
>
> (2000, p. 26)

This idea of natural law is therefore understood as being unchanging and applicable to the whole of humanity. As Curran (1988) argues, the idea that Catholic moral teaching is rational and universal allows it to be positioned as applying to all human beings, regardless of any faith position. This is one reason that many activists deem it appropriate to attempt to impose their beliefs about abortion onto others. As Peters (2018) explains, the natural law understanding of abortion is that:

> …elective abortion interrupts the natural progression of a pregnancy. Natural law also believes that pregnancy is the natural and right outcome of sexual activity, that sexual activity is only moral when located within a marriage, and that people engaging in sexual activity ought to welcome any possible pregnancy and child as part of God's intention for their life and the world.
>
> (Peters, 2018, p. 129)

The activists' sacred commitments are very much derived from traditional understandings of the sacred as connected to church hierarchy and authority. Because of how they understand their behaviour as religiously rooted, anti-abortion activists automatically assume that their activism is sacredly endorsed by God; this connectivity to a higher power makes a claim to transcendental authority. Such sacred claimsmaking – where the traditional authority of God is channelled through the apparatus of the church – aligns with traditional understandings forged between Christianity and the sacred, and is a form of sacred connectivity that has led to the erroneous assumption that the sacred is always tied up with the religious (Lynch, 2012a).

This model of religiosity based on rigid authority and conservative scriptural interpretations is falling out of favour, evidenced by the higher numbers of individuals claiming no religious identity (see Introduction). The idea that the church has inalienable moral authority has been seriously challenged, not only in terms of individuals engaging with religion differently, and subjectively living out their religiosity on their own moral terms (Heelas & Woodhead, 2005), but trust in the authority of various religious institutions has been eroded through the shockwaves caused by the various abuses enabled through religious institutions. As Lynch (2012a) argues, whereas the authority of the church as a sacred form has historically been dominant and wielded much power, in contemporary society, its saliency is questioned and other sacred claims – such as human rights and the care of children – act as challengers. As Lynch's (2012a) work demonstrates, and in line with the perspectives of lived religion scholars such as McGuire (2008), lived religion – and the sacred commitments that comprise lived religion – should not be simplistically viewed as good, wholesome or benign. Instead, adhering to one's sacred commitments can result in highly negative outcomes, such as the aforementioned harassment and even murder enacted by anti-abortion activists in other locations. As Lynch argues,

> To claim that harmful expressions of sacred commitments are simply inauthentic performances of the sacred form neglects aspects of it that allows for such destructive performances. Sacred traditions cannot therefore be assumed to be unambiguously good, but are complex phenomena that require careful cultivation.
>
> (2012a, p. 130)

This recognition of complexity therefore becomes highly applicable when analysing the entanglements of religious motivations and practices amongst anti-abortion activists. As we shall see, they understand their actions only in positive terms; they understand themselves as doing God's work, and this is seen as inherently good and worthy. Lynch's (2012a, 2012b) conceptualisation of the sacred allows us to understand them as having a sacred commitment, which they invest with much positive meaning, but it does not mean that, sociologically, the outcomes are beneficial. As the Introduction outlined, their actions have a significant negative impact for clinic staff, those accessing abortion services, and local residents, with there being broader public consensus for the enactment of bufferzones, particularly around clinics with heightened and sustained activism.

Ultra-Sacrificial Motherhood as a Sacred Commitment

Traditional sacred forms are maintained through the approach the anti-abortion activists take in relation to gender roles; in particular, the status accorded motherhood. More generally, ideas about 'good motherhood' are still highly influential in the construction of gender norms, despite fundamental changes in gender roles in the UK. Women are still expected to make the 'right' choices about their fertility, whether that is through preventing pregnancy at the 'wrong' times or refraining from consuming certain foods and drinks. Within contemporary post-feminist discourses, motherhood is still seen as the most desirable outcome for women; having a child is posited as the object of women's happiness (Millar, 2017). As Lowe (2016) has shown, motherhood norms underpin ideas about what women should and should not do with their bodies, whether or not they are pregnant or have children. The central feature of motherhood norms is the idea of maternal sacrifice, that women, regardless of their personal preferences, should always put the welfare of actual or future children first:

> The idea of maternal sacrifice, an often embodied requirement that appears to arise from a natural instinct to protect the young, has an important symbolic function in ensuring these social relationships are maintained. Maternal sacrifice as a symbol is used to both reassert gendered relationships and to promote a broader sense of community order. The good mother is always positioned in opposition to the other/bad/nominal mother who is a danger to the reproduction of the community. Women who fail to feel the right emotions endanger not just their developing foetus, but also the moral order.
>
> (Lowe, 2016, p. 203)

Maternal sacrifice has therefore operated as a broader sacred value at the societal level. This can be constituted through religious discourses, but is not singularly rooted through a religious positioning. Maternal sacrifice has a long history in governing women's bodies, but the norms of 'good motherhood' change over time (Lowe, 2016). In the current era, understandings of intensive motherhood are often central to the working of maternal sacrifice, with child-centred care by mothers seen as essential (Hays, 1996; Lowe, 2016). Intensive motherhood is entwined with risk consciousness (Lee, 2014; Lowe, 2016). As Lee (2014) has argued, risk consciousness operates through shifting the definition of risk from a balance of possibility to an issue of concern. She argues that it incorporates moral concerns, operates at both individual and generalised levels and is clearly linked to the surveillance of family life. In reproductive terms, risk consciousness often operates through the ways in which different reproductive options are developed, articulated and presented to women, often with a moral positioning related to their 'suitability' for motherhood (Lowe, 2016).

In the area of abortion, the legal and social framing of some abortions as acceptable, and others as less acceptable or problematic, even by those who support abortion, relates to notions of good motherhood. Those who are culturally positioned as potentially 'bad mothers', often women in marginalised positions, can be seen as responsible for electing to terminate a pregnancy, due to judgements made regarding their mothering capacity. In contrast, having no 'good' reason for abortion is stigmatised (Kumar, Hessini, & Mitchell, 2009). Moreover, as Millar (2017) argues, when those who support abortion frame it as a difficult, but necessary choice, they are drawing on a maternalistic position where maternal desires can be achieved through necessary abortions. This overlaps with the notions of maternal sacrifice used by those opposed to abortion. For them, women should always continue with a pregnancy, regardless of the personal cost (Ginsburg, 1989; Lowe, 2016). This is particularly evident in the valorising of women with serious health issues who continue with a pregnancy even when the outcome is, or could be, their own death (Lowe, 2016). This anti-abortion position is rooted in ideas about the naturalness of motherhood.

Ideas about maternal sacrifice have been entwined with religious discourses, particularly within Christianity. For example, in 2015, Pope Francis reaffirmed the idea that altruism and sacrifice by women as mothers is of societal importance as it provides a challenge to self-centred individualism which he argues is detrimental to society (Page, 2016). Yet as Page (2016) points out, whilst the ideal of maternal sacrifice is seen as a sacred endeavour, the everyday practical work of caring for children is usually not seen in these terms. The sacredness is thus in the *idea* of the role, rather than in the mundane activities that it consists of, for which mothers obtain little credit (Page, 2016).

As Llewellyn (2016), amongst others, have argued, the ideology of motherhood in Christianity is embedded in scripture, ritual and doctrine. There is a strong expectation for women to have children regardless of the broader changes which have reshaped women's lives (Llewellyn, 2016). Llewellyn argues that:

> From the biblical call to 'Be fruitful and multiply' (Gen. 1:28), the declaration that 'women will be saved through childbirth' (1 Tim. 2.15), to the understanding in Roman Catholic teaching that motherhood is the 'fundamental contribution that the Church and humanity expect from women' (*Evangelium Vitae*, para. 19), the normative message for lay women is that they are 'supposed' to be mothers and their Christian identities are fulfilled by becoming mothers.
>
> (2016, p. 69)

Early church theologians such as Aquinas and Augustine were influential in setting out the limited role for women as wives and mothers, and this was often centred on the symbolism of the Virgin Mary (Furlong, 1991; Lloyd, 1993; Warner, 1978). These ideas are not, of course, exclusive to Christianity, but it was particularly important in why sacrificial motherhood became entrenched within Christian-majority countries. Understandings of the role of the Virgin Mary have been particularly influential in providing the ideal role for women to follow. As Warner states:

> [Mary's] purity and submissiveness and poverty became quintessential motherliness (...) she is obedient, respectful, humble, quiet, and modest, simple in her tastes and demeanour,

compliant and gentle. Even her silence in the Gospels is turned to good account, becoming an example to all women to hold their tongues.

(1978, p. 190)

The significance of Mary as the ultimate sacrificial mother is particularly important (Forna, 1998; Llewellyn, 2016; Page, 2011; Warner, 1978). Within Catholicism, she is venerated as the ideal role model for women, with the virgin birth elevating her to sexual purity, a position unobtainable for ordinary women, who by engaging in procreative heterosexual marriage as the avenue for family building forgo their esteemed virginity (Forna, 1998; Warner, 1978). Mary's virginity is positioned in opposite to Eve, who developed illicit sexual knowledge, leading to the downfall of men. These oppositional positions of purity/danger, mother/whore, sacred/profane have long provided templates for the way that women, their bodies and behaviour have been culturally interpreted, and have had a significant impact on the ways in which women are perceived (Warner, 1978). In relation to motherhood, Page (2011) argues that women are left with little room to manoeuvre; the only way to achieve the sacred position of motherhood is through sex, which is positioned as a profaning process. The valorisation of an immaculate conception thus removes Mary from this dilemma (Page, 2011). Consequently, heterosexual marriage is positioned as the only divinely ordained space for sex; women's sexual behaviour outside this framework is deemed to be illicit (Hall, 2000; Lowe & Page, 2020).

The sacred endorsement of sacrificial motherhood within the anti-abortion movement is a value that can be located in UK society more generally, and has traditionally garnered theological support. Yet whilst public opinion has combined 'good' motherhood with 'responsible' motherhood enabled through abortion access (Millar, 2017), anti-abortion activists deem abortion as in conflict with good motherhood. Their assumption is that all women are destined to be mothers; this is their sacred calling – motherhood is deemed an essentialised role that all women will ultimately excel at. As we will later demonstrate, their notion of maternal sacrifice goes much further than society values in general; women's identities are assumed to be based on passive femininity, where sexual activity for women is confined to married, heterosexual sex (Lowe & Page, 2019a, 2020), and where, explicitly in Catholicism, married couples should 'always be open to maternity' (Kamitsuka, 2019, p. 109), facilitated through a papal ban on artificial forms of contraception. Women are also required to give over their bodies, and potentially their lives, in this discourse, through accepting maternity and taking a pregnancy to term, whatever the consequences. Such ideas about motherhood are therefore very conservative and limiting, with these beliefs fostered through drawing on traditional religious teaching. The lived religious identity of anti-abortion activists is therefore invested in these understandings, which position motherhood in ultra-sacrificial terms. In short, it is not merely sacrificial motherhood, but *ultra-sacrificial motherhood* which becomes a sacred commitment for anti-abortion activists.

Pro-Choice Sacred Commitments

Anti-abortion activists retain a strong investment in residual sacred forms, which are falling out of favour more broadly in society (Lynch, 2012a). Taking an anti-abortion stance and acting on this through, for example, clinic activism, is one strategy in upholding traditional church teaching and simultaneously endorsing their sacred commitments; their lived religious identity is oriented around this positioning. Their deep moral purpose is concentrated in their understanding of abortion, which is deemed to be irreligious and sinful. Yet this castigation has been challenged by religious pro-choice activists. For example, Tom Davis (2004), an American religious leader who, prior to the legalisation of abortion, helped facilitate the *Clergy Consultation Service on Abortion* (which assisted women to obtain abortions), critiques the sacred commitments of anti-abortion activists, and their use of sacred symbols. Whilst recognising the weight accorded the alignment of religious symbols with the anti-abortion stance, Davis resituates the sacred, and instead applies it to the obtaining of reproductive justice for women. He calls this 'sacred work', endorsed through his interpretation of scripture. Like many others, he accords abortion with positively ascribed sacred meaning, and challenges how scripture and other religious symbols have been weaponised against women seeking abortion. Such an example indicates the diversity in the relationship between religion and abortion, with many counter-arguments made against situating abortion as a sin (Kamitsuka, 2019; Peters, 2018). As we saw in the Introduction, given how many religious individuals agree with access to abortion in at least some form, many religious practitioners are closer to Davis' view than the anti-abortion activists.

Like Davis (2004), the pro-choice activists encountered in this book typically deem hierarchical and traditional formations of religion as highly problematic; attempts by anti-abortion activists to impose their religious values onto others is seen as an affront on the freedom of others. Their sacred commitments differ markedly to the anti-abortion activists, and rest on the principles of bodily autonomy and individual conscience, typically derived from feminist under-standings of equality. In order to understand the conflicts between anti-abortion activists and pro-choice advocates, it is important to recognise that both groups have sacred commitments, whether they are religiously grounded or not. These sacred commitments are ultimately in conflict with each other.

Linking the Sacred to the Profane

Thus far, we have expressed the importance of the sacred as a key conceptual framing for our analysis. Yet, to understand the sacred we must also pause to consider the profane. Lynch (2012b) argues that Durkheim lacked precision regarding what the profane was, it becoming a catch-all term to encompass anything that the sacred was not. It is perhaps for this reason that the meanings of the profane have been so easily displaced so that it is more usual to encounter the sacred-secular distinction over and above the sacred-profane distinction. Indeed, some authors slide from discussing the profane in one moment to the secular in the next. So does the profane equate with the secular? No. We have already outlined that sacred commitments remain central to a society whether it professes to be religious, secular, or a mixture of both (Woodhead, 2012). Therefore, equating the profane with the secular would undermine the idea that the sacred can be equally applied to religious and secular worldviews. For our purposes here, it is really important to disentangle the sacred, profane, secular and religious.

As the Introduction outlined, UK society cannot be neatly understood in terms of being wholly religious or wholly secular, and the UK operates on a complex mixture of both religious and secular entanglements (Woodhead, 2012). Along with greater religious diversity, rising numbers of individuals no longer identify with a religious tradition. But this does not necessarily mean that religion is cast in negative terms, nor does it mean that individuals abandon the asking of existential questions or remove ritual commitments from their life (Lee, 2015). Meanwhile many social institutions are connected to religious organisations, especially the Church of England (CofE), which retains an elite positioning in relation to government, royalty and the military (Brown & Woodhead, 2016; Guest, 2007; Guest, Olson, & Wolffe, 2012; Page, 2017). The public sphere can therefore be characterised as being diverse and pluralistic, containing various sacred commitments – some of which will complement others, and some that will be in conflict (Lynch, 2012a).

Understandings of the sacred and profane therefore emerge out of this complex interchange of the secular and religious. Rather than the profane being equated with the non-sacred or the ordinary, here we follow Lynch in understanding the profane as being rooted in a visceral reaction – as a pollutant that threatens the sacred (Lynch, 2012a). Lynch deems the profane as 'moral indignation' (2012b, p. 6) – something that is grievous to our sacredly held values. For anti-abortion and pro-choice activists, what was profaning to them differed markedly. For the anti-abortion activists, their 'moral indignation' was abortion which was deemed an outrage because it was understood as the killing of a person. But there were gradations within the anti-abortion response regarding *how* this was profaning. Whilst some rooted their moral indignation in terms of it being a sin, others took this further, arguing that abortion was not merely sinful; it was evil. There was therefore a sliding scale in how the anti-abortion activists themselves understood abortion as something profaning. As we shall later see, given the saliency of gender equality as a broader societal sacred commitment, the anti-abortion activists also attempted to incorporate elements of this in their campaign, oriented around the idea that abortion was fundamentally harmful for women. This demonstrates the complex ways in which sacred forms interact, often incorporating other compelling sacred forms that come to take societal prominence (in this case, gender equality). Despite trying to integrate gender equality into their sacred commitments, anti-abortion activists were deeply suspicious of feminism itself, and this ire towards feminism was directed at the pro-choice activists who came to oppose them. The counter-demonstrators were typically labelled in profaning terms, and deemed a significant threat to their sacred cause. Meanwhile, the pro-choice activists saw any assault on the hard-won reproductive rights of women as their moral indignation. For them, the anti-abortion activists threatened their sacred commitments of women's bodily autonomy and individual conscience – anyone curtailing these rights is deemed an infringement. In other words, each group viewed the other in profaning terms. Both groups are therefore set up for collision, because both groups have different sacred-profane registers. What one group considers profane, the other considers sacred, and vice versa.

For all groups, emotion was at the heart of it; it was through emotion that sacred and profane investments were made. Like others (e.g. Ahmed, 2004; Jasper, 2018, Lupton, 1998), we are focused on what emotions 'do' rather than internal bodily feelings. As Ahmed (2004) has argued, emotions can produce collective identities which differentiate between 'them' and 'us', aligning 'us' with positive emotions, regardless of intentions. Moreover, emotions inspire and sustain social movements, including through affective commitments which are the longer-term passions – both positive and negative – of activists (Jasper, 2018). Sacred commitments can thus be understood as both shaping the aims of the anti-abortion activists, as well as providing the emotional bonds that bind the movement together. Whilst sacred commitments were elevated and lauded, and constituted through a positive emotional register, the response to the profaning elements that threatened the sacred core was visceral. Sacred commitments and profaning threats therefore generate intense emotions for both groups. Both groups cultivated particular emotive capacities internal to the group, as well as an outward-focused public display of emotion, typically created through the use of particular material objects utilised during the activism. As Lynch argues, 'sacred forms of communication (…) typically focus on specific symbols, invite people into powerful forms of emotional identification, and are made real through physical and institutional practices' (2012b, p. 11).

Materiality

Material objects play a crucial role in the study of sacred forms (Lynch, 2012a). Sacred commitments are not just reflected through material phenomena – they are constituted through those objects (Morgan, 2010). As the sacred can encompass both the religious and the non-religious, this equally means that objects become salient for both anti-abortion activists and pro-choice activists. Meanings are generated and communicated through objects, and contribute to identity-building (Lynch, 2010). But the meanings invested into material objects are not static and different meanings can be applied to the same object (Hutchings & McKenzie, 2017). As our discussion in Chapter 7 regarding rosary beads and the Virgin Mary will later show, deep contestations arise when material objects are utilised in ways in which others profoundly disagree. Whilst there is individual investment in meaning, objects are also understood in a broader cultural context; they are not blank slates upon which any meaning is possible (Lynch, 2010). Some of the objects we are considering have a deep history – for example, the recycling of well-worn pro-choice slogans such as 'My Body, My Choice', or the heightened significance of images of Our Lady of Guadalupe for Catholic anti-abortion activists. Yet new meanings are continually negotiated and generated, demonstrated through the way

Our Lady of Guadalupe (a Mexican Marian apparition) becomes a key signifier of the anti-abortion movement, her connections to Mexican nationalism downplayed, and reworked as the Patron of the Unborn. As Lynch argues,

> ...the sacred subject is encountered as a force and presence beyond the immediate lives of the individual adherent or gathered community of the faithful. (...) Sacred subjects are subject to the ways in which adherents narrate and interact with them, but sacred subjects also set conditions in which such narrations and interactions take place. This agency is not simply the property of the sacred subject, then, but emerges through the interactions between adherents and the sacred subject.
>
> (2010, pp. 50–51)

The power of the image of Our Lady of Guadalupe is therefore rooted in her history, her influential position in Mexican society, and her status as the mother of mothers, tapping into the aforementioned ultra-sacrificial motherhood espoused by anti-abortion activists. This gives Our Lady of Guadalupe prestige and authority, from which a new narrative is woven, her being the protector of the unborn, and the idea that she can influence and push forward the agenda of the anti-abortion activists. Within the anti-abortion movement, Our Lady of Guadalupe therefore takes on a life of her own; she is invested with the power to intercede on their behalf. Mary is therefore accorded great agency by Catholic anti-abortion groups.

Considering materiality therefore offers a productive way of understanding how sacred forms are demonstrated, and how it contributes to the identity-work of groups and individuals. For pro-choice activists, this may be the meanings invested in the placards displayed. For anti-abortion activists, this may orient around the foetus dolls they use, or the brooches worn depicting a pregnant Virgin Mary. Going back to our concept of lived religion, this also enhances a lived analysis of the activists we are focused on. As Bowman (2017) argues, the study of material objects is important in extending our understanding of lived religion and how religious meanings are generated. At a surface level, it may appear that only focusing on the material objects utilised by the anti-abortion activists would enable attention on lived religion, but as we shall see, it is more complicated than that, given the multifarious nature of the public sphere, and how some pro-choice activists also deployed explicit religious meanings through material objects, whether that was through the symbolism of slogans, or bringing a Bible to a counter-demonstration (see Chapter 8).

Spatial Considerations

Sacred forms are mediated spatially in specific contexts (Lynch, 2012a). As Nelson (2006) has shown, places become sacred through investment by belief and practice. This creation is interrelated with socio-political identities of those who create them, and their meanings are not stable but have to be constantly reproduced. Often, this reproduction will be to confirm and preserve the sacrality, and thus reinforce, rather than challenge, the affective commitments of those who are creating the meaning of the space. Lynch (2012a) suggests that if the affective commitments to a sacred place are questioned or challenged, this is when the sacred form can erupt into focus, through what Lynch calls 'intense identification' (2012a, p. 134). An example of this is the outrage felt by anti-abortion activists that a London abortion clinic used to be a Catholic Chapel House and still has a plaque of Christ with St Michael the Archangel on the front of the building. This perceived profanation of a previously religious site added to the contestation. The meanings and interpretations given to certain spaces will also vary enormously depending on one's subject position.

In this book, we examine how sacred forms are enacted in the public sphere, primarily outside locations where abortions take place (hospitals and clinics) and where advice about abortion is offered. We will mainly be considering moments of 'intense identification', the moments when activists demonstrate their sacred commitments in the public sphere, in the space outside the clinic. By situating their bodies strategically at abortion sites, activists stake a claim to their sacred form, and carve out that sacred space temporally and spatially, often through the use of material objects. For the duration, activists publicly make representation to their sacred form through carefully chosen practices. Anti-abortion activists view the site of the abortion clinic as an evil and deathly location where lives are extinguished. Their sacred commitment is in trying to stop women from entering this destructive space. Practices and material objects such as prayers and holy water are utilised as a means of managing their perception of the clinic space. Meanwhile, for pro-choice activists, the abortion clinic is to be protected as a sacred site, where reproductive rights are enabled. Their sacred task is to stop those entering the clinic from being harassed by the anti-abortion activists. The space outside the clinic becomes contested terrain as both groups attempt for their message to take precedence.

These contestations occur in public spaces (hospitals, GP surgeries, abortion clinics and advice centres) that are read as healthcare settings, and constituted through notions of professionalism, clinical care and medical competency, typically funded through the National Health Service (*NHS*) – which itself is a sacred form as the provision of free healthcare is a deeply held value in UK society. The location for abortion is therefore deemed a legitimate medical site in the mind of the general public. Because of the saliency of the idea that abortion is a medical decision in the UK, which is embedded in the very abortion legislation, activism outside healthcare settings becomes an unwelcome intrusion, and a profaning act against the sacrality of the *NHS*. Abortion is often not consciously thought about, due to its public silencing (Bloomer, O'Dowd, & Macleod, 2017; Hoggart, 2017; Millar, 2017), so when abortion activism is encountered in the public sphere, it is disconcerting, causing grave discomfort. Furthermore, explicitly religious displays in the public sphere are viewed with concern. Generally speaking, public forms of religiosity are often understood as needing to be mediated in a particular way, and in a controlled form, such as the way religion is 'made safe' through the medium of tourism (e.g. cathedrals – Knott, 2010). Indeed Knott (2010) notes how the self-assured idea of a secular public sphere has been challenged in recent years by greater religious diversity and pluralism. This heightens the potential for tension regarding how religion is managed in the public sphere, meaning that:

> The fact that religion is on the rise, represented by faith, and that it has breached the boundary of what was commonly deemed to be a secular public domain has raised the stakes for everyone, irrespective of their ideological orientation.
>
> (Knott, 2010, p. 34)

Anti-abortion activism – and its increased and emerging presence in many locations throughout the UK – can be understood as fitting into this type of contestation within the public sphere. Whilst ritualised expressions of religiosity such as the National Service of Remembrance at the Cenotaph are treated benignly, anything deemed radical generates anxiety. This is underpinned by a well-established understanding that religious beliefs should be privatised, hence the anxiety caused when overt forms of religiosity emerge over a topic (abortion) that people are already uncomfortable with. These antagonisms reveal pertinent details regarding how space is constituted in relation to sacred and profane commitments, in a public space that is oriented around a complex mixture of religiosity and secularity (Knott, 2010).

Summary

This chapter has outlined our conceptual framing for this book. Starting with the concept of lived religion, we understand anti-abortion activists as undertaking their own interpretation of their faith and acting according. Whilst many activists identify as Catholic, and endorse the strict papal doctrines on abortion, they are not officially or formally representing the Roman Catholic Church; indeed as we will go on to see, the activists do not necessarily generate support from their broader religious communities. Their meaning-making is personally negotiated within the boundaries of the anti-abortion community. In particular, the adoption of ultra-sacrificial motherhood is significant. Ultra-sacrificial motherhood combines the broad ideas of maternal sacrifice generally expected of women with the traditional, conservative, religious views of this moral minority. A significant frame of reference we are utilising to understand activism around abortion is Lynch's (2012a, 2012b) idea of sacred and profane commitments. Both anti-abortion and pro-choice groups have different and conflicting sacred commitments. Following Lynch, we are not aligning the sacred with the religious – rather, a sacred commitment is a deeply held value that is non-negotiable, which may be religious in nature, but not always. Because the sacred commitments of each group are fundamentally at odds, this results in contestation and antagonism in the public sphere. In the next chapter, we will begin our analysis of anti-abortion activists, starting with their worldviews and motivation for activism.

Chapter 4

The Worldviews of Anti-Abortion Activists

Introduction

This chapter unpacks the worldviews and orientations of the anti-abortion activists. Activists typically had a traditional and conservative understanding of family life, objected to what they saw as a permissive society which encouraged sexual promiscuity, and sought ultimate meaning and value in essentialised understandings of motherhood. Religious perspectives informed their understandings of abortion. Their relationship to God, and their belief that God fundamentally opposed abortion, was crucial to their activism. We will emphasise why it is the case that anti-abortion activists often seek to downplay their religious identities in relation to their activism, with science being routinely used as a means of appealing to a broader audience, but ultimately, their Christian faith is pivotal to their involvement and their perspectives.

Situating the Anti-Abortion Activists: Devout and Devoted

The majority of those involved in the anti-abortion movement were Roman Catholic and were typically drawn from its more conservative wings, patterned by highly regular church attendance, a strong commitment to papal teachings, and regular religious practice such as praying the Rosary. For example, on undertaking a survey of participants at one of the early *March for Life* (*MFL*) events in Birmingham, one of the categories we asked was how regularly participants attended church. For some, the frequency levels depicted on the questionnaire did not represent their levels of engagement; categories were duly crossed out to be replaced with 'daily', to convey their highly-engaged church attendance. Such a faith-rooted perspective is long-standing in the anti-abortion movement. As Luker's study of United States (US) anti-abortion activists in the 1980s revealed, 'The pro-life world view, notwithstanding the occasional atheist or agnostic attracted to it, is at the core one that centers around God: pro-life activists are on the whole deeply committed to their religious faith and deeply involved with it' (1984, p. 186). Before examining their perspective of God and how this related to their activism, we will firstly outline how anti-abortion activists held conservative views on family life, and believed that society in general terms had become too permissive, with sexual behaviour being at the heart of their concerns.

Anti-Abortion Activism in the UK, 53–67
Copyright © 2022 Pam Lowe and Sarah-Jane Page
Published under exclusive licence by Emerald Publishing Limited
doi:10.1108/978-1-83909-398-220221007

Opposing Permissive Society and Endorsing Traditional Gender Roles

In the United Kingdom (UK), one in three women will have an abortion during their lifetime (Stone & Ingham, 2011). Abortion is a routine and everyday feature of reproductive health. In conversation with some anti-abortion activists, this statistic can sometimes come as a shock; they themselves being unaware that the levels of abortion were so high. For example, in a conversation with Toby, Derek and George – three young devout Catholic men – they were visibly impacted by this statistic, with Toby saying, 'But to say up to one third, if it is that much, (...) it is huge'. Some anti-abortion activists are therefore unclear of the parameters of their own campaign. But rather than using such a statistic to understand abortion as an everyday matter, this bolstered their view that there was a major fault line within culture itself, with Derek saying, 'There is a mist over the culture... The culture needs to change'. The levels of abortion were connected to a permissive and promiscuous society. In a town in the North of England,[1] Kathleen, an older activist, exclaimed that 'Some women are having their fifth or sixth abortion on the National Health Service (*NHS*)'. Promiscuity was connected to the numbers of abortions taking place, though how promiscuity was defined and understood varied. Typically, activists drew upon a mythologised nostalgic past, where they believed sex took place in marriage only, and if a young woman 'got into trouble', the man would do the 'decent thing' and marry her:

> What we have seen, of course, has been this explosion of promiscuity where young people, (...) For many years, from the late 60s onwards, it's just huge increase in sexually transmitted diseases, unwanted pregnancies and of course, increasing number of abortions all the time. If people are having casual relationships, very often the lad is not going to stick around. I mean in the bad old days a man got a girl pregnant, quite often he would actually marry her! (*laughs*) That doesn't seem to apply with a lot of them anymore. I don't think that society has been improved or helped too much by throwing around the contraceptives freely, making them very easily available (Rosie interview).

The assumption here is that being in a heterosexual marriage was a protection against needing an abortion, which is clearly not the case in practice. Moreover, their perception of what promiscuity was went beyond a sex-within-marriage-only

---

[1]In order to protect the identities of anti-abortion activists, we will not specify precise locations. However, in England, we geographically distinguish between the North (pertaining to counties such as Yorkshire and Lancashire), the Midlands (pertaining to counties such as Nottinghamshire, West Midlands, Leicestershire), the East (indicating counties such as Hertfordshire and Norfolk), the South East (encompassing areas such as Greater London, Hampshire, Sussex) and the South West (including Dorset, Gloucestershire and Devon).

understanding; it also included concerns regarding the use of contraceptives. George, in interview, concurred:

> ...more marriages end up in divorce now than ever (...) it all stem [s] from responsibility, from commitment, and obviously I don't want to put it all down to the pill or a condom, but it has a massive effect on people's responsibility to life.

George rooted his identity through traditional Roman Catholic teaching, where artificial forms of contraception are not permitted (despite this, as Harris (2013) shows many Catholics ignore the 1968 papal encyclical, *Humanae Vitae*). George's view was that heterosexual marriage provided stability to enable couples to commit to having children without needing contraception, with the implicit idea that contraceptives were to blame for greater levels of promiscuity amongst the unmarried. Whilst using contraception is typically understood as demonstrating responsible management of one's sexual activity (Allen, 2005; Campo-Engelstein, 2012), here, contraceptive usage is expressed as another example of sexual permissiveness.

The typical worldview of anti-abortion activists was one which evoked traditional formulations of society, centred upon clear gender roles, with women's primary role as mothers, and men as breadwinners, underpinned by children raised in married heterosexual families. For example, Christine said 'it's the woman who becomes pregnant and has the children, who is the mother. The father has a different but equally important role'. Motherhood was understood as a special god-given vocation, upon which all women's identities were pinned, and pregnant women were already understood to be mothers – at the 2016 *MFL*, one of the participants we spoke to outlined how,

> ...abortion hurts people and it always kills, and factually, it always kills a child. So it makes a mother, a mother of her dead child. A father, a father of his dead child, and at a spiritual level, these people do not ever lose their motherhood or fatherhood.

Therefore, in this individual's mind, one's identity as a mother was cemented not at a child's birth, but at conception, indicated by referencing the foetus as a fully-formed child. Because motherhood was understood in essentialist and fundamental terms, and was accorded a sacred, god-given function, motherhood was seen as the most esteemed role a woman could fulfil (Lowe & Page, 2019a). Whilst versions of sacrificial motherhood permeate UK culture (Lowe, 2016), these narratives emphasise that the activists engage with a more heightened and intense version of sacrificial motherhood, what we call ultra-sacrificial motherhood. The lack of reflexivity regarding the everyday experiences of women led to an inability to contemplate a woman intentionally and knowingly seeking out an abortion, and, as we will discuss in further detail in Chapter 5, women were instead understood as having been duped or coerced by abortion providers (Lowe & Page, 2019a).

Centrality of God

God was central to the anti-abortion activists' orientations, and the perceived opposition of God to abortion fuelled their activism. Maintaining a good relationship with God was crucial for them. Despite there being no firm biblical prohibitions relating to abortion (Kamitsuka, 2019), there was a certainty that God was opposed to abortion, as expressed in the following quotes:

> As long as we stick on the right side, that it's not our side, it's God's side (…) Victory is ours because victory is God's, you know (Jacquie interview).

> Paula said that the biggest sin against God is to deny life (field notes, South-East).

> It's an expression of truth, really, isn't it? That I believe the Creator, God is a creator of life and only God can take it away (Fr. Paul interview).

> On the opposite side of the road, there are more signs out than I have seen before. There are six in total (…) (the first says) 'Before I formed you in the womb, I knew you. God Jer 1:5' with an ultrasound pic of a foetus sucking their thumb (field notes, South-East).

Abortion was believed to be a sin against God, and a denial of God's will and purpose. This was theologically supported through their interpretation of sacred texts. The Jeremiah 1:5 verse, quoted above, was popularly referenced to situate God as opposed to abortion. Theologians have questioned the status given to this text in anti-abortion campaigns. For example, Kamitsuka (2019) argues that this draws on a very specific theory of predestination and requires much extrapolation to imply that one knows God's will. But anti-abortion activists endorsed this scripture to imply opposition to abortion, thereby believing that by being active in one's opposition, one situated oneself as being on God's side. The need for action was also mediated through God; frequently, we were informed that God had told the activists specifically and personally that they should oppose abortion:

> I asked Kathleen how she got involved and she said that 'God speaks to you' (field notes, North).

> Lawrence answered that he is more concerned with God's judgement (…) That is why we are here, because God has sent us (…) He said that 'this is the ministry that God has called us to' (field notes, Midlands).

> Joyce believed she had to stick up for the vulnerable, for if she didn't then she would not be doing what Jesus had asked of her (…) she says the Lord himself, in her interpretation, is being killed every

time an abortion takes place. And she was concerned regarding what Jesus would say to her and the little that we do, which in the grander scheme of things, is minimal. So there is a sense that they are fulfilling Jesus' word, and he would judge them harshly were he to not see pro-life activism taking place (field notes, Wales).

> My boss is God (...) the person who tells me what to do, I hope, and who I ask for help and guidance and inspiration is God (Rosie interview).

Anti-abortion activism was therefore deemed important in doing God's work, and was replete with sacred significance (Lowe & Page, 2020).

Doing God's Work

Anti-abortion activists understood their activism as a divine mandate; although it may go against societal expectations, it was justifiable because God's rules overrode secular ones. This divine inspiration was necessary for those moments when activists themselves questioned their involvement:

> Nora said that personally it came down to her faith and being motivated by God to come out and give her the strength and to participate, otherwise she said she would start to feel very conflicted and she wouldn't be able to feel peace with it. She then revealed that a woman had turned around to her and said 'You should be ashamed', and she said that comment had 'eaten her up' (field notes, East).

The divine was the key mechanism through which activists justified their actions, and they drew strength from what they perceived as a holy instruction. This held a huge amount of weight, because to not comply with God's expectations would not only result in the continuation of abortion but also God's displeasure at their own silence or inaction. Indeed, their own salvation was a motivating factor:

> Lawrence said that heaven is a longer period than jail. A need to answer to God (field notes, Midlands).

> God knows I don't like abortion, I'm against abortion, but I don't want him, when I breathe my last breath, the judge to say, "But what did you do about it?" I just go down to the abortion clinic, to satisfy my conscience really. I'm doing what I can. I could probably do more, actually, but at least I'm doing something (Fr. Paul interview).

The potential consequences of God's judgement at a later date loomed large for these participants, so that the impetus for activism was not just motivated by saving souls at the abortion clinic (whether understood in terms of 'saving' the woman or the foetus) but it also had implications for their own soul and salvation (Lowe & Page, 2020). Lawrence, an evangelical pastor, even indicated his willingness to break the law in order to fulfil his sacred commitment.

Given that God was seen as an all-seeing, all-powerful creator who could intervene to stop abortion, activists explained that petitioning on earth was required to ensure God was made aware of the issue:

> Simon explained that because of the fall, now God didn't necessarily have to listen to or intervene directly on earth, as we have free will. We need to make God aware of what needs to happen (field notes, Midlands).

> Alice says that they can't physically do anything to stop anything. Imogen then says but God can (…). Alice said that they asked God for his intervention. And their prayer did not stop here or over there, motioning towards the hospital. She said that their prayers intercede time and space (field notes, Scotland).

> We don't know what he wants to happen. We're not asking him to call down a flood or a fire or lightning or something to strike the building or people or anything like that. We're saying, the Our Father prayer, which is you know, 'Thou will be done on earth as it is in heaven.' Whatever he thinks should happen, at that point in time, at that place, we're praying that that will happen, that he will bring that about (Rosie interview).

They placed trust in God to address the issue of abortion but their activism was necessary for this sacred intervention to occur. These sacred understandings get to the heart of why they were so committed to the cause, and how their motivation was generated. A key issue was not about whether they were successful or not; rather it was about the crafting of a pious body, so that God could see that they were faithful, with potential reward in the afterlife. Despite Rosie's ambiguity regarding what God's will actually was, it was never countered that God might support abortion. In this way, their activism pivoted on the deep conviction they held that God not only affirmed what they were doing, but was instructing them to be active. As Chapter 8 will demonstrate, pro-choice activists who are Christian strongly dispute this interpretation of God's will, and make opposing claims regarding God's thoughts and intentions around abortion.

Another dimension to activists' relationship to God was the idea that God could heal. God as a healer was fundamental to them, and because they personally found this a useful resource, they extrapolated that this could also be used to support women who had had an abortion:

> Mike disclosed that although he and his wife had children, his wife had experienced a number of miscarriages. He said that there were

lots of babies that were not making it to life, such as those that are stillborn, and he said that this was for all the babies. Tina, his wife, says that it causes you a lot of pain, and it's not about standing here and judging people who are going through an awful time. Instead she linked the praying to healing, as only God can heal (field notes, Scotland).

When Beatrice became a Christian, she said 'I felt God lovingly showing me my worth, my value, my preciousness to him'. And it suddenly occurred to her, that the child she aborted was precious and valuable to him as well, because he put that child in her womb (...) 'I never got rid of the shame and the guilt' (...) about four-five years ago, she went to a healing weekend. She 'felt Jesus say to me, you have carried your burden, you have carried it long, now it is time to give it to me'. She said that Jesus forgives when we say sorry, but she hadn't forgiven herself (field notes, South-West).

For myself, I'm there because really as reparation for my own conduct in the past about which I am deeply ashamed. I was never knowingly involved in an abortion. I don't know whether there ever has been an abortion as a result of my impregnating a woman because I was never around to find out (...) It hurts, it rips your heart, oh please, give this child the chance of life. Give them the chance to go to God. Give them the chance to have the Beatific Vision. Just to kneel there and pray and say, I was part of that (...) once, I was part of that (Jeoffrey interview).

These very personal accounts reveal the pain and suffering that activists themselves had encountered in their reproductive lives, and how they were seeking both forgiveness from God as well as a form of transcendental healing and salvation. As Bacon et al., argue,

Within Christian theology more broadly, salvation has been imaged as reconciliation, liberation, healing, sanctification, justification, deification, revelation, satisfaction, victory, ransom, expiation (...). At the centre of most is an understanding that God's intended good for the world has been corrupted and that the world is thus now distorted and disordered. 'Sin' has commonly named the problem as personal rebellion against God (...) salvation is typically constructed as a movement towards the making whole of that which is broken, whether that be the restoration of relationship with self, God and other or freedom from the systemic and political 'powers and principalities' that conspire against spiritual, physical and mental wholeness.

(2017, p. 3)

The orientation of the anti-abortion activists was therefore firmly rooted in a specific theological understanding of being at one with God; having a good relationship with God was absolutely crucial to their sense of identity. All efforts were made to ensure they had God's blessing. This was undertaken by deeming abortion a sin, and being active, rather than passive, in their opposition to it. This also reveals the emotional struggles for the individuals involved; they were channelling their own agony and anguish into their anti-abortion activist work, and making sense of their activism through the lens of their personal experiences. This galvanised their motivation, and steered the parameters of their campaign (Jasper, 2011 – emotion is discussed in more detail in Chapter 9). Whilst those managing ongoing negative emotional states were using godly means as a method of managing that anguish, part of the emotional response in the first place was due to the way some of these participants felt they had badly let God down in the past, and were not living the lives God expected them to. Those who had had an abortion or whose behaviour had potentially led to one occurring, judged themselves through the prism of perceived godly expectations, and this resulted in inner turmoil, solace for which was sought through their activism. This sacredly-induced anxiety was rooted in an understanding that abortion was a grave sin (sin will be discussed in more detail in Chapter 5).

Relationship to Fellow Christians

As the previous sections have emphasised, anti-abortion activists fundamentally believed that God opposed abortion and they needed to actively challenge a permissive culture where abortion had become morally acceptable. Because of the direct link between their theological interpretation and their actions, they typically took a dim view of other self-identifying Christians who did not follow suit. Jeoffrey said, 'real Catholics don't do abortion'. This was a particular positioning strategy – those unerringly loyal to the faith – those who could properly call themselves Catholic – were those who were committed to the traditional teachings such as *Humanae Vitae*, where not only abortion is opposed but artificial forms of contraception too. It was therefore questioned whether those who did not follow papal instructions and who did not take an anti-abortion view could really call themselves Catholic. In one fell swoop, vast swathes of self-identifying British Catholics were dismissed by activists as being able to 'rightfully' claim the Catholic label. Being anti-abortion therefore became a strategy in identifying people as the 'true' Catholic faithful, therefore separating this identity from those who described themselves as Catholic but who were not fully committed to all its teachings. This positioning was evoking a very particular lived religion identity, premised on certain assumptions regarding faithfulness. And this commitment could be demonstrated through activists' participation in events like *MFL* and clinic vigils. This put into practice their beliefs and signified their 'true' Catholic commitment and identity. Yet this could cause conflict with their broader Catholic communities, especially those within their church who adopted an anti-abortion message, but who did not want to participate in prayer directly outside of clinics. Indeed some of their fellow Catholics were deeply opposed to the practice:

> Paula said a lot of people won't do it even if they are Catholic or Christian (...). Sarah-Jane asked whether it was because you had to be public with it, and Paula agreed. She said that her family looked at her as if she was bats. She said that her [children] had said to her, 'Mum, please don't do this' (field notes, South-East).

> Richard said a lot of people in the church do not really support them. They do not agree with abortion, but believe a woman should have the right to their own body. He seemed quite surprised that he got criticised from people from his own church (field notes, South-East).

> There are two kinds of responses I've got just from talking to people. One is yes, really agree with what you're doing; I think it's great what you're doing. But I couldn't do it; I would be afraid to do it. And I think that's quite worrying, that people feel they can't actually say what their particular beliefs are (...). And then, yes, there are people who disagree with the idea of standing outside an abortion clinic because of the idea that you're making it difficult for women who are in difficult circumstances anyway. And they may be very, very supportive of pro-life issues, but they don't agree with this particular approach (Christine interview).

However, a larger challenge for the Catholics we spoke to was regarding whether their priests were supportive or not, and how to manage a situation when priests were not perceived as being as committed to the anti-abortion cause as they were. Whilst some priests, like Fr. Paul quoted below, did get directly involved in prayer vigils and some were responsible for prayer vigil organisation and promoting the work, many others did not. Some anti-abortion activists were openly critical of the priests in their communities who had not physically supported the vigils:

> Sarah-Jane asks if their priests are supportive and Joyce says that priests have attended but they are always very busy. Linda says her priest is not so supportive. When asked about it, she said her priest had shrugged his shoulders, and said something akin to the idea that there are always extenuating circumstances. Sarah asks if Joyce's priest talks about abortion, to which she says sarcastically that he does, but not as she would. He mentions it in passing and if you were not listening properly you would miss it (field notes, Wales).

> I was absolutely scandalised (...) I was complaining [to another priest] about abortion. He said, there's worse things than abortion,

> I think coming from a priest, it's absolutely outrageous (Fr Paul, interview).

Many participants were cautious to not directly blame priests for their lack of action, expressing how busy their priest was, and excused their lack of presence through lack of time:

> Sarah-Jane asks if the priests ever come to pray at the site. They hesitate slightly before answering and Imogen says that they are so busy, and Alice confirms, also repeating that they are so busy (field notes, Scotland).

> Sarah-Jane asked Anne if she wished the priests were more involved in the campaign and she said yes, but they have a lot of other things to do as well, such as their involvement in schools, people calling the presbytery and demanding their attention (field notes, North).

As indicated above, some actively petitioned their priests to be involved, with an expectation that their priests would fully endorse the activism they undertook. When priests were not as involved as they would like, one way of mitigating this was through stressing their busyness, and downplaying any thought that they might disagree with their activism.

Downplaying Faith as a Motivator for Opposing Abortion

Anti-abortion activists often downplay the centrality of their faith position, arguing that their motivation for activism is rooted in something other than a commitment to a particular religious worldview. Instead, we regularly heard that one does not need to draw on religion to take a view opposing abortion, and that activists would be involved in their campaign work irrespective of whether they were religious or not. In an Eastern town, we experienced this exchange with two older women participating in a clinic prayer vigil:

> When Sarah-Jane said she was a sociologist of religion, Ruth said it was not necessarily about religion, it was about 'life' and the campaign was there for anyone who cared about life, and the fact they were religious was incidental (...) She wanted to emphasise that this wasn't solely about Christians and that she had heard that in London, non-Christians were involved outside clinics too (...) She said it wasn't about being a faith issue; it was about helping people. Grace concurred. She said that many people opposed abortion who weren't religious (field notes).

In an interview, Christine said 'obviously it's part of my religious belief, but even if I wasn't religious, I think I would still be really concerned at a society that doesn't protect unborn children' and one male vigil participant in Scotland said 'he had been involved with looking at ethics [in his work role]. He said you didn't need to bring religion into it' (field notes). By downplaying faith motivations, many people we spoke to evoked ethical commitments that could be situated away from religious frameworks, and any mention of sin, hell or damnation. Instead it was common for discourses of equality and human rights to be referenced (Lowe & Page, 2019b), situating the foetus in need of legislative protection, akin with other minority groups in society. For example, Maria, an interviewee, said 'it is about equality and it's about rights and right to life'. Meanwhile *MFL* 2020 drew heavily on the slogan, 'Equal from Day 1', with the *2010 Equality Act* being liberally referenced. Many speakers at *MFL* argued that the unborn were a clear omission from the *Equality Act*, and that being in the womb should not make a difference to the legal protections received.

It was very rare, however, for us to encounter individuals who were not religiously devout participating in the clinic activism. In five years of fieldwork, we only encountered two; many anti-abortion activists we spoke to mentioned that non-religious people were involved, but they were often referring to the same person. One individual's activism was rooted in ethical veganism, a belief system that, in England, has legally been deemed to hold the same protected status as a religion at least in terms of employment law.[2] Meanwhile, Sam, a self-identifying atheist, firmly understood the anti-abortion cause as a human rights issue. He said his opposition to abortion was rooted in science, not religion. Whilst Sam's linking of being anti-abortion with human rights is not unusual, his youth and his atheist identity certainly was. Sam perhaps located congruence with the specific dynamics of the campaign he participated in because it did not take an overt religious focus (the activist group he belonged to did not prioritise prayer as a form of activism). Despite the prevailing idea presented to us that opposing abortion did not need to be premised on a faith position, clinic activism was routinely organised for the religiously-committed. One vigil organiser told us that 'we know that there are people who are against abortion and don't have any faith and we're quite happy for them to come along, but only as long as they accept that there is a faith element there, you know, and are comfortable in that atmosphere'.

As we will later explore when we consider the specific vigil practices (Chapter 7), it was typically the case that activism encounters were specifically organised around the needs and understandings of devout Christians, especially with the prayer cycles utilised and the explicitly religious objects on display. As we have already demonstrated, despite being repeatedly told that anti-abortion activism was not specifically rooted in a faith position, overwhelmingly religious understandings framed participants' approaches to abortion. For example, at a vigil in a city in the South West, one woman told us that her motivation comes from her faith as she believes 'life is precious from the moment of conception to natural

---

[2]Casamitjana Costa v The League Against Cruel Sports (2020) ET (Case No 3331129/2018) [33]–[39].

death'. In his interview, Andrew said that the messages his local campaign conveyed included the idea that 'God loves you' and said 'It is a very explicitly religious campaign I should explain; I should add. Based on prayer and all that stuff'. Meanwhile Rosie in interview said the following:

> For people who don't believe in God (…) then a lot of my position doesn't make sense. I realise that. From the perspective of somebody who has no religious belief and thinks the world is only what they can see and touch and doesn't think of it as any spiritual realm, then the most logical thing from that perspective is, you do what you think is best for you at any point in time, what is best for you and perhaps best for the unwanted child. You get rid of the child if you don't want it, or it's not convenient or it's too difficult to bring it up on your own or you're under pressure from someone to get rid of it. If you believe, if you're a person who believes in God, you do what you believe God wants and what you believe is right. That is to not kill, to protect your unborn child or any vulnerable person. To nurture them and bring them up, even if it's inconvenient, even if it's difficult for you, even if it's going to interrupt your career.

For these activists, there was an understanding that their faith position offered something distinct regarding their perceptions. Despite attempts to align non-religious perspectives with an anti-abortion worldview, here, Rosie connects the traits of individualism, selfishness and 'convenience' as typifying both the non-religious and pro-abortion approach. To be religious is therefore to be anti-abortion. Other religious individuals dispute this, as we shall see in Chapter 8.

Appealing to a Broader Audience: Science and Religion

Those organising the anti-abortion campaigns had a challenging task: they concurrently wanted to convince those who were not religious that abortion was wrong, therefore changing general societal attitudes to abortion, whilst also keeping the religiously-motivated anti-abortion participants on-board. In order to avoid alienating either group, they explicitly brought together scientific and religious messages (we will discuss the internal and external messages in a later chapter).

The 2020 *MFL* took place online, due to COVID-19. The event therefore prioritised numerous speakers – many from the US. Sitting in front of a statue of Mary, Joseph and Jesus to one side, and an image of Donald Trump on the other, Fr. Frank Pavone, a Catholic priest representing the US-based *Priests for Life* (which claims to be one of the largest anti-abortion organisations in the world), was specifically asked about the relationship between faith and science by the *MFL* facilitator. He attempted to merge secular and religious perspectives by saying that the 'prolife ethic' is based in science but there is a religious dimension. He argued that one's 'prolife commitment' is rooted in:

> ...what our religion says (...) Catholic teaching holds human reason in the highest esteem and we come to know about how human life begins precisely from science (...) the religious approach to abortion starts with affirming that we make these arguments from science, we make them from reason, we can come to know even without any religious faith that tearing a baby apart limb from limb is wrong.

For Fr. Pavone, 'science' had decided when life began, and for him, this led to the inevitable conclusion that abortion was wrong – whether one was religious or not. He then specifically referenced human rights by saying, 'This we know from a human rights perspective'. This slippage from science and rationality to human rights was premised on emotive imagery of a 'baby' being torn apart. In contradistinction, the United Nations accords human rights at birth (Copelon, Zampas, Brusie, & deVore, 2005). A recent *United Nations Human Rights Committee* affirmed that access to safe and legal abortion is a human right, and a necessity to protect the right to life of women and girls (*United Nations Human Rights Committee*, 2018).

The importance of linking the scientific and religious together in official discourse is therefore an attempt to manage the dual messaging of the anti-abortion campaign. It attempts to appeal externally to those who are not religious, through evoking rationality and human rights discourse, which is seen as being inevitably rooted through a scientific understanding that opposes abortion. It also conveys an internal message to the religious faithful already part of the campaign to emphasise the 'value added' by their faith commitment and belief. In other words, the rational and reasonable position is for everyone to be anti-abortion, but religious individuals have additional resources that they can bring to the table. Indeed, Fr. Pavone went on to argue that religion motivated people to go out and save lives and had a core role to play in healing those who had had abortions. He stated that 'we do not reject those who have had abortions. We want them to find the peace, mercy and forgiveness of Christ'. Fundamentally, then, this narrative brought together messages which were understood to appeal to the in-group and the out-group. Its starting point is an understanding that everyone should believe abortion is wrong, whatever their (non)faith perspective. Fr. Pavone draws on emotive and inhumane imagery of limbs of a baby being torn apart to press his point, despite this representation being hyperbolic. It also emphasised that religious individuals are the ones who will shoulder the burden of the campaign, and offer healing through god-given means to those who have had an abortion, with an understanding that abortion will inevitably require healing interventions. This rejects the pervasive idea that access to abortion is a fundamental human right, how a denial of safe abortion leads to negative health outcomes for women, including death, and the variety of ways women understand their abortion experiences, which are rarely negative in the way that anti-abortion activists believe. Meanwhile in the UK, abortion is broadly understood as a healthcare matter, with the medical profession overwhelmingly supportive of abortion access (Cohen et al., 2021; Francome & Freeman, 2000; Savage & Francome, 2017).

When examining the literature utilised by anti-abortion activists, scientific claims remain interwoven with their religious beliefs. For example, the *Society for the Protection of Unborn Children* (*SPUC*) stall at the 2016 *MFL* in Birmingham had leaflets calling for activists to get more involved. Alongside the foetal right to life arguments and Christian exhortations to be more active, the leaflet declared:

> Biological Science agrees with the Bible that a new human life starts in the womb (see Psalm 139).

This statement is interesting in that although it clearly situates the Bible as the main authority to be agreed with, it does so by arguing that the science backs their religious position. Over the course of the five years of fieldwork, 'science says' arguments were articulated to us more frequently by individuals and by organisations in their public messages. These claims will be explored in more detail later.

As these example show, science claims are thus deployed to support the position that the anti-abortion activists already hold, that ending a pregnancy is harmful to women. However, this presents difficulties when considering the need to articulate why abortion in particular is considered more harmful than, for example, miscarriage. This question is extremely pertinent given that mifepristone and misoprostol are used for both miscarriage management and abortion. There is not generally a prohibition in the anti-abortion community on using these medicines in the case of miscarriage, and thus we would expect there to be an articulation of harm that takes this into consideration. However, few answers were forthcoming, even from those that had often used science as the basis of their argument against abortion. Although medical abortion is regularly denounced, and at the time of writing, there were legal challenges lodged against the development of telemedical services for medical abortion, we have not seen any attempt by anti-abortion groups to explain why the medicines are safe for miscarriage, but harmful for abortion. One of the anti-abortion activists told us the two could not actually be compared, because in a miscarriage the 'baby had already died'. This clearly indicates that, despite their claims to the contrary, many of the harms claimed about medical abortion are not about the risk from 'dangerous' medication, but from their wider moral objections to abortion.

The increasing use of science claimsmaking that we have detailed here could be seen as a strategic decision by anti-abortion activists to appeal to a non-religious audience, particularly in the context of the UK. As we outlined previously, in Britain, religious engagement is expected to be largely a private affair and there is a dislike of overt religiosity in public spaces. Yet as we have shown above, although they use scientific claims to back their position that abortion harms women, these are selective and underpinned by and through their religious beliefs. The everyday lived religion practice of anti-abortion activism underpins their interpretation of the scientific evidence. Moreover, as the general public understands anti-abortion activism as religiously rooted, the deployment of scientific claims of harm are largely unsuccessful and unconvincing. The lack of public traction for these claims occurs not just in relation to the issue of women's health but also in the narratives that are constructed about the developing foetus.

Summary

This chapter has demonstrated the key elements of the worldviews of UK-based anti-abortion activists. Anti-abortion activists are typically oriented towards a nostalgic and mythologised past, where gender roles were more clear-cut, advocating a clear demarcation between motherhood as an explicit vocation, and breadwinner-based fatherhood. Their belief was that permissive culture had undermined the values of traditional heterosexual marriage, and abortion was a key element in explaining the decline of morality in society. These views were buttressed through particular conservative Christian theologies. Their Christian – often specifically Roman Catholic – identities were fundamental to their orientations, endorsed through their strong commitment to papal encyclicals opposing both abortion and contraception. Yet to be active in directly opposing abortion took more than believing it was wrong. Cultivating an explicit activist identity was rooted in how they understood their relationship to God, and a belief that God was telling them to be active in their opposition to abortion; a God who they firmly believed abhorred abortion. Powerfully, their own salvation was understood as being dependent on this activism, increasing the motivation to participate.

Despite their activism being deeply rooted in their religious positioning, there was a recognition that this religiously-endorsed and conservative position would not appeal to society at large, especially given that the 'moral minority' comprises fewer than 10% of the population (Woodhead, 2013 – see Chapter 1). Indeed, some acknowledged that people belonging to the same faith position as them disagreed with them (although explaining the lack of support from priests was more challenging to negotiate). Therefore, activists try to make their stance more appealing by downplaying the faith element to their activism, and utilising scientific discourse. But science was always read through a religious lens, resulting in claimsmaking that go further than scientific conclusions themselves, such as when life begins, and inconsistences and omissions, as examined in the example of how drugs in abortion and miscarriage care were understood. Because of this fundamental belief that life begins at conception – which, in their interpretation, has scientific support – the status of the foetus was fundamental to them (these aspects will be address further in Chapter 6). The next chapter will examine their specific understanding of motherhood.

Chapter 5

Ultra-Sacrificial Motherhood and the 'Harms' of Abortion

Introduction

As we will show in this chapter, the claims about abortion as harmful rest on religiously-informed understandings of motherhood as natural for women. Pregnancy is believed to be a divine gift and the rejection of this is why abortion is deemed so harmful. Importantly though, as we will show, in much of the public messaging about abortion, the faith-based beliefs about abortion are minimised or absent; instead, the focus is often on descriptions of abortion causing physical and mental harm which increasingly utilise scientific discourse to make the claims. For example, ideas that abortion is inevitably the cause of mental health problems through the ongoing impact of abortion regret. This chapter will argue that although the non-moral narratives may seem be a strategic necessity when trying to be persuasive within secular public spaces, the underlying religious context is clear. Finally, and linking with the religious grounding of their campaign, the chapter will outline the framing of abortion as causing spiritual harm, a risk that can spread from women seeking abortion to abortion clinics and beyond. We argue that this arises from, and underpins, their understanding of abortion as profaning.

Motherhood as a Sacred Commitment

As we set out in Chapter 3, motherhood is sacralised generally in society, with women expected to put the welfare of actual or potential children first. This maternalist position is rooted in ideas about the 'naturalness' of motherhood for women. Whilst this is not always rooted in a religious position, Christianity also maintains that motherhood is sacred with a strong expectation that women should have children (Llewellyn, 2016). These ideas are amplified within the worldview of the anti-abortion activists and, for them, motherhood is not just compulsory, but all women *are* mothers whether or not they actually have children. This position shapes their understanding of women and abortion as the following example illustrates:

Anti-Abortion Activism in the UK, 69–89
Copyright © 2022 Pam Lowe and Sarah-Jane Page
Published under exclusive licence by Emerald Publishing Limited
doi:10.1108/978-1-83909-398-220221010

> Tessa said that although she knew some people got upset about
> them being there, she was doing the right thing, because they
> would come to regret their abortions. So it was important to try
> to prevent this, or offer hope and healing afterwards. She spoke
> about the 'unnaturalness' of abortion, and that science says that it
> is unnatural to have an abortion. Tessa talked about abortion
> regret as a universal problem. She said that this could take a
> long time to emerge, and said she knew of women who had
> suppressed their feelings for twenty years or more. Pam agreed
> that some people might wish they had decided differently, but said
> that most women did not regret their abortions. Tessa didn't
> accept that. Pam suggested that some women regret motherhood
> and she looked completely shocked. This was not something that
> she had ever considered and after a few moments, dismissed it
> utterly as a thing that could happen (field notes, South-East).

In this extract, we can see how abortion is positioned as something that is
'unnatural' and it is because it is unnatural that it will inevitably lead to harm.
Moreover, the idea that some people could regret becoming mothers is not
something that had ever been considered previously, nor could it be contemplated. This was not the only occasion when the idea of regretting motherhood
was completely rejected. It was women's sacred role to have children, and this was
a double gift. Pregnancy itself was, as Derek stated, an 'empowering beautiful gift
that women get to have' and, as commonly recited in a prayer at clinic sites, the
anti-abortion activists 'recognise each life as a beautiful gift from God the
Father'. Hence, in line with this understanding of ultra-sacrificial motherhood, it
is beyond comprehension that having children could ever lead to regret. This was
not an unusual position to take as the profaning character of abortion has long
been seen as an assault on the sacred commitment of motherhood. This has been
the bedrock of the anti-abortion position for centuries.

That womanhood and motherhood are intimately connected is a taken-for-
granted notion and thus, when considering abortion, it is the impact abortion has
on *mother*s that the anti-abortion activists think is crucial to consider. This would
often rely on essentialised notions that women are 'biologically made' for pregnancy, and abortion fundamentally interferes with this, as can be seen in the
following accounts:

> ...it must be the most obvious violation of motherhood, the
> mothering instinct to destroy your own child. It's intensely
> harmful. Not just physically, but emotionally and spiritually as
> well (Jeoffrey, interview).

> I think it harms women, you know, because women – they are
> biologically, mentally and emotionally ready to bring, to give life,
> whether they have chosen to or not, so to have that life either
> chemically ended, or dissected or sucked out or whatever (...)

I think there are problems. So they are not biologically made to be terminated (Derek, interview).

In Jeoffrey's account, we can see that it is *motherhood* that we need to consider in relation to abortion. That women may have lives *beyond* motherhood does not need to be considered, because it is *conception* that creates mothers. He sets out a number of aspects that can cause harm that we will unpack in more depth shortly. In a similar way, Derek relies on the biological inevitability of harm being caused, because women are biologically programmed 'to give life'. For him, like many others, this is the divinely-ordained position. That women may not want to 'give life' is against the natural order of traditional gender roles that he subscribes too. Moreover, the idea that, biologically speaking, 'giving life' is what women's bodies are designed for, overlooks the frequency in which pregnancies end through miscarriage (see Fig. 1 depicting an anti-abortion sign signalling abortion as exploitation).

The notion that Jeoffrey referred to, that there is a maternal instinct that would naturally lead to women continuing a pregnancy, also occurred in the accounts of other people we have spoken to. At an anti-abortion event in the Midlands, Brenda says that women have 'a natural instinct' to protect, but that this was 'under threat'. She states that:

> Most women don't want abortion but don't feel that they have a choice. Women would 'choose her baby over abortion in a heartbeat'.

Fig. 1.   Abortion as Harmful to Women Sign.

Similarly, Gordon drew upon these notions of maternal instinct and uncon-
ditional love and sacrifice. In his interview, he referenced a child, saying:

> The responsibility of any adult towards a child during the
> development of the child from start to finish is one of protection
> and support.

In Gordon's view, abortion was both the destruction of a life, and contra-
dicting what a 'mother' should do. Whilst mostly these ideas were just presented
as 'facts' without the need for any further justification, on some occasions, anti-
abortion organisations went further and deployed scientific discourses to explain
this 'natural' occurrence.

For example, at the 2020 *LifeStream*, a speaker set out the 'science of
pregnancy'.[1] Despite this billing, the presentation made religious analogies, such
as thinking about the placenta as Michelangelo's painting, the *Creation of Adam*,
in the Sistine Chapel. This speaker suggested that new scientific knowledge is
uncovering evidence that shows pregnancy should be seen as a co-operative 'dyad'
of 'mother' and 'prenatal child' and that this indicates that seeing pregnancy as a
'clump of cells' or 'parasite' is now outdated. One of the central arguments made
was about the impact of foetal-maternal microchimerism (transferred cells that
remain after pregnancy ends):

> It speaks of some kind of mysterious co-operation at the cellular
> level between mother and child (…) what is amazing is that these
> cells act, they can help mum heal, protect her from cancer, so we
> can think of these cells as someway benefiting the health of the
> mother, it really speaks of the radical mutuality at the cellular level
> between two people that really only serves to enhance our
> understanding of the beautiful maternal child bond (Dr Kristin
> Collier, *the Science of Pregnancy*).[2]

The speaker does acknowledge the current gaps in understanding about the
implications of this process. However, the use of the word 'mysterious' in this
quotation, we suggest, may speak to the mainly religious audience as part of a
creation 'wonder' rather than just scientific uncertainty. Moreover, although there
was one brief mention that there could be harmful effects, the overall message is
that science has shone more light on the beneficial impact of pregnancy to
women's health through the permanent cellular level changes during pregnancy.
Although it is not mentioned directly, the implication suggests that abortion is
detrimental to women. This position is reinforced by the use of the term 'prenatal

---

[1] *LifeStream* featured online replacement workshops which would have normally been held
alongside the annual United Kingdom (UK) *March for Life* (*MFL*) that had to be cancelled
due to the COVID-19 pandemic.
[2] Field notes 13 June 2020 from online stream also available here https://www.
marchforlife.co.uk/lifestream-20-all-the-videos/.

child' throughout the talk and the emphasis on the 'naturalness' of bonding. This latter element aligns well with their sacred commitment to ultra-sacrificial motherhood.

But situating motherhood as a *natural instinct* means that the anti-abortion activists need to have explanations for why abortions take place. As we have outlined elsewhere, the notion that women are always pressured or coerced into having abortions from partners, family, friends or wider society is a crucial part of the anti-abortion activists' worldview (Lowe & Page, 2020). It is how they explain why so many women have abortions when it is clearly not in line with the 'natural' decision they would make. It also means that anti-abortion activists can position themselves as the people that are 'really' offering choice. Their understanding is that the pressure on women is so great that they are almost inevitably led to prioritise other things, above their 'natural calling' (Lowe & Page, 2019a, 2020).

The claim that women do not really want abortions could often be seen to be resting on an understanding of pregnancy as a unique time whereby women may not be able to think clearly. This was sometimes deemed to be caused by the biological changes that occur in the body. For example, in a pavement counselling guide (for people situated outside clinics persuading women to not have abortions), it gives specific advice about what to say to men:

> Many boyfriends/husbands will say that they will support their girlfriend/wife in whatever choice they make. (...) Be prepared to explain to the man that this is not fulfilling his role as a loving partner. Inform them that the woman's hormones can be making her feel very vulnerable and anxious at this time so their role is to be strong for the baby and protect their partner from making a decision that will be damaging to both herself and their relationship (collected at a Midlands clinic).

In this extract, women are positioned as potentially incapable of making a rational decision – which, for the anti-abortion activists, is always to continue with the pregnancy. Moreover, the role of putative fathers is also clearly in line with the conservative views on gender roles in which men are, or should be, the protectors of women. Moreover, it is part of the role of anti-abortion activists to make them understand this, because, in the minds of the anti-abortion activists, the traditional married heterosexual couple is the natural form that family life should follow.

This notion that women may be unstable emotionally and/or misguided in their thoughts often occurred in the materials that were designed to be handed to them as they entered an abortion clinic. In the North, a leaflet (no author) which we collected on three occasions outside a clinic across a number of years, was folded, and had the words 'Think About Yourself' on the front. Inside, it exhorted women to 'be sure of their true feelings' and encouraged them to consider the information it contained that they may not have been told. Clearly, the 'true feelings' are assumed to be those of a 'natural mother'. The idea that the 'real' harm of abortion is hidden from women was also found on other leaflets. A leaflet (no author) used outside a clinic in the Midlands, for a number of years was entitled 'Has the clinic told you?'; it was replaced recently with one of a similar design with the message 'Do you know?'. This message was also frequently conveyed in posters such as 'Abortion HURTS women and kills babies; Pray for the end of abortion' and 'Love them Both' that are regularly displayed outside abortion service providers. The underlying message in these, and other examples, is not just that abortion is harmful, but that abortion service providers mislead clients about abortion. This is in line with the broader anti-abortion movement claims that abortion service providers are an 'abortion industry', and routinely do not seek fully informed consent as they are motivated by profits (Amery, 2020; Lowe, 2019). There is no evidence that this is the case, not least because in the UK, abortions are largely provided through National Health Service (*NHS*) funding. Within this context, anti-abortion activists regularly told us that they are the only people who routinely inform women about the risks and harms of abortion. This is similar to other studies (for example, Cannold, 2002; Lee, 2003; Saurette & Gordon, 2015).

The idea that women are always coerced into abortion was buttressed through the narratives of activists who had previously had abortions, especially as personal testimony delivered at anti-abortion rallies. As long as they were dutifully remorseful for their actions, those who had had abortions could be welcomed into the anti-abortion campaign, by framing their decision in terms of intense regret linked to perceived coercive practices. As we also mention in Chapter 9, this narrative is one promoted by the post-abortion groups run by anti-abortion organisations (Husain & Kelly, 2017). The source of that coercion ranged from various family members, partners and friends, as well as wider society that have moved away from traditional values (we explore this latter element in Chapter 9). Rosie in her interview said that 'I know girls who have been marched in there by mothers, clutching their arms, saying, "You're going in"'. Maureen, outside a clinic in the South-East, said:

> It was sad because no woman ever wants to have an abortion. It is always coerced. Often by 'their so-called boyfriends' [she made scare quotes with her fingers in the air at this].

This positioning of women as unknowingly and unwittingly seeking out an abortion, or being subject to coercion, enabled anti-abortion activists to situate women seeking an abortion as someone in need of education, practical help or support, and meant they did not have to situate them as someone who has 'killed' their 'child'. This therefore was a powerful rhetorical device in softening their message to those seeking abortion services, without them apportioning blame to service users directly. Yet in the process, women were understood as ignorant, emotionally unstable and lacking in their own judgement or agency. And when one dug deeper into how women were perceived, there was still an underpinning tendency for women to be judged, especially through the way activists linked the problem of abortion to unmarried sexuality – indicated by reference to their 'so-called boyfriends'. Moreover, the anti-abortion activists' understanding that abortion was against women's 'natural inclination', a notion which arises from their religious understanding of ultra-sacrificial motherhood, was an important element in their construction of abortion harms.

Harmful to Women

As we detailed earlier, anti-abortion activism can be seen as a moral regulation movement. Hunt's (1999) conceptualisation of moral regulation movements is useful as it explains the broader shifts over time in how social actors seek to constrain the 'immoral' behaviour of others. In particular, he identified a shift from using the concepts of 'vice' and 'sin' to using ideas about science, health and risk. This can be clearly seen in the anti-abortion movement, who now typically use health and/or science to 'prove' abortion 'harm'. Moreover, risk narratives have become a central frame of family policymaking in the UK (Lee, 2014). This includes assigning an 'at risk' status to individuals to allow policy interventions, whether or not their current behaviour is a cause of concern, and the extension of potential harms to a wider population that may be deemed to be at risk (Lee, 2014). Thus, the adoption of understandings of harm, health and risk by anti-abortion activists are in line with broader societal trends.

Many of the leaflets that are routinely handed to those entering abortion clinics contain a range of adverse health issues which are claimed to be caused by abortion. Some of the claims related to the physical risks of the procedure itself (often infection, haemorrhage, and incomplete abortions), or future physical harm (such as breast cancer or infertility), whereas others make claims of a long-term impact on mental health. However, although abortion was often portrayed as presenting a physical risk to women's health in the materials we collected, this was mentioned much less frequently by the anti-abortion activists themselves. When we did encounter this narrative, it often relied on vague claims rather than listing issues in detail. These different forms of risk can be seen in this encounter:

> Paula said that in Poland they have gone the other way and pretty much stopped abortion and the health of women improved pretty much immediately. She said that the best medical results for women throughout the world are Poland and Ireland, and this is because they don't support abortion.[3] She said that abortion 'mucks up your innards' and there is a link between breast cancer and abortion. She said that if you get pregnant and then you stop it, you are muddling with your system. But she said that the medics don't give you all these facts (field notes, South-East).

In this extract, we can see one direct claim, that abortion is linked to breast cancer. This claim has been widely discredited, which maybe why it was unusual for activists to mention this to us specifically. This extract also outlines two other

---

[3]This encounter preceded Ireland's change in abortion law.

claims that relate to physical health that occurred more often. First, a general sense that abortion was physically harmful (it 'mucks up your innards') without naming any particular condition.

The second element, which again we were told fairly regularly, was the claim that places where abortion was heavily restricted were paragons of good reproductive healthcare for women. None of the activists gave any specific evidence about where the claims that abortion restrictions were good for women really emerged from, it was just repeated as a fact. In the materials, this type of claim was more muted and they were more likely to say that abortion did not improve maternity care:

> Effective action to reduce maternal mortality requires better pre-natal care (...) and improved access to emergency obstetric care when problems arise in labour. This is why mothers and babies die, and promoting abortion will not save lives (*Society for the Protection of Unborn Children* [*SPUC*] leaflet collected at *MFL 2016*).

In these types of claims, there are a number of issues that seemed to have been overlooked. Most obviously, they are ignoring that people who live in countries where abortion is legally restricted, still have abortions. People buy abortion pills online, including from international health organisations that specialise in tele-medicine across borders. Pregnant people may also frequently travel to access abortion in other places, or have abortions by other means, which may be unsafe. Crucially, it also ignores cases where women die, even in Europe, such as Savita Halappanavar, whose death was linked to the legal restriction of abortion in Ireland at the time (Berer, 2013).

Whilst reports of physical harm were referenced occasionally, it was much more common for the anti-abortion activists to highlight their belief that abortion had a negative impact on mental health:

> A lot of the women, what do they do afterwards? Well some of them come out and seem jolly and (...) but maybe they are feigning that. And also there are women who go, and you probably know this as well, multiple-abortive women who go maybe five or six times. And they turn to drugs or alcohol, and promiscuity (Robert, interview).

> Judith emphasised that abortion was a traumatic event and that the women who were angry at them being there had probably had abortions themselves and not got over it. The word 'trauma' was used over again. The idea that women were unable to recover from abortion (field notes, Midlands).

In Robert's account we can see specific claims made about the harm that abortion can cause. He mentions the idea that women sometimes seem to be fine but explains this as them in denial about the consequences. Robert also presents a picture of a cycle of desperation, with abortion 'causing' addiction and 'promiscuity' which 'inevitably' leads to more abortions. The emphasis here on illicit sex is aligned with the traditional worldviews about appropriate sexual behaviour. Judith also firmly believed that abortion was a form of trauma, from which women would struggle to recover. This fits in with the narrative of 'abortion regret' which we repeatedly encountered in other narratives too:

> Tessa talked about abortion regret as a universal problem. She said that this could take a long time to emerge, and said she knew of women who had suppressed their feelings for 20 years or more (field notes, South-East).

> They have a lifetime of regret, shame, guilt and 'what ifs' (Alicia, field notes, South-West).

> Both Victoria and Wade are keen to tell me about the 'reality of abortion'. That it leads all women to regret and suicide 'even those who have been raped' (field notes, South-West).

> Caroline said abortion leaves women 'broken'. She mentioned mental health issues (field notes, North).

The emphasis on abortion regret as a constant ongoing problem from which women never recover has become a common narrative in anti-abortion accounts (Ehrlich & Doan, 2019). Ehrlich and Doan (2019) have argued that it builds on the narrative that abortion causes grief and this will have long-term consequences.

In the accounts given to us, the regret was frequently connected to using various milestones of the aborted foetus as a constant reference point:

> Alicia said that every anniversary of when that child was aborted, you will be thinking about what the child would be doing now. Would my child have had children, would I have grandchildren? (field notes, South-West).

> Fran is very concerned about women who carry the burden of having an abortion with them their whole lives, saying things like 'she would be five now'. Some things you can put right later on but with abortion, it is not one of those things. If someone does have a religious belief and they can go to a priest and say they've done a terrible thing, they can seek forgiveness. But if they're not religious, they often can't get that forgiveness and they blame themselves (field notes, South-West).

In these accounts, we can see the projection of an 'imagined future' which rests on the fundamental idea that the foetus was a child from conception in the minds of activists, so much so that it was presumed that women, as *mothers*, would continue to reflect on their decision for the rest of their lives, at various key moments. Moreover, some of the anti-abortion activists we encountered who had previously had abortions named the 'children' whose lives they had terminated, even if this was at a very early gestation. At least in one case, this practice was encouraged by an anti-abortion support organisation.

The positioning of women as mothers of specific children from conception was thus a central element in their perception of harm. It is as *mothers* that women will have ongoing grief and mental ill-health issues. Moreover, as Fran's account explains, this understanding was underpinned by religious beliefs and a concern that in a secular society, the woman would be unable to seek any sort of solace. Indeed, in Fran's mind, it was forgiveness that was required, ultimately situating abortion as a mortal sin. Her religious positioning was foregrounded as she highlighted the key role of the priest in making amends and absolving one of that perceived sin.

The ideas of grief and trauma are congruent with broader societal discourses where women are deemed to always be regretful and are discouraged from expressing positive emotions towards abortion (Ehrlich & Doan, 2019; Millar, 2017). But these common understandings are pushed further by activists; women are expected to experience abortion within a narrow frame of reference, often hinged on the idea that women should feel guilt for their actions, as a means of punishing their sexual behaviour, which is often presumed to be illicit. The idea that deteriorating mental health was an inevitable consequence fitted with their worldview that abortion was inherently damaging, and always and inevitably led to negative consequences. Evidence suggests that reactions to an abortion and the emotions experienced vary enormously – there is no singular response, but this will be influenced by the particular factors and context (Millar, 2017). But negative emotions are read through a particular lens of post-abortion syndrome (PAS). As Millar argues,

> The slippage between different emotions works to construct abortion as loss and, specifically, the loss through death of an autonomous, material foetus. The merging of severe psychological conditions (trauma) with commonly experienced emotions (sadness) gives post-abortion grief the broadest reach possible while constructing the loss involved as profound and external.
>
> (2017, p. 139)

For the activists we spoke to, abortion *inevitably* leads to negative consequences; the idea that a woman might be relieved or positive about her abortion was not countenanced. If women are not demonstrating negative emotions, then this is seen as a result of them being in denial (Lee, 2003). Indeed, if a woman were to experience a 'happy abortion', in Millar's (2017) terms, she would be deemed cold and heartless, and as we will explain later, spiritually harmed. In other words, as someone who had not taken full responsibility for her actions, she was positioned as wounded.

Medical Claimsmaking

Of all the public materials produced and circulated by anti-abortion activists, the health advice given to women seeking abortion is often the most contested. For example, identical leaflets (no author) collected from outside abortion clinics were part of the evidence presented in the successful campaigns to introduce the first two bufferzones in London. The argument made by pro-choice campaigners was that the inaccurate information about health risks was part of a broader approach of misinformation and intimidation by the anti-abortion groups who regularly targeted the clinics. Although, as we have previously shown, religious ideas are the bedrock of anti-abortion beliefs, in line with the trend identified by Hunt (1999), in the public information aimed at convincing women not to have abortions, there is very little overt moralising about the 'sin' of abortion. Instead, as we have outlined above, the claims made in public often rely on the position that abortion is a risk to women's immediate and future health. An increasing reliance on medical and scientific discourse has been a trend for a number of years and it is not our intention to assess the veracity of all the health claims made by anti-abortion groups. Instead, this section will focus on the evolution of the claims of harm made in leaflets from a specific site in the Midlands. We have chosen this as it is a useful illustration of the shift towards a scientific framing of claimsmaking within the anti-abortion movement, particularly over their use of evidence.

Both the earlier and later leaflets used at this Midlands clinic had the same light pink paper, with a picture of two white women on the front. It also included the personal number of a local anti-abortion activist as well as details of a local anti-abortion crisis pregnancy center (CPC). Whilst they do not have a named author, the similarities and local details suggest that they were designed by and for the local network that have held regular vigils outside a particular abortion clinic for decades. The busiest time for vigils at this clinic were the two *40 Days for Life* (*40DFL*) periods, but vigils would regularly occur on other occasions. The only other place we found this leaflet in use was by a new *40DFL* group that appeared in another city in the Midlands area. We are not certain of the exact date or reason for the updated leaflet. However, as the new version was collected after leaflets were used as evidence in the successful imposition of the first bufferzone, and the local city council had passed a motion condemning the presence of anti-abortion activists outside this specific clinic, we suggest that a likely reason for the change was a concern to ensure that the leaflet could not be used as evidence to support the introduction of a bufferzone in the area.

The overall message in the earlier leaflet constructed the harm as coming from abortion as 'unnatural', similar to the claims that we outlined above. The inside of the leaflet states:

> Abortion violates something basic in a woman's nature. She is normally the giver of life. When she is deprived of her natural role as a mother she usually reacts with bitterness and feelings of resentment with those who led her to the abortion.

This message is clearly in line with the sacred commitment to ultra-sacrificial motherhood in that it posits ideas about universality of feelings and a pre-ordained order that is harmful to disrupt. It is clear here that women are 'led' to abortion, and it is not an option that they freely choose for themselves. This is followed by details of foetal development, claims that abortion causes physical and psychological harms, religious messaging and helpline numbers. The physical harms of abortion listed on the leaflet include statements about infection, pain and heavy bleeding. It also includes some less-common claims such as 1 in 4 women being unable to succeed in a future pregnancy, that about 5% of abortions lead to loss or damage of other organs, and that there is a risk of coma. No additional commentary on these risks is given. In addition to the physical risks, the leaflet lists a wide range of adverse psychological effects, including depression, suicidal thoughts, substance misuse, eating disorders and 'damage to maternal instinct, feeling incapable of motherhood'. It contains a section headed 'beliefs and values' which claims all main religions are against abortion. It states that the 'child' was 'created by God in His image' and it has an 'immortal soul'. It suggests they should pray and trust in a divine plan. The leaflet also claims that 90% of relationships will end after abortion. Some of these claims are supported by a couple of small unattributed quotes which appear to be from people who regret their abortions. Unusually for anti-abortion material, the leaflet has some acknowledgement that pregnancy can be difficult in that it suggests that feelings of 'depression, anxiety or fear' can occur in any pregnancy. In this case, it exhorts women not to mistake these 'natural' feelings about pregnancy as a reason to have an abortion.

In the updated version of the leaflet, the messages of harm are presented very differently and some of the specific claims have been changed. It retains the initial message that all pregnancies can induce anxiety, but, significantly, apart from this initial statement, the newer leaflet no longer speaks with its own authoritative voice. Instead it presents evidence of harms from other sources. It does this in two distinct ways. First, the evidence of harm is now attributed to medical sources through the use of footnotes. These sources include the *NHS*, named doctors and articles in medical journals. The second change is that the unattributed quotes are more prominent. Also significant is the absence in the newer leaflet of any reference to religion. Overall, the number and range of harms in the newer leaflet is significantly reduced. Although we cannot be sure of the reason, we would suggest that this is likely to be because they could not find medical sources to verify the previous claims.

In terms of physical harm, the issues mentioned on the newer leaflet include the risks of infection, incomplete abortion, cervix damage and 'failed' abortions. The source that these are linked to is the *NHS* website, a highly respected and trustworthy source. However, whilst the types of health risks are in line with *NHS* information (at the time we believe that the leaflet was produced), for some of the claims, the additional commentary inflates the risk. For example, the probability of damage to the cervix was listed as a 1% risk on the *NHS* website. However, the leaflet adds to this claim that this will impact 1,900 future pregnancies a year, which is not *NHS* information, and it is not clear where this number came from.

Thus, it may be misattributed to the *NHS* in the way that it is presented. Similarly, the number stated for incomplete abortions on the leaflet was the same as from the *NHS*, but the broader claim on the leaflet that 'the foetus/baby is still alive' is very different from the *NHS* website that instead states that further treatment is needed if the pregnancy continues. Despite the inclusion of these types of statements, it is clear that the physical risks portrayed have been dramatically reduced, and the more extreme claims, such as coma and organ failure, are no longer included.

The changes are even more dramatic in terms of the presentation of the risk of future psychological harm. The long list of psychological effects presented in the earlier leaflet are now largely absent. The newer leaflet instead focuses solely on the risk of suicide and presents two evidence-based claims, both from reputable medical journals. The first that pregnancy is a protective factor against suicide, and the second that a study found that women who have abortions are six times as likely to commit suicide than those who continue pregnancies.[4] Whilst clearly suicidal thoughts are a serious and significant element of pregnancy mental health issues, it is thankfully rare. Moreover, the underlying reasons for the suicide attempts are not given, and it is not mentioned as to whether it was the abortion or something else that was the important factor. Also, now absent from the 'facts' included on the leaflet are any claims that abortion damages 'maternal feelings' and all other, more common, mental health issues. The latter is, however, still represented in one of the quotes that claims that the 'grief' of abortion has continued for years. The leaflet now also claims that 'for me, abortion was harder to get over than the rape'. Whilst the claim about rape is clearly contentious, by using a quotation, the leaflet does not seek to generalise the experience, thus also removing any need for further evidence. This indicates why personal accounts became more prominent in the second version of the leaflet. It allowed dominant understandings of abortion to be portrayed without need of further evidence. This was the only leaflet we encountered that had undergone such a radical shift in the way that it presented the harms of abortion and we were unable to interview the author about the changes. Nevertheless, it is illustrative of broader trends that we observed, about the increasing use of anti-abortion groups making (questionable) claims that science 'proves' the harms of abortion and using general sources as a reference rather than evidence produced by anti-abortion organisations themselves.

The emphasis in the earlier leaflet on a wide range of mental health issues that are claimed to be caused by abortion clearly fit with the narrative construction of PAS. As Lee (2003) has clearly shown, the notion that women are 'victims' of abortion was an important contrast to moralised frames which focused on claims about the foetus' right to life. She argues that the concept of PAS originated in the United States (US) and was then adopted by anti-abortion groups in Britain in the 1980s and 1990s. Because in Britain access to abortion is achieved on health

---

[4]Interestingly the source, Kendell (1991), for this 'fact' actually suggest that access to contraception and abortion is likely to be a factor in the decreased suicide rate amongst pregnant women.

grounds, claims that abortion was harmful were clearly attractive to anti-abortion organisations (Lee, 2003). Yet, as Lee (2003) sets out, in contrast to the US, the UK response to claims about PAS was largely muted, and there was little publicity or engagement by medical professionals. Thus, although the attempts at restricting abortion through the development and deployment of PAS is in line with the trend from 'sin' to health identified by Hunt (1999), it failed to generate the wider concerns which would have been needed for this to be successful. The limited public attention within the UK may also explain as to why, although a risk of mental health issues was frequently mentioned by activists and on leaflets seeking to dissuade women from having abortions, the term PAS was largely absent. Nevertheless, we suggest that the shift towards medicalising abortion harms was an important step in the increasing trend towards the adoption of scientific claims as detailed in the changing leaflets outlined above. Whilst these claims may seek to address a wider public and convince them of the harm of abortion, it is clear for the activists themselves they remain rooted in their religious understanding of abortion.

Spiritual Harm

As mentioned in the quotation from Jeoffrey at the beginning of this chapter, alongside the issues of physical and mental health, anti-abortion activists have concerns that abortion causes spiritual harm. This is an important element because it underpins the other assumptions of physical and psychological harm. Although references to religion appeared much less often that the other claims of harm to women (and foetuses) in public materials, it was often articulated when we spoke to the activists themselves. Whilst, in most cases, those who are spiritually harmed are women themselves, the risks posed by abortion are deemed to potentially have a wider impact, as this section will illustrate.

At the most basic level, spiritual harm is caused by the notion that, in having an abortion, women are rejecting their sacred role. As we have described, for the anti-abortion activists, women's 'natural' role is motherhood, and pregnancy is a 'sacred gift'. Consequently, it is not surprising that a rejection of a divine plan for motherhood is seen as spiritually harmful, as the following leaflets illustrates:

> Before the physical abortion takes place the unborn child has first been spiritually aborted so a conversion of the heart must come before the mother makes a positive decision for life (Pavement Counselling Guide, collected from the Midlands).

> In order to agree to abort our child we first have to let go of its place in our heart, or perhaps never let it live there in the first place (*Post Abortion Support for Everyone* (*PASE*) collected in the South-East).

As these extracts show, abortion is harmful in a 'spiritual' way. The spiritual harm occurs not just after the procedure, but it is a necessary part of the process of seeking abortion. In other words, it is only really possible to contemplate abortion through a process that has the effect of spiritually harming yourself. The symbolism of the heart here is important, as it signifies both a belief in divine love for all people, and the love that a mother would 'naturally' have for a child. The understanding that changing someone's mind is an act of 'conversion' rather than just persuasion is also illustrative of the religious symbolism of the act.

Perceptions of spiritual harm can arise from beliefs about a divine plan for every foetus that is conceived. This links to the idea of predestination in religiously presented foetal stories which we will discuss further in Chapter 6. As a leaflet (author unclear) collected in Northern Ireland (NI) sets out:

> He is the creator of all human life, and therefore the only one who gets to decide when and how it ends. This is what makes abortion-on-demand so wicked and sinful: Human life is not ours to take, but to cherish.

The understanding that, as one leaflet stated, 'abortion is the sin of murder' (*The Street Preacher*, collected in the Midlands), was not uncommon amongst the anti-abortion activists. However, what was notable was that references in the public materials varied. In Britain, anti-abortion activists associated with Catholicism tended not to mention this in materials aimed at those seeking abortion, but it was present in materials developed for an internal audience. In contrast, anti-abortion materials distributed by anti-abortion groups associated with evangelical Christianity often included references to sin and/or murder in both their internal and external messaging. In NI, there was not such a marked difference between different denominations.

Although it was not in the British public materials, the Catholic activists themselves did explain the importance of understanding abortion as the sin of murder, and its role in causing spiritual harm. In an interview, Fr. Paul, a Catholic priest-activist explained:

> ...it's a very serious sin; it's against the Fifth Commandment, 'Thou shalt not kill,' they put themselves outside the church with that sin. They have to reconcile to get back in again (...) God is infinitely just, but He's also a God of infinite love, compassion and mercy. On account of this, Holy Mother Church has always taught, no matter the gravity of the sin, if a sinner should be truly repentant and have a firm purpose of amendment, then through confession and reparation, the sinner will always find forgiveness. After asking God with a humble and contrite heart, [they] will be restored to a life of union, grace and peace with God, his Creator (...) [If a woman does not seek forgiveness] it would be a serious impediment to their eternal salvation. It would be taking a risk. Hell or heaven is for eternity, to be condemned for an eternity, you've only got one chance in this life; you don't get a second chance.

There are a number of important elements here. First, abortion is such a serious violation that it *automatically* places people 'outside the church' and thus risks their 'eternal salvation'. The spiritual harm caused by abortion is both during their lifetime and 'for eternity'. Yet, as indicated here, there is a way to recover from this harm and risk and that is through 'forgiveness' and 'reparation'. Failure to seek forgiveness was understood as putting women's very salvation on the line.

In this interview, Jeoffrey, who is also Catholic, also emphasised the religious need to seek forgiveness in the correct manner, in order to not compromise one's soul:

> ...abortion is a sin of such gravity that it has to be forgiven by a bishop (...) a woman who is penitent can go to a priest, can get faculties from a bishop or go to a bishop and have that sin forgiven and they're forgiven. That's it. Then there's nothing to stop them going to heaven... I can't judge a soul because a soul is known only to God. Only God can possibly judge whether this person is in the state of mortal sin or not.

Yet his account went further than solely focusing on women seeking abortion. Jeoffrey described his activities as attempting to make reparation for abortions that he may have caused in the past. He took vicarious responsibility for this, absorbing the 'sin' of others, in his act of reparation. In his prayers outside of the clinic, he infused his own identity as an activist who 'saved' those entering the clinic in the here and now. However, Jeoffrey still emphasised the personal consequences for women who had had abortions. Thus, even though he was penitent about his past behaviour as a potential cause of pregnancy, it was women who had had abortions who he believed ultimately needed to obtain godly forgiveness.

This conviction of the idea of abortion as a grave sin often informed activists' beliefs when they were outside clinics. At one site in the Midlands, we were told the following:

> They were praying for the lives of the unborn, and for women having abortions because it was a sin and they needed 'repentance'. They were also praying for the staff involved in abortions and to change hearts and minds in society; this included praying for those against them... Simon said that abortion was a mortal sin, but to be a mortal sin, there were three important points: It was a really bad thing. You have actively chosen it and not been forced; rather, you understand your actions (field notes).

In his definition of a mortal sin, Simon was following Catholic doctrine about not just the gravity of the offence, but also that it needed intention. Singer describes mortal sin as:

> ...a serious breach of God's law, mortal sins are actions that imperil the violator's soul. To be deemed a mortal sin, an action

must be intrinsically evil, the violator must know that what they are doing is immoral, and they must freely choose to commit the behavior. For the Catholic Church, seeking an abortion meets all of these conditions.

(2018, p. 18)

The emphases in these definitions of mortal sin raise interesting questions in relation to the assumption that most abortions happened from ignorance, pressure or coercion. If, as many of the anti-abortion activists told us, women are unknowingly, unwittingly or subject to pressure or coercion, the numbers committing a mortal sin are clearly limited. In this way, the sin of abortion could be displaced onto others, such as abortion providers.

The notion that abortion was always understood as a result of coercion mean that a more palatable message could be presented in their outward-facing activism, but this could have the effect of reducing claims about the seriousness of abortion. It was important therefore to find a way to reconcile these positions. This could be done through evoking wider understandings of 'sinfulness'. For example, at the closing prayers at one *MFL*, a bishop said:

Have mercy upon every man and woman in this land. Those who have intentionally sinned against life, those who in distress did not know what they did. Those who failed to offer support and love when it was needed most. Lord, none of us is without sin. We have all failed you in many ways. Have mercy upon us, forgive us. Reconcile mothers and fathers with their unborn children. Heal their grief and their guilt and their sorrow. Heal our society of the trauma of abortion (field notes).[5]

Therefore, whether or not a mortal sin had been committed, it was clear that activists still understood even women who were seemingly coerced to be in a sinful state as well as suffering from trauma caused by abortion. Here we can see abortion as a cause of both mental and spiritual harm being reaffirmed. But the notion of abortion as sinful was ameliorated by positioning *everyone* as being in a state of sin.

Thus, within Catholic responses, sin and redemption were underpinning ideas of both spiritual and mental harm. Whilst the gravity of abortion was seen as an incredibly serious sin, it was understood that if the 'correct' attitude was formulated, forgiveness was possible. Because it was women seeking abortion, this was gendered, and women were associated with this 'sin', even when men's culpability was referenced. These ideas foreground traditional understandings of women's sexuality and the inference that they should be obedient to a higher power in managing the 'danger' of their sexuality (Jantzen, 1998; Peters, 2018; Ruether, 1990). This is in line with their ideas of ultra-sacrificial motherhood

---

[5]Speeches at MfL were often made publicly available after the event allowing full transcription.

which focus on traditional and conservative gender roles. Whilst these conservative Catholic understandings situated women's behaviour as sinful, there was a route to atonement, even though this involved submission to male clerical authority, reorienting their understanding fully as a sin, and undertaking a confession and reparation. This 'appeasement' approach was presented more harshly and bluntly in the evangelical rhetoric we encountered:

> Laurence said that we [the activists] could convince a 'lady' to not go through with this and to instead have the child, but ultimately, they are still dead in their sin and going to hell, and so would their child, unless they repent and put their trust in Jesus (....) Lawrence says they are here not just to stop abortions but to more importantly 'to turn to Jesus Christ, submit to him and be born again' (...) He emphasised that hell is a real place (...) whether you believe it or not, you will end up in hell or heaven (Lawrence, field notes Midlands).

As an evangelical, Lawrence emphasised being 'born again'. As Woodhead outlines:

> Evangelicals affirm the supreme authority of the Bible, the sinfulness of humanity, full and perfect salvation through the work of Jesus Christ on the cross, the necessity of giving one's life to Jesus and being 'born again', the importance of a strict Biblical morality that affirms family values, and active evangelization (...) [Evangelicals put] emphasis on the importance of direct experience of the sacred (particularly in the experience of being 'born again' in the Spirit).
>
> (2004, p. 94)

Lawrence's idea that even if a woman chose to proceed with a pregnancy, both her and the child would be so sinful that they would go to hell was one of the most caustic and abrasive ideas that we encountered throughout the whole project, but was read through his understanding of the need for everyone to commit to Christ and therefore be 'born again'. At the point of being 'born again', the proclamation of faith in Jesus transforms the individual through the means of the Holy Spirit and one is 'saved' (Foubert, Angela, Brosi, & Fuqua, 2012), with this being a necessary process for anyone wanting to enter heaven. Therefore, although the theological work underpinning their ideas were different, both Catholic and evangelical anti-abortion accounts were premised on notions of sin, God's judgement, and taking the necessary steps to ensure that one was on the 'right side' of God. Yet the evangelical messaging came across as far more abrupt and damning.

Whether through confession, forgiveness, reparation or being 'born again', it was clear that you needed to be 'saved' from the spiritual harm caused by the 'sin' of abortion. Abortion is a rejection of the divine plan and therefore also a rejection of ultra-sacrificial motherhood idealised by anti-abortion activists. This position is heavily entwined with the claims of trauma and abortion regret. Recovery from these claimed mental health harms was through a religiously-informed process that focused on forgiveness for the sin of abortion. As well as risking their immortal soul, failure to embark on this road to recovery was deemed to leave women both spiritually and mentally bereft. This position was encapsulated in the idea of women being 'abortion hardened'.

As we have already described, many of the anti-abortion activists believe that abortion means that women are no longer able to be their true selves following abortion, because they have acted against the 'natural' role for women (Lowe & Page, 2020). This separation from the self is understood religiously as being alienated spiritually. It is the rejection of their divine role as mothers that is said to cause 'abortion hardening'. It is possible to recover from this position, but only through undergoing penance and seeking forgiveness for what they have done. This is an essential element of post-abortion recovery programmes as organised by anti-abortion organisations (Husain & Kelly, 2017).

Whilst it was never directly articulated by the activists, it appeared to us that 'abortion hardening' was the spiritual manifestation of abortion regret. It was deemed to be a serious and widespread problem. Indeed, many of the anti-abortion activists believe that those who campaign for abortion do so because they have not recovered from their own abortions (Lowe & Page, 2020). This belief also appeared to extend to us as researchers, with one anti-abortion activist stating that she believed Pam was 'post-abortive' as an explanation of her position on abortion. Seemingly, they could only explain why so many people support abortion by assuming that they were living with 'spiritual harm'.

The spiritual harm believed to be caused by abortion was not only limited to individuals but also had a broader impact, especially in the area surrounding an abortion provider. Anti-abortion activists themselves were told to be careful of the environment that they would be entering if planning to stand outside a clinic. The preparation section for pavement counsellors had a prayer which stated that:

> Protect us and our precious families, and all the brothers and sisters we will meet today. Help us to be the voice of those who cannot speak as we prepare for our work in the pro-life movement (...) We put on God's armour so that we can resist the devil's tactics and schemes (collected in the Midlands).

This need to be protected when in the vicinity of an abortion clinic was reiterated by others. At a meeting we attended for those about to undertake a *40 Days for Life* (*40DFL*) in 2015, the types of preparation needed to be in the space of an abortion clinic were spelt out in detail. The speaker, described as a Catholic hermit nun, stated that it was a risk being outside of the clinic, and anyone doing this needed to 'live a life of holiness'. Our field notes recorded that she stated:

> If praying outside of a clinic, you need to protect yourself against evil. Take holy water and sprinkle it on yourself at the beginning and the end. Don't sprinkle it on others, as they have good

lawyers. Take communion, go to Mass and use your rosary. It is spiritual warfare and this is your armour.

On this occasion, the speaker also described in some detail the involvement of Satanists and witchcraft in abortion, claiming that abortion clinics held Black Masses[6] and other 'evil' ceremonies within clinics. She attributed these stories to an account given by a former wizard in America who had converted to Catholicism.[7] There was no sign in the audience that this information was questioned. Nor were her other claims challenged about the link between Star Trek and child possession, or the spiritual danger of entering a New Age shop. She was introduced as someone who undertook deliverance ministry (cleansing people from evil), so presumably was deemed to be an expert on these risks.

The need to contain or reclaim abortion clinics from the 'evil' that dwelt within them could also be seen in other materials. Many standalone abortion clinics are housed in buildings that had been converted from other uses. At one clinic in the South-East, the abortion clinic was situated in a building that had previously housed a hostel run by an order of Catholic nuns. One of the leaflets given out by the *Good Counsel Network* (*GCN*) which sought to recruit people to pray outside this clinic featured two photos, one of the outside of the abortion clinic today, and the other of a picture of a chapel which the leaflet claimed was taken inside in the 1960s. The leaflet was headed in red block capitals 'End abortion in London and reclaim the building for our Lord and our Lady'. The GCN was also at pains to point out that another abortion clinic nearby had previously been a Chapel House and drew attention to the depiction of St Michael the Archangel engraved on the front of the building. The use of previously 'Christian' buildings was deemed to be particularly profaning and symbolic of the spiritual harm caused by abortion.

A dramatic example of concerns about the spread of evil was found in a leaflet advertising *MFL* in 2016. On the back of the leaflet, it explained the rationale for holding the event in Birmingham.[8] It stated:

> The largest single abortion provider in the UK is the British Pregnancy Advisory Service (BPAS) originally known as the Birmingham Pregnancy Advisory Service. Birmingham lies at the heart of the UK and has helped spread evil throughout our nation (...) Join us at the geographical roots of this evil to shower it with our witness of truth (*MFL UK*).

---

[6]A ritual associated with Satanism, based on an inversion of the Catholic Mass (van Luijk, 2017).

[7]Much of her speech seem to derive from the claims of Zachary King, who, around the time of this event, was marketing his story and conversion through appearances, YouTube and a book. His claims were readily accepted by some, but many others within the Christian anti-abortion movement questioned or dismissed them as untrue.

[8]Initially, MFL was held in the centre of Birmingham However, in 2018, the event relocated to London.

As it is described here, the spiritual harm of abortion is not contained in either the body of the women seeking abortion, or the place that abortions take place, but can have a national impact. In Chapter 9, we will outline in more details the claims that anti-abortion activists make about the wider cultural impact of abortion.

Summary

This chapter has outlined the ways in which the perception of women, as mothers, inevitably leads to specific claims about the harms of abortion. It began by outlining the idea that abortion is harmful to women and illustrated how these claims arise through their devotion to ultra-sacrificial motherhood. Their sacred commitment to the notion that all women are 'naturally' mothers, and that a pregnancy is a divine gift means that it is inconceivable that abortion would not be damaging. Their focus on claims about science and health in outlining the risks of abortion are in line with the broader shift from 'sin' to health in moral regulation movements and the ways in which risk narratives are a major framing of UK family policy. However, what remains clear is their religious understanding of abortion is a key influence in the adoption and presentation of health claims. Their claims of science are chosen, moulded, and shaped by their sacred commitments. Moreover, their understanding of abortion as a sin which causes spiritual harm underpins the claims that abortion inevitably causes trauma and regret, and this is informed by their understanding of the foetus. The next chapter will analyse further the centrality of the foetus to their campaign.

Chapter 6

Foetal Stories

Introduction

In this chapter, we build on the religious understanding of the anti-abortion activists and unpack how this influences the ways in which they, and the materials they distribute, construct a fixed discursive meaning of the foetus, utilising a mixture of religious and scientific narratives and where personhood was accorded from conception. We begin with outlining some of the central themes in the narratives about foetuses and how these are largely made possible by eliminating acknowledgement of pregnancy as an embodied state. Next, we will consider the ways in which the activists use the idea of uniqueness to construct potential foetal futures and therefore what is, or might be, lost. We will then examine the account of foetal death and show how the construction of these 'victims' of abortion remain crucial to anti-abortion framing and thus sacred claimsmaking. Finally, we will look at the anti-abortion activists' absolutist position in relation to foetal anomaly, sexual crime and threat to life and illustrate how building on the ideas of ultra-sacrificial motherhood we have already outlined, women were expected to be sacrificial in their decision-making, even, in some cases, to the extent of giving up their own lives. Hence, although the foetal stories could be read as contrasting with their emphasis on motherhood, they remain interrelated through the religious beliefs of the anti-abortion activists, as we will go on to show.

The Status of the Foetus

As detailed in Chapter 2, public images of the foetus have been used since just before the introduction of the *1967 Abortion Act* by anti-abortion groups to try to dissuade people from supporting abortion reform. Since then, as Lupton (2013) has shown, the meaning of the public foetus has expanded significantly. Lupton argues that:

> Human unborn organisms – embryos and foetuses – have become powerful and suggestive figures in contemporary scientific, legal, philosophical and popular arenas. They are entities invested with many different and often contrasting meanings and emotions, all

Anti-Abortion Activism in the UK, 91–111
Copyright © 2022 Pam Lowe and Sarah-Jane Page
Published under exclusive licence by Emerald Publishing Limited
doi:10.1108/978-1-83909-398-220221013

of which are highly contextual and constantly shifting in response to changes in medical science, technologies and popular representations (2013, p. 2).

Lupton (2013) describes how images of the embryo/foetus are no longer contained within the pregnant body; we have become used to seeing images in different contexts; however, their significance is contingent rather than fixed. A foetus in an advertisement for a car does not have the same meaning as a first ultrasound scan of an intended pregnancy shared with friends or family. As Eades (2019) argues, in England, the 24-week foetus is an example of this complexity in that it can be located in a womb, incubator or abortion clinic and its location will shape the social imaginary. She argues that the social practices surrounding it go beyond its pure biological existence. In other words, the foetus holds a complex subjective meaning at the cultural level that is shaped by the time and space which it occupies. At an individual level, pregnancy is also contingent and subjective, especially for those who are pregnant (Ross, 2016; Schmied & Lupton, 2001). Indeed, even women with an intended pregnancy often have a shifting understanding of the developing foetus as part or not part of the self (Lowe, 2016; Lupton, 2013).

This wider cultural ambiguity of the understanding of the foetus is not shared by anti-abortion activists. For them, the foetus is a sacred commitment, which constructs it with particular meanings. Conception is divinely ordained, and this sacred status positions the foetus as an objective 'fact'. The idea that its meaning could be contingent on other factors is unthinkable as this could challenge its sacred status. This produces a moral certainty for anti-abortion activists that abortion is wrong and underpins their conceptualisation of abortion as always harmful. Moreover, as we have argued elsewhere, their perception that life begins at conception, rooted in their religious beliefs, is now often bolstered by the adoption of scientific claims (Lowe & Page, 2019b).

A typical example of the foetal stories used by anti-abortion activists was found in a leaflet we collected in 2017 at a *40 Days for Life* (*40DFL*) vigil held outside a hospital in the South-East which hosts an abortion clinic. The leaflet (no clear author), which also appeared elsewhere, was A4 in size and has white and orange writing on a dark background. On one side of the leaflet, there is a free-floating Caucasian skin-coloured foetus in a sac attached, via an umbilical cord, to a similarly coloured piece of tissue representing the placenta. The shape of the face and limbs of the foetus are clearly visible. The image takes up just under a quarter of the page and is next to a list of foetal 'milestones' between conception and 12 weeks (e.g. the claimed appearance of heartbeat, brain waves, fingerprints). Whilst purporting to represent biological reality, the image has clearly been aestheticised, which is common practice for foetal images (Lupton, 2013). Above the image, the text reads:

> Before we can begin to look at whether abortion is right or wrong we need to go back further and ask, 'what does it mean to be pregnant?' Scientifically speaking, at conception a genetically

complete, living human being is created (...) Human life begins at conception, it is entirely arbitrary to choose any other starting point; this is the only tenable, scientific position to take.

In this quote, the scientific understanding of pregnancy does not seem to consider the pregnant body at all. The free-floating foetus is detached and is the only element in this narrative. However, it is important to remember that these ideas are held in a context where women are understood as mothers, and women are perceived as ignorant, pressured or coerced into abortion (Lowe and Page, 2019a, 2020). This means that the anti-abortion activists are starting from a position where they take for granted that women are 'naturally' inclined to continue a pregnancy; therefore, the implications of the status of the foetus for women does not need to be considered.

The leaflet mentions a central overriding belief of the anti-abortion activists we spoke to, that life began at conception, and needed to be protected from that point onwards. Indeed, the tag line for a number of the *March for Life* (*MFL*) campaigns, featured on the wristbands distributed and shouted during the marches, was 'Life from conception, no exception'. In our data, we found three approaches (not mutually exclusive) taken towards the foetus, all of which put the foetus in high esteem and on an equal par with the status of a fully-fledged, born baby – *equal rights*, *foetal independence* and *personhood*. Though the emphases differed, this equality status underpinned all three approaches. Firstly, some activists emphasised an *equal rights* positioning, emphasising dignity and respect, along with the sacredness for life, as the following quotes indicate:

The activists outline there is a baby involved and human life is sacred. They are defenceless; we have a duty to be there for the babies (field notes, Midlands).

I think the main thing about being pro-life is upholding the right of every single human being, whether that be the smallest of foetuses to the adult. So there is no difference, there is no argument to be made about an adult, a baby, or a foetus. All human life deserves their dignity (Daniel, *MFL* participant).

These data illustrate how unborn foetuses were frequently discussed in terms of being a 'baby' or a 'child'. And this status meant that they had an equivalent status to a born person. A slight variation on this first approach was through emphasising developmental processes:

...from the moment of conception, right the way to the person's last breath, everything is sacred (Toby interview).

I want a society that protects human life from the moment of conception right through to natural death (Christine interview).

This idea of development through the life course further emphasises the position of the foetus as being accorded equal status. This drew on a particular conservative Christian understanding of life that has contemporary origins. As Luker outlines, the conservative Catholic view is that 'an embryo is a child from conception onward and that abortion therefore ends the life of an innocent child' (1984, p. 128). A foetus is therefore accorded moral equivalence and is deemed to be in the same 'moral category' as a woman (1984, p. 156). This understanding of equivalence and equality was therefore bound up with a religious worldview, where the foetus is given sacred status that is equal to that of an already-born person. But this ignores the historically contingent ways in which personhood has been understood religiously – for example, in the Catholic Church, the idea of ensoulment *potentially* taking place at conception was only officially ratified in the mid-nineteenth century (Kamitsuka, 2019; Sjørup, 1999; Tauer, 1988).

The equality argument enabled the anti-abortion activists to challenge the idea that a woman has a 'right' to abortion. By giving equal status to the foetus, rights-based arguments for abortion based on the status of the woman as having full personhood, as opposed to the *potential* personhood of the foetus, were under-mined (Copelon, Zampas, Brusie, & deVore, 2005; Luker, 1984). Furthermore, this position removed the right of the woman to decide on the status of the foetus and her relationship to it. A contextual understanding of personhood is more aligned with the lived experiences of pregnant women, where the woman makes a decision, or not, to recognise the status of the foetus through continuing with the pregnancy (Kamitsuka, 2019; Keane, 2009; Maguire, 1988). Personhood from this perspective is not biologically determined, but is relational, and is achieved only when the broader community (initially through the woman carrying the foetus) recognises it as such (Maguire, 1988).

The second approach emphasised the *independence* of the foetus – that its existence was separate to that of the woman. In buttressing this point of view, both science and religion were utilised:

> ...it is not just a women's body; we are carriers when we carry children. It is in our body, our body but it is a completely separate living entity with its own human DNA, its own bloodstream. It relies on the mother for life, yes. In the same way as a new born baby relies on the mother or people around it, for it in order to live (Lucy, *MFL* participant).

> Dominik says that his goal is to change hearts and minds about abortion and to make people realise that the baby that is growing inside the woman's womb is a separate human being. It is growing in her womb but it is a separate life, and it is not only about a woman's right to choose because a woman wouldn't have the right to kill a random person on the street (...) Barry says that it is certainly a Catholic point of view. He says that life is sacred from the moment of conception (field notes, Midlands).

Lucy's quote not only emphasises the idea of pregnant women as incubators, but builds on the developmental narrative that gives equivalence between a new-born baby, who requires care for survival, with a foetus in the womb requiring support to survive. These narratives also emphasise something else – that the foetus is a wholly separate entity to the woman.

We also found this position in the leaflet described above from the South-East. It outlined in detail what is commonly explained as the 'SLED' argument. 'SLED' stands for size, length of development, environment and degree of dependency and is used to make a claim that there are no significant differences between a foetus and a baby. In relation to the size, development and dependency, for example, it is common to point out that children grow and develop throughout childhood. This particular leaflet states that the foetus is just a stage of size, development and dependency, just like toddlers are different from teens:

> 'Fetus' designates a particular stage in development in the life of a human being (....) Saying an unborn child is not human, because she/he is a 'fetus', makes as much sense as saying a 15yr-old is not human because she/he is a 'teenager'.

The position adopted is that having unique DNA from the moment of conception is what makes someone both human and alive, and the fact that the foetus is contained within the pregnant body is irrelevant. The foetus is 'genetically complete' and therefore an independent person. The last element of the SLED argument, environment, clearly reduces the pregnant person to the status of an incubator (Lowe & Page, 2019a). Indeed, prioritising the science of DNA not only enables an alignment between humanness and personhood in the minds of anti-abortion activists; it is also seen to support the full independence of the foetus. Biologists, meanwhile, critique this understanding, with maternal cytoplasm required for cell division to take place, irrespective of the foetus's individual genetic material (Kamitsuka, 2019).

The idea that there is no real difference between a foetus and a baby was also often underlined by some of the activists who informed us that actually 'foetus' is just the Latin word for 'baby'. We occasionally suggested to them that language is not fixed, and thus even if this had been the case originally, it is largely irrelevant now because it no longer carries the same meaning. This was not something that many of the anti-abortion activists could contemplate. For them, language is, or should be, fixed and unchanging. Some even suggested that using the word 'foetus' was a deliberate strategy to mislead people as part of a broader agenda to enable abortions to be culturally permissible. Due to their sacred commitment, for them, the foetus is an objective entity with equivalence to a baby; widening the understanding of the fixed meaning of the term as 'baby' would help solidify this position into wider culture. There was no recognition that the foetus could be contingent and subjective either individually or more broadly.

The third approach more overtly draws upon scientific language to denote what Luker (1984) calls 'real' *personhood* to the foetus, rather than 'potential' personhood. In all three positions, scientific perspectives are prioritised, rather than theological ones:

> Ian also went to see an [embryology expert] who told him that we are formed from the genetic material. From this he concluded that personhood begins from conception. This was the scientific position, not one from faith (field notes, North).

> When he was younger Nathan used to think it was just a couple of cells, but then he was educated (…) Since then he has learnt more about 'the facts' and he watches videos online, although he declares that some are rubbish. He tells me that they discovered that there is a flash of light when the sperm goes into an egg (field notes, North).

Participants stressed that personhood was a non-negotiable 'fact' that was not premised on levels of development but was there from conception; Ian asserted not that humanness begins at conception, but that personhood did. They therefore rejected outright the idea of *potential* personhood, more commonly aligned with a pro-choice viewpoint and where personhood is contextually negotiated (Keane, 2009; Luker, 1984). Participants were keen to express their own learning on this topic and their attempts to secure knowledge from credible and trustworthy sources. They also highlighted the non-theological dimensions of their viewpoint. Ian even emphasised he had consulted experts in the field, though whether they would share his conclusions is impossible to say. Ian utilised unique DNA as the issue that denoted personhood, contributing to an understanding of the foetus as equal. Meanwhile Nathan's knowledge is not as assured. His main source of knowledge is YouTube videos, and although he tries to be discerning, he had been led to understand that at the moment of conception, a flash of light occurs, giving it an awe-inspiring status. It was not the only time we heard such a claim. But it is likely that this is a misunderstanding in relation to a scientific experiment using chemical fluorescence.[1] This idea was appealing to Nathan, as the idea of there being a flash of light corresponds with the religious concept of ensoulment. This is rooted in the idea that along with a life being created, a soul is formed (Lowe & Page, 2019a).

In ascertaining the status of the foetus, three key claims are made amongst anti-abortion activists: firstly that the foetus has equivalent status to a baby, child or fully grown adult, and this gave it specific rights. Secondly, that it has independent status and its total reliance on the bodily systems of the woman is irrelevant. And thirdly, that personhood is accorded to the foetus, linked in some cases with the religious idea of ensoulment. These are not mutually exclusive ideas, and as the data above indicate, the ideas are overlapping. The evidence base for the status accorded the foetus also include a mixture of religious and

---

[1]Public accounts exist of this misunderstanding, for example, the National Catholic Register (www.ncregister.com/blog/trasancos/pro-lifers-there-is-no-flash-of-light-at-conception).

'scientific' claims, with particular emphasis accorded to unique DNA. As Elsdon-Baker and Mason-Wilkes (2019) argue, the relationship between religion and science is complex. Despite an assumption of an antithetical relationship between science and religion, especially for conservative religious groups, the reality is that scientific ideas can be readily drawn upon and accommodated. Here, science-like arguments forge two key purposes: an appeal to rational-sounding arguments are an attempt at making the anti-abortion case more palatable to non-religious audiences, but they also establish an outward-facing group identity that show-cases progress and advancement, given that scientific narrative is understood in these terms (Elsdon-Baker & Mason-Wilkes, 2019).

Foetal Futures

Through the emphasis on DNA, ideas about the uniqueness of each future foetus could also be found in the activists' accounts and written materials. The narratives about foetal lives often contained an emphasis on the potential contribution they could make to society. These notions were visible in the theme of *Irreplaceable* for the *2019 MFL*. The programme for the event stated:

> ...we hear stories of well known people whose mothers were offered abortions which they courageously refused: these babies grew up to be musicians, celebrities, even a pope – this helps us see more clearly what (...) we are losing with every abortion. But it is important that we don't value people based on what they do (...) Every unemployed man, every woman in a psychiatric hospital, every bedridden old lady, every homeless teenager is unique, of value and irreplaceable.

This extract reiterates the idea that abortion is usually a result of coercion or pressure as it suggests that women who decided not to have abortions have 'courageously refused'. In it, we can also see a common element in the foetal future narrative that abortion could be responsible for the loss of many 'great' people, such as musicians or a pope. This idea rests on an individualist narrative in which societal developments are the result of singular 'heroes', rather than ideas, events and 'progress' as being the outcome of collaborations and collective learning over time. The abortion could kill a 'great man' theory was also illustrated by a speaker in a previous *MFL* (2016) when a claim was made that the iPhone only existed because Steve Jobs had been adopted rather than his birth mother choosing abortion. This simplistic narrative clearly overlooks the complex and multiple factors that are behind all technological innovations and how adult lives are not pre-destined, but entwined with the circumstances in which they are raised.

However, unlike the iPhone example, the fact that not all lives are destined for 'greatness' is acknowledged in the *MFL* programme through the portrayal of the list of more marginalised positions that are also presented as unique lives. The particular categories chosen for this list is interesting in the way that they fit with other broader ideas of the anti-abortion movement. The first is the 'unemployed man'. As we have outlined in Chapter 4, much of the anti-abortion movement believes in the 'ideal' family where women are mothers and men are providers. If men are unemployed, they are clearly not able to fulfil this 'natural' role. As a leaflet by *Post Abortion Support for Everyone* (*PASE*) states:

> The father of the baby can find himself unable to influence the decision being made (...) many men feel confused and devastated (...) their instinct to protect has been thwarted (...) a man who perhaps welcomed abortion originally as a 'sensible' option, may only many years later appreciate that it was their son or daughter that died (collected in the South-East).

As this extract illustrates, men can be divorced from their role as protectors in relation to abortion. Here, like in other accounts, this is believed to arise from a lack of understanding as to what abortion 'really' is, the 'death' of their child. For many of the anti-abortion activists we spoke to, the position of men often seemed ambiguous. On one hand, part of the 'problem' of abortion is men abandoning their 'natural' responsibility towards their pregnant partners. They may encourage abortion as a 'sensible' option, which leaves women unsupported, or even worse, men could exert pressure on them to have abortions. Yet at the same time, some argued that men have been emasculated from their 'natural' role in society, not least by positioning abortion as a women's decision. This complex mix of potential male positions in relation to abortion has also been found in the United States (US) (Arey, 2020). In the United Kingdom (UK), as in many other places, anti-abortion attempts failed in obtaining a legal right for putative fathers to stop abortions. The judgements have clearly stated that men cannot prevent women terminating pregnancies.[2]

The focus on the '*unemployed man*' in the *MFL* programme is thus an interesting one. It could be read as an example of a 'failed' or 'emasculated' provider. This position is likely to have a particular resonance for those who believe in the traditional view of fatherhood. Moreover, it fits with broader narratives of the 'dangers' of feminism as articulated in the religious critique of what is called 'gender ideology', a notion that the 'natural' gender roles and sexuality is under threat (this will be discussed in more detail later). Yet at the same time, the programme is articulating the idea that ordinary lives have value and, specifically, that the anti-abortion movement values them. As Arey (2020) argues, positioning men as potentially a 'deadbeat' but also calling on them to 'step-up' and become a supporter of a continuing pregnancy creates a mixture of masculinity discourses that reinforce men as potential 'heroes' that can 'save' women from abortion.

The second category of marginalised people is the '*woman in a psychiatric hospital*'. As we described in the previous chapter, the idea that abortion is linked

---

[2]For example, see *Paton v. United Kingdom App. No. 8416/78, 3 Eur. H.R. Rep. 408, 1980.*

to mental health issues is widespread. Although there is no direct claim made to women who have had abortions, given the widespread association, it is likely that many anti-abortion activists who read this would associate this as an outcome of abortion. As a leaflet by *Abortion Recovery Care and Helpline (ARCH)* explains:

> Many women spend years in a confused state of denial, guilt and regret using misplaced energy in trying to discover and remedy what is wrong with them. Many turn to alcohol, substance abuse and promiscuity to deaden the lingering pain from this unrecognised experience (collected at the 2016 *MFL*).

As this extract illustrates, and in line with Lee's (2003) earlier findings, there are two themes within the understanding of post-abortion syndrome (PAS). The first is that it is a serious mental health issue with multiple possible symptoms, and the second is that it is unrecognised or denied. This has the effect of allowing anti-abortion activists to be able to attribute any mental health issue to a previous abortion; any challenge to this position is dismissed as denial. As Ehrlich and Doan (2019) have shown, the abortion regret narrative is 'laced with a sacralised conception of women's essential maternalism' (2019, p. 92). Moreover, the cultural trope of the 'mad woman' who fails at her pre-destined motherhood (Chesler, 2005) is much broader than the anti-abortion movement. Consequently, the figure of the *'woman in a psychiatric hospital'* aligns with both the positioning of women as victims of abortion and the broader general understanding of women as irrational beings, especially if they have been thwarted from becoming mothers for any reason.

Whilst the third category in the *MFL* programme, the *'bedridden old lady'*, appears to be less embedded in anti-abortion narratives, it is worth pointing out that this is an offensive description. Whilst the anti-abortion movement often claims to be supportive of disability rights, this leaflet indicates some may have a limited understanding rather than holding an inclusive approach. The final example, *'homeless teenager'*, returns to the idealised family, in that 'troubled teens' are often presumed to be at risk of 'undesirable' sexual activity and thus unintended pregnancies. In the UK generally, abortion seekers are often stereotyped as young, unmarried women, despite statistics clearly indicating that abortions happen throughout reproductive lives; neither marital status nor the presence or absence of existing children have an impact on abortion trends, although they may be factors of individual decision-making (Purcell, Hilton, & McDaid, 2014).

The emphasis on these four categories of marginalised people who are still worthy, and *irreplaceable*, alongside the more positive futures of 'great' people, suggests a pre-destined future foetus that is fixed in its development and outcomes. Moreover, it also resonates with other concerns that many of the anti-abortion activists have that abortion is a 'gateway' to other problems in society. These broader concerns of the impact of the 'abortion culture' will be discussed in more detail in Chapter 9. Next, we turn to their understanding of abortion as a form of murder.

Foetal Death

The overwhelming majority of the materials we collected from anti-abortion groups focused on pictures of aestheticised free-floating foetuses designed to draw attention to 'child-like' elements such as facial expressions and feet, assigned behaviour such as waving and thumb-sucking, or the future potential of the foetus by aligning it at a development stage similar to being a toddler or teen. In presenting these foetal stories, the aim was to focus on the imagined future in order that, as we have previously described, women recognise their 'true' maternal feelings and continue with the pregnancy. It was only a minority of sites and materials that sought to situate the foetal abortion story as largely one of death rather than future hope, mainly through the use of graphic images. As we will later show, this was a contested issue amongst the anti-abortion activists in Britain, with some openly speaking out against them. Graphic images were more commonly used in Northern Ireland (NI).

It is important to recognise that even though the 'foetal death' narratives are the opposite of the 'future hope' framing, they often rested on similar understandings. For example, in December 2017, the *Centre for Bioethical Reform UK* (*CBR*) set up their abortion education project in a Midlands city centre. They were there as part of their *Awakening Tour*, a specific campaign visiting different towns and cities that they developed for the 50th anniversary of the *1967 Abortion Act*. They constructed their display in front of an empty shop on a pedestrianised street. The street was busy with Christmas shoppers, and market stalls competed with the Christmas shop window displays for attention. Nearby, in the middle of the thoroughfare, in front of the anti-abortion display, was a street entertainer. Every 30 minutes or so, he started his show, playing loud music whilst performing a tumbling display through hoops that were on fire. Each time this happened, a large crowd gathered around him; it became really difficult for shoppers to just walk past the anti-abortion display.

The anti-abortion display consisted of two large images, approximately two metres by two metres in size (see Fig. 2). In the first, is a picture of a black slave, kneeling in chains, who is labelled as a victim of the transatlantic slave trade. Across the top of the display it says: '#Our Blind Spot – THEN'. The other image, with a matching message, '#Our Blind Spot – NOW', is an image of a dismembered foetus, who is labelled as a victim of the 'abortion Industry'. The text states that the foetus was 11 weeks. It is in pieces, and this means at first glance, it is not immediately recognisable unless you read the text. In the busy street, many of the passers-by do not give it a second look.

Alongside the display, there are leaflets that the anti-abortion activists hand out to the few passers-by that engage with them. This gives more detail about the comparison of these two images as well as containing other graphic images of bloodied foetuses. It argues that slavery existed because slaves were 'dehumanised' through language, attitudes and from being 'hidden from view', and it is similar trends that allow abortion to take place. This relies on the personhood narrative outlined above. Another leaflet handed out on the same day states:

Fig. 2.   Slavery Comparison.

> Cloaked in euphemisms they [abortion industry] fail to adequately
> inform the mother that her developing baby is torn apart inside her
> then suctioned out. The embryo or fetus is the most vulnerable and
> defenceless of all people and yet is denied the most basic of human
> rights: the right to life (*CBR*).

As we can see in this extract, and we have described elsewhere (Lowe & Page,
2019a), the rationale for the use of graphic images of abortion is that women in
particular are misled about it, and if they, and society more generally, are shown
the 'reality' of abortion, it will end.

During the demonstration, the organisers undertook a live video recording
where the following message was conveyed:

> They [pro-choice counterdemonstrators] are trying to say that a
> woman has the right to murder a child because they are in their
> own body, which is the same argument we used for slavery. If a
> slave was on our land, we said we had the right to do what we
> want.

There is no language amelioration or attempts to 'tone down' their public
messages. A woman accessing abortion is starkly aligned with being a murderer
and akin to slave owners. However, an implicit message here is also the idea that
the general public will come to its senses and understand how appalling abortion
is, like they came to understand slavery as unjust and inhumane. Thus, although
women are deemed murderers, implicitly, it was not intentional, as they lacked
education and understanding. Moreover, by comparing themselves to the anti-
slavery campaign, anti-abortion activism is contextualised as progressive and
ahead of its time, rather than a backward step in curtailing women's reproductive
rights. Their campaign strategy, like the foetal development images, assumes that

images have a single meaning and that once people are 'awakened' they will see and automatically understand that abortion is wrong. Yet as Eades (2019) describes, displays of graphic abortion images provoke a range of different reactions in passers-by, and many repudiated the narrative the anti-abortion activists project.

There is not room here to fully explore the claims about slavery, but it is worth noting a few salient points. Despite their idea that images have a fixed and objective meaning, the impact of the use of grotesque images within social movements is complex. Whilst they hope to convey a moral certitude about right and wrong, the impact may be different depending on whether the viewer is already a supporter or not (Halfmann & Young, 2010). The use of slavery itself as an analogy as an obvious wrong has a long history. For example, in the nineteenth century, it was used in relation to a broad range of causes including workers' rights, child rights and the protection of animal welfare (Kim, 2011). The focus on the transatlantic slave, particularly by evangelical anti-abortion groups, positions the abolition of slavery as a white Christian movement in which the dehumanised slave was finally seen as a person (Guenther, 2012). The British MP William Wilberforce is often referred to and a quote from him was found on the campaign leaflet given out at the display. This framing completely ignores the pivotal work of Black abolitionist campaigners in ending slavery. Moreover, it is important to recognise that the racialised framing inherent in this discourse weaponises Black women's painful history of reproductive coercion to deny abortions to both them and others (Guenther, 2012; Luna, 2018). Moreover, in the context of a colonial legacy in which British abortion law was exported globally, taking the stance that (white) Christian values on abortion are universal needs to be understood as a neo-colonial standpoint (Malvern & Macleod, 2018).

In general, the language of taking a life, killing, and murder was more muted at the vigil sites, where, as we will explore later, there was a concern not to alienate those seeking services. The exception to this in Britain was campaigns underpinned by an evangelical Christian approach, where women seeking abortion were specifically called out as murderers:

> Lawrence said 'we are here to preach the gospel of Jesus and to encourage women and men not to kill their kids'. Pam asked their motivation and Lawrence stated that it was that they didn't want 'live babies to be murdered', and it was the glory of God ultimately. As Christians, mankind was made in God's image and there was value in life, to end it was murder (field notes, Midlands).

Meanwhile, prayer vigils such as *40DFL* were far more subtle in their messaging; indeed, many deemed the messages conveyed by groups like *CBR* unhelpful. Maria, for example, said that, 'personally I don't like their tactics'. But at the same time, while the prayer vigil activists were motivated to position themselves very differently – through prayerful practices and offers of help – this was still underpinned by a fundamental belief that a child was being killed (Page

& Lowe, 2021a). This understanding was occasionally conveyed in situ at clinic sites, as detailed in the following encounters:

> William [an activist] is currently talking to someone (...) we presume it is a passer-by (...) As we went past we heard the words, 'it's murder' (field notes, South-East).

> Anne says that the *40DFL* prayers are helpful in addressing people from different religions. She says that they pray in an informal way as well. And if there is someone who isn't sure as they are going in, they will pray that they will change their mind. And God doesn't want them to 'kill their baby'. But she said God won't come down and turn people away from the clinic – so 'we are doing His work' (field notes, North).

Therefore, despite the focus on prayerful witnessing, the rhetoric of killing and murder was very close to the surface. Indeed, in in-depth interviews, which often took place away from the clinic sites, participants explained more fully their views about abortion as a form of killing:

> I always had this very strong feeling that 'Thou shalt not kill,' that commandment is sacred to me (...) When my second child was on the way our GP who knew our circumstances, my husband [was] on a very, very low grant and we were struggling a bit, and he [GP] actually offered me an abortion. I hadn't thought of doing that (...) When I registered what he was saying, he didn't say, 'I could kill your baby', he said, 'I could terminate it for you right now' (Rosie interview).

> [Abortion is] an intrinsic evil, no matter how it's packaged, it is always morally wrong. It's murder. It's the taking of an innocent life and to destroy an innocent life is always morally wrong (Jeoffrey interview.

> ...if you accept these are children who are being killed, then we need to do something (Christine interview).

Therefore, although the outward messaging was packaged very differently, and many of those participating in prayer vigils were deeply opposed to the tactics of groups who utilised graphic images and directed the term 'murder' at clinic users, it was still the case that this was also their underpinning belief. But there was an understanding that calling out clinic users using such language would not endear them to the message, especially as women were positioned as not being fully responsible for their actions. Hence at many clinic sites, the tone was softened and made more palatable. As Chapter 7 will emphasise, one key aim of the prayers was to ask for God to intervene to stop women from having abortions – thereby reducing the need for shock tactics. Constructing their message as embodied through prayer – associated with being peaceful, helpful and sacred – enabled them to downplay any rhetoric such as taking a life, killing and murder. Yet fundamentally, this very rhetoric was embedded in their understanding of abortion and connected to how they conceptualised the foetus. Moreover, this was, they believed, the underlying cause of the mental and spiritual harm to women, as no *mother* could countenance causing harm to their 'child'.

Graphic images were also largely absent in materials we collected, even when abortion is described in similar terms. For example, a small leaflet collected in a Northern English city in 2016 has a prayer on one side to 'save a child from abortion', with, on the other, an image of an intact foetal sac, in a tear-shaped image, with an outline of the foetus visible within the amniotic fluid. It states:

> On the right you see a *living* baby which was surgically removed (…) due to an ectopic pregnancy (…) This baby (…) was no more than 6 weeks old and was vigorously moving in the sac (…) At 6 weeks the skeleton is established and at 8 weeks she is sensitive to light and pain (…) ***In England & Wales alone it is estimated that 600 babies are killed EVERY DAY by abortion*** (…) ***Please pray for the protection of our people and our country!*** (Human Life International Ireland, emphasis as original)

Although this leaflet contains a similar 'foetal death' narrative story to the large graphic displays by emphasising that abortion is 'killing' a 'living' baby, it combines this with the 'foetal development' story. It again narrates a fixed understanding of the sacred form of the foetus as a 'child already living' whose life could be curtailed because of a lack of comprehension of the foetus, along with foetal death due to a perceived ignorance of the 'reality' of abortion. Less commonly than in other materials, it combines this with both religious exhortation to pray and a concern about the wider impact of abortion. Moreover, the decision to use an image from an ectopic pregnancy, where the foetus is implanted in the fallopian tube, rather than the womb, is particularly interesting, given this is a life-threatening condition. In the next section, we will explore how the activists explained their absolutist stance in relation to this and other serious circumstances.

The Absolutist Stance

The idea that some abortions are more excusable than others is deeply ingrained in cultural understandings and can occur even amongst those who support abortions (Baird & Millar, 2019; Weitz, 2010). Taking an absolutist stance – where abortion in any circumstance is wrong – meant that the anti-abortion activists needed to carefully navigate abortion for reasons of foetal anomaly, sexual crimes and if the pregnancy was life-threatening, given that even those who are against abortion being available on request often think access should be available in these cases (Clements, 2014; Scott, 1998). For some anti-abortion activists, the exception was when a woman's life was in danger, and some did concede that this would be a legitimate reason, but they deployed the doctrine of double effect, as we will explain below.

Firstly, foetal anomaly. There were a number of ways that anti-abortion activists argued that having a foetal anomaly was not grounds for abortion. Typically speaking, activists downplayed any medical diagnosis of a foetal anomaly by arguing that the tests could be wrong:

> Fran then recalled a story of a woman who was told her baby had a 'deformity' but when she (...) had the baby, it was fine. Staff put that fear and doubt in people's minds for no reason. The scans can be very imprecise (...). She also recalled a friend who was diagnosed with precancerous cells when pregnant and they wanted to give her a course of radiotherapy to destroy the cells, but this would damage the baby. She pressed on with the pregnancy and the baby was born fine, and they investigated again and the precancerous cells had gone. She reiterated her position that it's very difficult but if you get onto that slippery slope where you say abortion is right in some circumstances, where do you draw the line? (field notes, South-West)

Another issue raised was the general leniency towards what was classified as a disability, arguing that abortions were allowed for 'trivial' reasons and that the abortion law was far too relaxed:

> Kathleen said that women now have abortions for trivial things like 'clubfoot, harelip as well as Downs' (field notes, North).

> Charlie then raises the issue of disability and how it is wrong that disabled babies are given less worth. He thought this was a terrible situation (field notes, Scotland).

By emphasising equal status and minor reasons for disability as a route to abortion, these individuals were able to resituate such cases under the same remit as any other foetus and did not see this as a special case. Just like in the programme detailed earlier, many of them used offensive language to describe disability. A more challenging issue to maintain was disability cases where life outside the womb was not viable. But even here, the emphasis was on the importance of allowing the baby to be born:

> Pam asks if they think there is a difference between a case when you could live with a disability and one that could not survive outside of the womb. Alicia says that if the child is loved, because they want the child and then they find out it is disabled, why not bring that child to birth. 'Isn't it better to see your child, and to love your child, rather than to say I want to end my child's life'

(...) Theresa says that she knew someone in that position; their child only lived a few hours, but they loved that child throughout. They healed and became pregnant again with twins. 'It was like God was saying, here is one to heal your loss and another one' (field notes, South-West).

Roger says he doesn't agree with terminations for disability. Pam asks what if it will be fatal. He says that it is better for women to spend that time with their child, and for it to be treated better when it dies. It is a human life. He says that children should have a chance (field notes, Midlands).

Alicia and Theresa believed that it was God's decision to make regarding when a life ended, and this informed both their position that abortion in the case of a fatal foetal anomaly should not be allowed, as well as the idea that God was at the core of the healing process too. By leaving the situation to God, in their mind, it meant that everything would work out. This investment in transcendental intervention also allowed them to give great weight to the perceived imprecision of foetal screening, and the 'miraculous' outcomes when cancer disappeared and babies were born without any disability. But what Alicia's, Theresa's and Roger's position ultimately means is that they would wish to remove the right for a woman to end that pregnancy, thereby potentially putting her through a full-term birth of a baby that will not survive. It is assumed by them that taking such a pregnancy to term is always in the best interests of the woman; but this ignores women's lived experience. As Lalor et al.'s (2009) study found, even for those who did not terminate their pregnancy, receiving a serious anomaly diagnosis was often experienced as a bereavement, and the journey to acceptance of the situation was complex, with some women articulating that they had hoped for a stillbirth to remove the decision from them.

Similar to foetal anomaly, abortion after a sexual crime is also not typically considered a good enough reason for abortion. In analysing the data, the most 'pro-choice' view we could locate on this was in speaking to Bill who was participating in a vigil in the Midlands. He argued that

...he could understand that women could be very traumatised by rape, and affirmed the view that it was still up to the women to decide but they should consider the issue deeply, and the woman should not take it out on the child, and there is always adoption (field notes Midlands).

While sympathising with the gravity of a situation like rape, and also unusually arguing that the woman herself should be able to make the choice, there was a lack of reflexivity regarding how women themselves would manage this situation – first an assumption that they may not give the issue enough thought, secondly that an abortion should be understood in terms of 'taking it out' on a 'child' and the idea that adoption was a solution. As Triseliotis, Shireman, and Hundleby (1997) note, after the *1967 Abortion Act* was passed, women were far more likely to choose abortion over adoption. The idea that adoption becomes the solution to an unwanted pregnancy ignores the lived experiences of women – the relational dimension to pregnancy and the feelings invested as the foetus gets nearer to full personhood; giving a baby away at birth is therefore a significantly different experience to abortion (Peters, 2018).

Meanwhile for others, the numbers of abortions needed due to sexual crimes was downplayed:

> He did feel sorry if there was a question of rape or incest, and he described this as a difficult issue. But he said that 99.9% of abortions have nothing to do with that (Steve, field notes Midlands).

> [In cases of rape] the only victim is the child, the only innocent person is the child; it's an absolutely innocent (Tara, *MFL* 2016).

It is striking that in both of these encounters, there was an absence of reflection of how the woman experienced the situation; instead there was a minimising of how prevalent the issue of pregnancy due to rape was (which also subtly undermines the significant levels of rape and sexual assault in UK society) and an apparent prioritising and centralising of the foetus over the woman. For other activists, women's experiences were considered, but with the conclusion that women would always be better off by continuing with the pregnancy and taking to term and birthing the child of her rapist, which linked both with fundamental understandings of women's mothering responsibilities, as well as the idea that abortion was always a traumatic event:

> I know that, if I were a woman and I became pregnant, say as a result of rape, I know it would be absolutely the greatest challenge for me, the most difficult thing in my life to do, will be to give birth to that child (...) rape is always wrong, but abortion is always wrong too. Two wrongs don't make a right (Jeoffrey interview).

> Rape isn't necessarily, to me, a reason to have an abortion. The baby hasn't done anything wrong. The man has done something wrong (...). But why should the baby be punished by being killed? Then the mother's body, in a way, is violated twice. First of all she's raped and then a baby is ripped out of her. Even if at that moment she wanted that, later on she may well grieve for that child she's lost because that would be her basic instinct (Rosie interview).

> ...Miriam said that if you have an abortion, it doesn't unrape. It doesn't take away the rape. But it does add another dimension to it, when you have taken away a life (...) others have given them up

for adoption, so that other loving couples can make a home for them (field notes, South-West).

Jeoffrey's account recognises that to ask a woman to birth her rapist's child might be something that is difficult to do. However, his belief is that she should proceed with the pregnancy, and despite these challenges, there is no room for abortion. Meanwhile Rosie's and Miriam's accounts foreground women's experience more fully, but they come to the conclusion that women themselves are harmed by terminating a pregnancy due to rape, and abortion regret will be the outcome. Again, adoption is hailed as a panacea for women who do not want to keep the child, with little reflection on the lived experience of handing a baby over to adoption services. Meanwhile, for Miriam, the child is imagined as being adopted into a childless family. Implicitly here, partnerships without children are deemed as lacking, and this 'failure' to meet heteronormative expectations is addressed for Miriam through being able to adopt a child born of rape. The extent to which this is reflexively from the raped woman's perspectives varies significantly. But even in cases where more weight is given to the considerable ask of a woman birthing her rapist's child, there is an assumption that the woman should come to the 'right' decision and not proceed with an abortion. In short, the prevailing view amongst activists was that having an abortion did not undo the wrongfulness of the rape; therefore abortion was not justified. Their perception of ultra-sacrificial motherhood is evoked as a means of supporting this perspective.

The most compelling reason for the legitimation of abortion is often considered to be when the woman's life is in danger (Gray & Wellings, 2020; Scott, 1998). This could therefore be considered one area where anti-abortion activists would concede that abortion was necessary. However, the discursive strategies utilised by activists were complex, and it was not the case that abortion was readily accepted as necessary in such situations. We have already emphasised Fran's 'slippery slope' argument, holding an absolutist position, outlining that if abortion was allowed in certain circumstances, 'where do you draw the line?' And some activists did imply that women should be willing to sacrifice their own lives for the sake of their child:

> Bill then recited a story about a woman who was sainted in the 1960s (St Gianna Molla). She took a pregnancy to full term even though she had ovarian cancer; she had the baby, died and was later sainted (field notes, Midlands).

This draws on the ultimate notion of maternal sacrifice (Lowe, 2016), but goes further in what we call ultra-sacrificial motherhood, where women should be prepared to die so that their child can live. But other strategies revolved around minimising the likelihood of such a medical emergency occurring in the first place, along with understandings that any medical intervention needed was not strictly required. Some insisted that the necessity of abortion due to a medical emergency was overplayed and that this rationale for abortion was overblown by pro-choice advocates:

Obviously, there's a few extreme circumstances like ectopic pregnancies where the mother and baby would both die anyway if it wasn't removed, but mostly, in modern medicine I think there's very, very few medical conditions where the mother's life would be at risk if she goes ahead with the pregnancy (Rosie interview).

Roger says nothing in the church harms women's lives. Pam says that women can die because they need abortions. He says that if a woman's life is at risk, then procedures can be taken to save her life. It is a myth that if it is a Catholic country then women will die (field notes, Midlands).

A woman's life being in danger was therefore understood as an exceptional event, which modern medicine could successfully manage. Even high-profile cases where women had died from lacking access to a timely abortion, such as Savita Halappanavar in Ireland, were downplayed and minimised by activists, with a perception that it was incredibly rare for a woman's life to 'really' be in danger. Rosie referenced ectopic pregnancy to acknowledge the 'life in danger' argument. But great discursive work could be deployed to articulate that this was not 'really' an abortion, as Jeoffrey outlines:

God's law comes first and therefore I would have to say that no civilised country should permit abortion at all. The only time in which a child of the womb can be killed is if it happens as a by-product of some procedure to save the mother's life. It can never be intended (Jeoffrey interview).

Jeoffrey therefore saw issues such as the extraction of the foetus from the fallopian tube as a 'by-product' activity and not an abortion per se. This is called the doctrine of double effect and is official Catholic doctrine (International Theological Commission, 2002). Whilst this might appeal to the anti-abortion movement, it is not generally recognised by the general public. Thus, their claim there is no medical need for abortion is seen as, at best, disingenuous. The pro-choice community's frequent chant 'Pro-life, that's a lie. You don't care if women die' indicates how this absolutist stance against abortion is more broadly inter-preted, as one in which women's deaths are seen as preferable. Meanwhile, the doctrine of double effect means that anti-abortion activists themselves can deny that abortion restrictions are ever responsible for maternal deaths because if followed properly, medical intervention is possible (Lowe & Page, 2020).

The discursive strategy of reframing a medical intervention to be primarily about something else (saving a woman's life), and away from the idea of abortion, allowed Jeoffrey and other activists to concurrently hold the position that abor-tion was always wrong, alongside the position that a woman was not being asked to sacrifice her own life. In general terms, this enabled Catholics to take a less draconian view, when, as Luker argues, 'the present Catholic position on when life begins means that abortion in all cases implies the death of a full human being'. (1984, p. 60). This anti-abortion position is ameliorated to some extent, given that the idea that a woman's life should not be saved would be anathema within the broader context of UK society.

Learning Opportunities for Activists

The discussions we encountered among activists were formulated in a particular environment. Key events such as *MFL* were used as opportunities to convey specific messages on how to manage difficult questions around abortion. This was a recurrent theme at the online *MFL* 2020.

One panel involving medical professionals explicitly discussed risk to life, articulating similar viewpoints to the ones we have already outlined. One doctor, for example, drew upon the exceptionality argument – that abortions to save a woman's life was incredibly rare, and countered that 'To intentionally end the life of the child is usually not medically necessary'. Another doctor on the panel went on to support this viewpoint, saying 'If everyone opts for termination all the time, [we] don't get to know how we can manage [difficult conditions]'. The prevailing view was that medical professionals were too quick to turn to abortion as a solution, and far more emphasis was needed on medical interventions that supported the continuation of pregnancy, even though the implication was that this was untested. The risk that this might pose to women's health was not foregrounded. However, in the context of their beliefs about the serious harm posed by abortion that we outlined earlier, presumably this is deemed to be a safer option.

Setting up a panel of medical professionals situated this discussion as authorised and expert-sourced knowledge, giving it credibility, despite such viewpoints not being held by the majority of medical experts. This can have a powerful impact on anti-abortion activists, as such knowledge is treated as trustworthy and reliable, and useable in their own public-facing activist encounters. This links with Foucault's (1976) power-knowledge nexus; the intimate connectivity of power and knowledge is impactful in making something intelligible through discourse. *MFL*, therefore, offers a key space where anti-abortion discourses are forged and authorised, acting as an important resource where legitimacy for anti-abortion views are operationalised through knowledge-power relationships.

This messaging also occurred in a more digestible form for the children of anti-abortion activists. The inclusion of a youth stream foregrounded *MFL* as a learning opportunity specifically for young people, where anti-abortion messages were framed as a form of education. The specific issue of a woman's life at risk was discussed; anti-abortion activists were therefore socialising their children into specific frames of thinking, endorsing the anti-abortion cause. Indeed, young people were implored to take these anti-abortion messages back to their friends.

The discourses presented at *MFL* therefore perform a particular function. Like those activists who compared abortion to slavery, by evoking scientific knowledge, anti-abortion activists are conveying an identity asserting that they are not backwards or old-fashioned in their thinking – rather, they understand themselves as being ahead of their time. Ultimately, the anti-abortion activists believe that life begins at conception, and it does not matter, to them, whether one draws on scientific or religious understandings, as in their minds, the same conclusion is drawn – that abortion is wrong. This also meant activists could try to appeal to a secular audience by not fully relying on religious reasoning in their opposition to abortion. But in reality, scientific claims were embedded in religious frameworks; they were enmeshed together, to formulate a worldview the activists invested in and which was non-negotiable (Lowe & Page, 2019b). Any challenge to the status they accorded the foetus was immediately dismissed – there was no middle ground to occupy, and no weight was given to the idea that personhood may be constructed or negotiated (Keane, 2009), hence the antagonisms that occurred between anti-abortion and pro-choice activists, as Chapter 8 will illustrate.

Summary

Most of the foetal stories we encountered adopt a narrative of hope in which the divinely given foetus is pre-destined for a particular role. The idea of uniqueness could be applied either to a future 'great man' or a still-valued ordinary person. This was particularly the case when the activists were involved in prayer vigils outside clinics. The narratives of equal rights, independence and personhood also occurred in the accounts of foetal death. This overlooks the foetus as situational and contingent on the particular time and space that it is occupying. The foetal stories presented here also draw attention to the ambiguous position of men as either a cause or solution to abortions, and the racialised narratives of a white Christian movement who claims to save black bodies, but actually articulate a neo-colonial position.

Viewing the foetus as having full personhood from conception was dependent upon undermining the rights of women's bodily autonomy, and by seeing the foetus and the woman as two separate entities, this devalued the woman's fundamental role in sustaining the pregnancy. It was generally believed that women should take a pregnancy to term in cases of a sexual crime or foetal anomalies, even if it was a fatal condition. Many believed a woman should sacrifice her life if it was required. Adoption was understood as better than abortion, with little recognition regarding women's own decision-making or that pregnancy is embodied. Ultra-sacrificial motherhood was therefore upheld; the foetus was centralised over the woman, with women expected to make the necessary sacrifice. A key issue which tied these various contexts together was seeing themselves as forward-looking and progressive. They understood their activism, as being ahead of its time, rather than being rooted in traditional, conservative values. They drew concurrently on religion and religiously informed scientific discourses to come to the conclusion that abortion was a form of killing, and that, rather like the issue of slavery, the general public would eventually come to understand abortion as an abhorrence. Yet in order to uphold these idealised views of women and the naturalness of motherhood, the perspectives of real-life women were often downplayed.

Chapter 7

Being an Activist: Material Religion, Embodiment and Spatiality

Introduction

This chapter investigates the very specific ways anti-abortion activists engage their campaign in public spaces, with particular emphasis given to locations in the vicinity of abortion services (e.g. standalone abortion clinics and hospitals). The first part of the chapter examines the forms of lived religion engaged with, the material objects utilised and how a pious body is cultivated through embodied practices. Material forms of lived religion were crucial to how the activism was conveyed, and we will examine in some detail the material objects connected with anti-abortion activism, comprising various artefacts, including prayer books, miraculous medals, shopping bags depicting the Virgin Mary, and hand-made items of clothing. Specific emphasis will be given to the status accorded Our Lady of Guadalupe as the icon of the anti-abortion campaign for many Catholics. One of the most significant material objects used was rosary beads. The prayer practice of the Rosary centralises Mary. It started around the fourteenth century, at a time of Marian prominence, and remains a popular practice amongst all varieties of Catholics, from liberal to conservative; historically it also played a significant part in marking out a distinctly Catholic identity as opposed to Protestantism (Mitchell, 2009). We will argue that the Rosary was utilised so readily at vigil sites because it is related to the significant status accorded Mary in the anti-abortion campaign. The very explicit religious positioning of their activism – using prayer, prayer books, rosary beads, and invoking powerful allies like the Virgin Mary and Jesus – emphasises how this was specifically grounded as a religious exercise, and a means of engaging their godly commitments in a belief system which understood God as being fundamentally opposed to abortion (see Chapter 4). The second part of the chapter focuses on the geographies of activism and how space was specifically utilised for their campaign. We will give specific attention to the kinds of practices engaged with, such as pavement counselling, which is an explicit tactic in trying to dissuade people from utilising the clinic services.

Anti-Abortion Activism in the UK, 113–139
Copyright © 2022 Pam Lowe and Sarah-Jane Page
Published under exclusive licence by Emerald Publishing Limited
doi:10.1108/978-1-83909-398-220221017

Material Religion as Lived Religion: Prayer Practices

Chapter 4 emphasised the faith-based motivations of anti-abortion activists, and how their worldview was underscored by a belief that God opposed abortion; they had a fundamental desire to please God through opposing abortion directly. In this chapter, we will detail more fully how the anti-abortion activists enacted this piety, and the forms that their lived religiosity took. A key dimension to this was the deployment of material objects. Because the activism outside clinics mainly comprised Catholics, this chapter will predominantly focus on the materiality of the campaign of Catholic anti-abortion activists. Despite protests from activists that this was not a religious campaign (see Chapter 4), the design and nature of their activism continually referenced religious practices, religious objects and religious icons. We will frame this through the idea of material religion. As discussed in Chapter 3, material objects are an important focus for study, in order to understand the sacred commitments of groups and individuals; they can help tease out the symbolic forms embedded in their endeavour. Here we will pay particular attention to objects such as prayer books written for the anti-abortion cause, and the Virgin Mary as an icon for the Catholic devotees to the anti-abortion movement.

With the exception of a few groups like the evangelical-based *Centre for Bioethical Reform UK (CBR)*, who typically downplayed any overt religious positioning in public, prayer was often fundamental for the Catholic-dominant campaigns (e.g. those belonging to *Helpers of God's Precious Infants [HOGPI]* and *40 Days for Life (40DFL)*, where prayer underpinned the activism). Whilst they are significant umbrella organisations, on the ground, anti-abortion activism is largely organised by local grassroots groups. In addition, it is important to recognise much variability in the styles of activism, it being highly individualised, with those involved bringing their personal objects for the duration of their activism, which would then be taken away. So although individuals were affiliated to specific groups like *HOGPI* and *40DFL*, this did not produce uniformity in the activism, with much individualism encountered in practice.

40DFL was a prayer initiative started in Texas, United States (US) in 2004, and focuses on a biannual targeted prayer practice over 40 consecutive days, with a commitment to pray for 12 hours per day, whether the clinic is open or not (sites have to pay a fee to be an official campaign—https://www.40daysforlife.com/en/resources-faq.aspx). During our observations, few sites managed to achieve this full remit, with most United Kingdom (UK) groups doing selective hours every day or undertaking the activism on specific days. The inability of groups to be able to achieve the full number of hours is, we feel, an indicator of the lack of support for anti-abortion clinic vigils. Many of their signs feature the message, 'Pray to End Abortion', and over the 40-day period a daily devotional is provided, including elements such as scripture, reflection and prayer. It is claimed to be an ecumenical campaign. Lent is one of the chosen periods, as well as a campaign in the autumn. Meanwhile, the *HOGPI* initiative was started in New York in 1989. The Virgin Mary (Our Lady of Guadalupe) is their emblem and features on their branding. Whilst one person is typically designated the role of pavement counsellor, other participants join in prayer. *HOGPI* has its own prayer book to follow, oriented around and dedicated to saving 'babies' from abortion. The prayer practice is fundamentally oriented around Catholic identity; the sequence includes praying the Rosary and features hymns. In Britain, *HOGPI* directly organise monthly processions to abortion clinics and support individuals to set up grassroots groups in order to hold regular year-round vigils. Both *40DFL* and *HOGPI* suggest the use of pavement counsellors to directly approach women entering the clinic, to try to dissuade them from having an abortion, although whether or not this happened seems to be dependent on the individual activists present at the time. The numbers of 'saves' made were often counted and shared and celebrated amongst the activist community. We will focus more on the activities of pavement counsellors later in the chapter, but here we examine the prayer practices.

The complicating factor is that because at the local level, the activists can support different campaigns, there is not necessarily a neat divide between them. For example, we routinely saw the *HOGPI* prayer book being utilised at *40DFL* vigils, so there emerged a melding of practice – praying for 12 hours, thereby following the *40DFL* directive, but using the *HOGPI* prayer book as the focus:

> They show Sarah-Jane the *HOGPI* prayer booklet, and Mike says that there are lots of prayers in here (...) Mike explains that they pray through the book, and they start at the beginning and work their way through. He says it lasts two hours, and the idea is to do this for 12 hours a day for Lent (...) He says the prayers are specifically relevant for praying for the unborn, with prayers to Our Lady of Guadalupe specifically for the unborn child (field notes, Scotland).

The *40DFL* campaign was therefore often used as a period of intense activity over 40 days. Whilst some sites centred solely on the *40DFL* campaign, at other sites, this complemented engagements throughout the year. Therefore such participants were used to the *HOGPI* approach, and simply adopted this for 40 days. The appeal of the *HOGPI* prayer book was explained to us as follows:

> Sarah-Jane asks about the significance of the *HOGPI* prayers, which takes you through Jesus' life and resurrection. She asks how that relates specifically to abortion. Alice says that these prayers are used for all occasions but that the *Helpers* have made up some of the prayers themselves for the purpose of being outside abortion clinics, or wherever you locate the 'culture of death'. She says that they call it the culture of death, and Imogen repeats this as if in agreement (field notes, Scotland).

> There are two copies amongst the four of them. Joan says it is a good book. Sarah-Jane mentions *40DFL* also have the daily prayers, and Joan says they liked the *HOGPI* book because it's about praying the Rosary for the unborn (field notes, Midlands).

The appeal of the *HOGPI* prayer book therefore related to the way it was specifically addressing the issue of abortion, but was filtered through the familiar prayer practice of the Rosary. As we will later explore, this is significant due to the centrality of the Virgin Mary to the prayer practice. From our observations, the prayer book also focused their practice:

> We observe them for some time; they don't make any eye contact with anyone passing by, or with each other. They are fully immersed in concentrating on following the prayer book, taking it in turns to lead the prayer. This is absolutely their focus (field notes, South-East).

In both cases, situating themselves outside of clinics, hospitals and non-directive pregnancy advisory services was important for activists aligned with *HOGPI* and *40DFL*. As both campaigns endorse pavement counselling, being there when they were more likely to encounter people seeking abortion was important:

> Sarah-Jane asked if there was an abortion clinic that morning, and whether they timed their visits with the clinic. They said that they explicitly tried to time their visits with when the abortion clinic is running, but they were considering changing to Thursday as this was becoming the more typical day for the abortion clinic (field notes, South-East).

But even when approaching women was not their aim, there was still something symbolically significant about praying at a clinic, rather than at home or at a church. Ellen in the South-West said that 'being here showed that you cared', whilst Joyce in Wales said it was about 'bearing witness'. Rosie said in her interview that 'It's a way of saying, there's something happening here that we don't think is right. Just being there physically is a way of showing that'. Meanwhile these interviewees explained this commitment to their physical presence at the site of abortion in more detail:

> Even if we weren't allowed to talk to people (...) I would still think it would be good to be there. And from a Christian point of view, I think that that is the witness we've been given from the gospels and you know, to a certain extent I feel that there is the parallel there, this, you know, Jesus being an innocent victim sentenced to death. And we believe that these children are innocent that are dying there. And to witness to that I think, it's really important to be there to witness to it (Jacquie interview).

> I remember my uncle explaining central heating to me; he said that you put the radiators near the window because you attack the cold at the coldest point. I was just thinking about that. Yes, we go to the abortion clinic because that is the darkest place around here.

That's where the demons are gathered and we go to pray and invoke the powers of our Blessed Lady and our Lord and the good angels and so on, to protect the vulnerable people that are going there and the people in the area and so on. What would be an absolute nightmare to me would be living (...) next door; I would not want to be there. We attack the darkest place (Jeoffrey interview).

Jeoffrey's evocative materialisation of the clinic site underscored again the spiritual help and intervention required in order to remove the perceived demonic influence at the abortion site that we outlined in Chapter 6. The physical space of the abortion clinic was invoked in terms of evil, destruction and death, with Jeoffrey conveying this in terms of a battle between good ('our Blessed Lady and our Lord') and evil ('the demons'). In order to manage this spiritual battle, specific resources were utilised by activists, such as marking out the space with particular physical objects (e.g. miraculous medals in trees outside the clinic or having bottles of holy water to hand).

The body of the activist was therefore at risk and precautionary measures had to be taken. The way the body was utilised at clinic sites expressed the physicality of the demarcation of space as good versus evil. For example, at one site, the Stations of the Cross were performed around the block on which the clinic was situated, with someone at the head of the procession bearing a large wooden cross. Beyond the material objects of rosary beads, miraculous medals, wooden crosses and holy water, specific spiritual practices were also important. Prayer was a key means through which God's power could be harnessed, and was a crucial embodied practice (Page & Lowe, 2021a):

...we pray before we get there, that God will be with us and help women (...) we are there as a prayerful witness (...) and we do pray. We are praying with the intention that, and we don't hide it, we are praying with the intention that people will change their minds (...) So we feel are there before and afterwards, try to soak it all in. In prayer and in compassion (Toby interview).

Toby's prayer practice enveloped his activism, in that prayers were said before arriving at the clinic, prayers were said at the clinic, and he also reflected on his involvement afterwards. This was goal-oriented, and Toby emphasised a clear purpose – he was praying so that women would change their minds, and he was utilising God as a channel for this. As Genova says, 'a prayer is an attempt to communicate with the divine in an attempt to influence: some form of outcome is expected from a prayer' (Genova, 2015, p. 11). The centrality of God to prayer was frequently mentioned, as these data demonstrate:

The activists emphasised petitioning God/getting God's help through prayer. And seeking God's help for everyone involved in abortion, e.g. the workers too (field notes, Midlands).

We're praying also for the people who work in there. We pray that they will see the reality and the truth about what they're doing. Many of them seem to me to have blinded themselves, maybe they don't even know the aftereffects because they don't see the women afterwards (...) If somebody says, "What's the use of praying? What does that do?" I can't explain, you cannot explain, it's a totally mystery. It's a bit like when you have a portable radio and you tune it in, if you get at the right point when you're tuning it in, you get a programme don't you? You get on the right wavelength, the right broadband or whatever. To me that's what prayer is like. It's like trying to tune in to a spiritual realm and whatever you believe in. If you believe in God or in Jesus, you're trying to get on to that wavelength, that deity's wavelength so that you can communicate with them and they can communicate with you. If you're not tuned in or you don't believe that person exists, then obviously it doesn't do anything (Rosie interview).

Who was being prayed for could also be far-reaching and could go beyond focusing on the women seeking abortion (see Chapter 5) or the foetus (see Chapter 6). Praying for clinic staff was deemed important, in order to get them to change their minds about working in abortion practice. Rosie gave intimate details regarding how she connected with the divine through getting on the right 'wavelength'. This was a two-way process, and she was seeking assurances from the divine in return. Indeed, many activists were focused on harnessing the power of prayer, and the best way to secure divine intervention:

When I ask them to describe what they believe the witness is doing, they say that they 'believe in the power of prayer'. This has the capacity to help women (Shirley and Gill, field notes, South-East).

Ruth said it was about asking the Holy Spirit to come to people to get them to see the value of life (...) She reaffirmed the power of collective prayer saying that Jesus had said that when two or three or more are gathered in his name, he's there, so you feel the power of it when you pray together (field notes, East).

For Simon, the Rosary was essential, and this united the Catholic community. The Rosary allowed people from different languages to pray together, he spoke of Lithuanians, Columbians and Polish people (...) Simon spoke of how the Catholic community would be united after death, so it was ongoing connections (field notes, Midlands).

It's one of the things I still find quite awe inspiring at times is suddenly realising that this has been going on for hundreds, possibly thousands of years in some cases (...). People have been saying that (…) in the same way, with the same intention, with the same sense behind it across all those radically different cultures (…) it is something that speaks to every human being. And which I suppose encapsulates the relationship with something, namely God, who is so far different that the relationship seems a strange concept to have, and yet it works (Gordon, interview).

Many involved in activism believed in the power of prayer, and how the prayer needed to be harnessed to be effective in mobilising that divine power. God was centralised as the all-powerful who could effect change and get women to reverse their decision. However, what we are also starting to unpack is the strategies through which participants were getting the attention of the divine. Ruth points to the importance of the collective nature of the prayer – that this made the prayer more effective and more likely to be heard. The solidity of the Rosary prayers as being homogenous and repeated across the globe also emphasised a united collective, also unlocking the power of the prayer activism. Whilst Ruth referenced her understanding of a particular biblical verse, Simon focused more on the collective power of people praying the Rosary to end abortion as a global endeavour. Meanwhile Gordon emphasised the history of the Rosary – its power was generated through its repetition down the ages. At vigil after vigil, it was the Rosary prayer that was specifically foregrounded:

> The Rosary is understood as a powerful symbol; at this site, their main prayer practice is the Rosary (field notes, North).

> Sarah-Jane asks if she prays the Rosary here, and Anne says she does as that is the most powerful prayer (field notes, North).

Given the centrality of the Rosary, it was therefore unsurprising that rosary beads were a ubiquitous presence at prayer vigils (see Fig. 3):

> At about 14.00, a woman arrived (…) She had a rosary in her hand and also had literature. She prayed for a while silently, fingering her rosary and holding a folder with a leaflet on the top (field notes, North).

> Philip is stood next to the clinic entrance with Eric next to him (…) I can see their lips moving from over the road (…) Occasionally they start to sing a hymn (…) When they sing, Eric sways in time with the music and it is louder than the prayers (field notes, North).

> They held candles (…) [the holders were] made of cardboard, with crosses around the sides and a fake flame inside. The prayer was entirely silent. There was no hymn singing, there was no reciting of prayer. Many had rosary beads (field notes, Scotland).

Fig. 3.   Praying with Rosary Beads.

It is also notable from the quotes depicted here, that although the rosary beads were centralised, there was diversity too. Some prayer vigil activists were silent; others mouthed the prayers. Others took up singing with enthusiasm. Some were solely focused on the prayer practice whilst others were carrying other objects, such as anti-abortion leaflets or candles. Despite an understood uniformity of the Rosary, as Giordan (2015) emphasises, prayer is socially constructed, and will elicit different norms depending on the context. Here, local cultures created different emphases and focus, such as the insertion of other material objects. Indeed, the activists often emphasised individualised elements in their prayer practices. Greta, for example, has Christ's head on a necklace and additional prayer cards. She, like some of the others, drew on Christ alongside Mary in her prayer practice. Janice referenced Mary, Joseph and Jesus who, as Harris (2013) point out, epitomise Christian family life. Meanwhile Jeoffrey emphasised the power of prayer to ensure that the abortion clinic was 'healed by goodness'.

Often the rosary beads had special significance. Ellen's had been blessed by John Paul II. Richard's had come from Fatima, the Catholic Marian pilgrimage site, with the words 'Fatima' written in black against the dark wood, whilst Janice's were purchased in Medjugorje, an unofficial Catholic pilgrimage site in

Bosnia and Herzegovina centred upon an apparition of the Virgin Mary. As we will later explore, investment in these sites consolidated communities of belonging through belief in the vision, especially in a context where the status accorded Marian apparitions is contested amongst Catholics (Maunder, 2016). Both Christine and Judith's were made of wood from Bethlehem. Indeed, if a prayer vigil participant did not have their rosary beads visible, when asked about them, they reached into their pockets to retrieve them. Activists also sometimes had rosary beads available for distribution as part of their campaign. However, in stark contrast to these personal rosaries, these beads were made from cheap plastic and were usually either pink or blue, to depict the colours associated with newborn girls and boys. Sometimes these were on display as part of the anti-abortion material presentation (typically alongside leaflets), with the intention of handing them out to any receptive individuals attending the clinic.

The special rosary beads and other objects symbolised a prayerful body that situated the participant as pious and opposed to abortion, often, as we will later explore, through reference to Mary. For many activists, an intimate knowledge of the Rosary was literally formed of their habitus in a Bourdieusian sense, embedded since childhood (Bourdieu, 1984). For example, Judith was keen to emphasise to us that she knew the Rosary off by heart; its formulation was embedded in her being. It was therefore easy for vigil participants to align the body in an appropriate configuration, and such forms of habitus contributed to a broader understanding of the correct and appropriate behaviour expected at a prayer vigil (e.g. by vigil organisers), with one's head bowed in prayer (some extended this piety to also include kneeling). This was understood as the piety required to demonstrate one's faithfulness, so that Mary would intercede on one's behalf. These embodied engagements were therefore for Mary's benefit as intercessor.

Some sites had explicitly banned eating at the vigil; such an earthly engagement was seen as compromising the cultivation of 'appropriate' piety. The necessity to convey pious embodiment was apparent at moments when the guard slipped; our arrival at a site where participants had been casually chatting prompted them to quickly adjust their behaviour to engage in prayer, thereby accommodating their new audience. As Mahmood (2005) argues, the cultivation of the pious subject is a continual process; one's exterior display is expected to convey one's interior morality, but this takes explicit work. Whilst the Rosary prayer practices were typically embedded from childhood, the navigation of the pious body at the vigil site itself was continually worked at, including appropriate emotion, demeanour and comportment. Focusing their attention on Mary assisted many vigil participants in engendering the 'correct' habitus, emphasising the perceived Marian virtues of humbleness, obedience and submissiveness (Warner, 1978).

The rosary beads became emblematic of the whole anti-abortion campaign, therefore situating anyone in the vicinity of a clinic with beads as an anti-abortion activist, thereby potentially inadvertently labelling Catholics who had no association with the campaign. Colour-coding the plastic beads on display in relation to newborn babies reaffirmed such associations between their anti-abortion stance and the beads themselves. Indeed, the rosary beads came to be read in a particular way and take on a specific meaning in these contexts, such that pro-choice activists involved in counter campaigns reflected that it was the rosary beads they looked for in order to situate whether someone was an anti-abortion activist or not:

> Emma-Louise then says she feels sorry for the ordinary Catholic going about their everyday business as she says it is true that if they spot rosary beads in their car, or on their person as a pedestrian, they will immediately think, is this an anti-abortion activist? Is this 'one of them'? Therefore, Emma-Louise suggests that the rosary beads themselves come to symbolise something more, as a signifier of the whole anti-abortion movement, which many ordinary Catholics disagree with (field notes, North).

In the vicinity of a clinic, rosary beads, as a pervasive material object, have become attached to a particular meaning – they signify opposition to abortion. This symbolism means that, in the minds of pro-choice counter-demonstrators, anyone with rosary beads is stereotyped in these terms. This had an impact on the meanings generated around the material object itself. Despite the diversity of potential meanings surrounding rosary beads, at particular spaces and times, the rosary beads invoked a principal meaning, signifying an anti-abortion position.

The rosary beads fed into a collective identity that contributed to a specific embodied practice that prioritised Mary.[1] Yet at the same time, the prayer practices were pliable and constructed. It did not look the same at different sites. It was mediated through individuals who all had slightly different meanings and understandings, as per a lived religion approach. Some prayed the Rosary but did not display any Marian imagery. Some gave equal weighting to Christ and Mary in their prayer practice. Others invested heavily in Marian understandings; some not only had posters and prayer cards featuring the Virgin; they also had her embedded on their clothing through brooches and other garments. These participants generated constant attention and devotion to Mary, demonstrated through regular pilgrimages to Marian apparition sites such as Lourdes and Medjugorje. This contributed to a broader emphasis on the Virgin Mary as the key emblem of the whole anti-abortion campaign. The centralisation of the Rosary was therefore a dual devotion; the Virgin was repeatedly symbolised and invoked, in prayers, imagery and protections sought. We will now examine the importance of the Virgin Mary in more detail.

---

[1]Technically, the Rosary features elements of Christ's life (to which Mary is integral) and on which one meditates (Mitchell, 2009). But in our research, the emphasis that vigil practitioners gave to Christ and Mary varied; a good number elevated the Marian elements of the practice. Meanwhile, a small minority of activists opposed the Marian focus.

The Significance of the Virgin Mary

Mary is introduced in the books of Matthew and Luke in the New Testament scriptures. She is understood as a virgin who became pregnant through the Holy Spirit, and gave birth to Jesus, the son of God. At the *Council of Nicaea* in AD 325, she started to be referenced as the Mother of God (Rubin, 2009). Her virginity status has been upheld as a marker of her purity and being free from sin, as depicted in the Catholic teaching of the Immaculate Conception. Whilst Protestants have downplayed Mary's significance, Catholic teachings such as the Immaculate Conception and the Assumption of Mary have emphasised her importance (Johnson, 1989; Warner, 1978).

Vigil participants invested heavily in Mary's story and her experience as a mother, and held an intense connection to her. This was demonstrated through reference to the pilgrimages taken to sites where apparitions to Mary are believed to have taken place and also the use of objects like miraculous medals.[2] Their understanding of Mary was one of intense piety and purity, a woman obedient to God, who they feel would never have contemplated abortion despite her challenging circumstances. They thus liken her experiences to the real-life clinic users, and extrapolate from Mary's story that unmarried mothers, however difficult the situation, should never need an abortion, as these examples illustrate:

> Sarah-Jane asks about the significance of Mary. Jennifer said that she was important as the mother of our Lord and that we ask her to intercede. Bernadette then expands on the significance of Mary, going back to the biblical story of the angel announcing to Mary that she was pregnant and how she would not have felt ready but the angel affirmed that she was blessed by the Lord. Bernadette explains that Mary expresses confusion, saying that she has not known any man, so how is this possible? The angel confirms it is the work of the Lord – 'the power of the Most High will overshadow' Mary (quote is taken directly from the Bible, Luke 1:35), and she will give birth to a child, and this child will be significant – he will be the Messiah and will serve his people. Bernadette then directly linked this to the situation of pregnant women who were seeking an abortion, saying it was possible to move to a position of supporting life. Whilst they may not feel ready or may not feel a baby is possible, they will be able to accept the pregnancy with the support of others around them, such as the surrounding community. She said that pregnant women seeking an abortion 'could borrow from the attitude of Mary' to therefore 'be brave enough to give birth to the child'. (...) She therefore said Mary was an important intercessor, to

[2] A miraculous medal, which depicts Mary, is worn devotionally to remind one of one's faith and piety, and foregrounds Mary as an intercessor for prayer.

intercede on behalf of young girls to accept anything that comes their way, and to give birth to, love and nurture the child (field notes, Scotland).

[W]e love women, especially Our Lady (...). But the idea of pregnancy being a burden, I think, for me, it is the most empowering for me, men we are never going to have that experience. It is an empowering beautiful gift that women get to have (...). We live in a culture now where it is about me. And a person can be a burden to me and a baby can be a burden to me and it is looking, it is very self-centred culture that ends nowhere but death. And that is what we are talking about. Life and death (Toby interview).

There was therefore an expectation for clinic users to be like Mary – to always proceed with the pregnancy, no matter what the circumstances, with Toby rejecting the idea of pregnancy as a burden. This is one of the key reasons why Mary is invoked as pivotal to the Catholic-inspired anti-abortion campaigns. On the one hand, Mary enables compassion to be foregrounded – Mary is deemed sympathetic to one's plight and seen as truly understanding of what it is to experience an unexpected pregnancy. But on the other hand, the only outcome on the table is fully sacrificing one's body to the pregnancy (Kamitsuka, 2019). In this narrative, women are instructed to 'take up their cross and carry an unwanted pregnancy' (Kamitsuka, 2019, p. 207). This alignment of ordinary women with Mary not only promotes maternity as women's essentialised role; it implores women to recognise the sacrifice they are expected to make, whatever the consequences, and with little consideration for their own needs. This is why Toby is so quick to judge women seeking an abortion, and equating this with a broader culture of self-centredness – this taps into existing expectations for women to make the necessary sacrifices and to put themselves last. These expectations typically encourage feelings of guilt and blame amongst women in general terms, but what the anti-abortion activists are asking goes much further than general sacrificial motherhood (Lowe, 2016). Instead, their use of Mary – whilst presented as a benign and compassionate role model – endorses ultra-sacrificial motherhood, where women's ultimate altruism and obedience is expected (Lowe & Page, 2019a).

Mary is accorded significant status through the carefully chosen embodied prayer practices and the use of particular material objects, which constructs Mary in a very specific way, emphasising her obedience, compliance and sacrifice. Using the saintly and submissive virgin mother as their key reference point meant that vigil participants lost sight of the embodied realities of those very women they were claiming to help, and they could not understand that abortion could be freely chosen with a positive outcome. Indeed, using Mary as a stand-in to understand the lives of contemporary living and breathing women had significantly negative consequences for those accessing clinic services; not only was there a failure to recognise the lived realities of women's lives and the part abortion could play in positive decision-making; they also positioned women who did not follow Mary's sacrifice as inherently sinful and in opposition to God.

Underpinning these narratives, therefore, was clear judgement of women who sought abortions, and a valorisation of ultra-sacrificial motherhood.

Key Apparitions of Mary: Our Lady of Guadalupe – Protectress of the Unborn

We now focus on the way a very specific apparition of Mary was utilised and embedded in much of the prayer vigil activism we witnessed. Thus far, we have outlined the significance of Mary to the prayer practice. But one form of Marian veneration was far more pronounced – the apparition of Our Lady of Guadalupe (see Fig. 4). Her centrality to the anti-abortion campaign was due to her given status as the protectress of the unborn. Given that this particular envisioning of Mary depicts her as pregnant, this is seen as particularly significant to the anti-abortion prayer vigil movement. It is clear that Our Lady of Guadalupe is not always referenced in this way, and Our Lady of Guadalupe has generated varying interpretations. Other meanings given relate to her centrality to Mexican identity; Mexican prisoners have adorned their skin with Our Lady of Guadalupe tattoos

Fig. 4.   Lady of Guadalupe with Holy Water.

(Blackwell, 2019; Blake, 2008; Lozano & River, 2016). She has also featured as an emblem of queer desire (De Alba, 2011). But for the anti-abortion activists, Our Lady of Guadalupe took on a very specific and conservative meaning – she was an emblem of their campaign, with her apparition backstory making her appropriate as their key image for veneration.

Prayer vigil activists could easily recite the detail of Our Lady of Guadalupe's apparition in Mexico in 1531, as these quotes reveal:

> Roberta explains that Our Lady of Guadalupe is a manifestation of the Virgin Mary and is depicted as pregnant, at a site in Mexico where the Aztecs had previously practised child sacrifice. So it therefore becomes a signifier for converting Mexicans to the 'true' religion, stopping child sacrifice, and esteeming the life of the unborn. She comes to represent a protest against child sacrifice, and is why it is deemed an appropriate image in this context (field notes, South-East).

> Imogen starts to explain that in Mexico, Our Lady of Guadalupe appeared on a cloak of a peasant and that tilma was still there in Mexico. She said that the Mexicans recognised her as a pregnant woman because of the clothes she was wearing, as she had a bow around her waist, indicating a pregnancy. Over the next nine years, all the human sacrifices stopped amongst the people who worshipped the Sun God, the Aztecs, so she is now considered a patroness of the unborn (field notes, Scotland).

It was not just their understanding that this apparition of Mary depicted a pregnant Virgin that was significant. Abortion was specifically linked to human sacrifice, as practised by the Aztecs (we will discuss in Chapter 9 how child sacrifice was conveyed by evangelical groups). Given Mary's apparition was seen as powerful enough to Christianise Mexico and end human sacrifice, the inference was that this particular manifestation of Mary could be petitioned to stop abortion in contemporary times. Whereas Our Lady of Guadalupe is understood as an emblem of national identity in Mexico, being a uniting influence in converting the country to Catholicism in the sixteenth century, for the anti-abortion activists, Our Lady of Guadalupe was *the* anti-abortion reference point. A whole culture had developed around this, such that special images of her (e.g. blessed by the pope) were sent around the country, for veneration at Catholic churches. Indeed, at one *March for Life* (*MFL*) event, the church for the pre-march Mass utilised an image of Our Lady of Guadalupe, becoming the focal point for March participants to venerate before setting off:

> There was an initial speaker who said prayers, invoking the Lady of Guadalupe (who was referenced three times in total) (…). Lady of Guadalupe's image is situated to the left of the main altar, and after the service around 20 people were queueing up to venerate the image (field notes, *MFL*).

Therefore, Our Lady of Guadalupe was a significant reference point at key events, and this was further developed through specific clothing that participants wore:

> A woman has a halter neck dress with an image of Mary. It is Our Lady of Guadalupe. Interestingly, around the edges of the dress are the roses associated with this particular apparition. She said she had purchased it from Etsy, after seeing someone with a similar item of clothing with the same pattern last year (field notes, *MFL*).

> A woman has a t-shirt with an image of Our Lady of Guadalupe. There are printed baby feet at the edge of the image. This is accompanied by her wearing a miraculous medal around her neck, which utilises the exact same image. Sarah-Jane asks if she bought it from somewhere but she says she made it herself (field notes, *MFL*).

As these quotes indicate, clothing signified one's anti-abortion stance, demonstrating much personal investment, even making the clothing themselves; this labour was understood as a form of pious engagement with Our Lady. Clothing practices at one *MFL* event would be reinforced in future years, as people were inspired to personalise their fashion to venerate Our Lady, therefore creating a form of anti-abortion brand identity. Our Lady of Guadalupe was therefore sought out in novel spaces; Etsy is a space for bespoke and unusual crafted items, therefore enabling these clothing identities to be forged. As Entwistle argues, 'Conventions of dress attempt to transform flesh into something recognizable and meaningful to a culture' (2000, p. 8), therefore these investments in bespoke items enabled the very cultivation of an anti-abortion sub-culture, which, along with brightly cultured 'Life from conception, no exception' wristbands, hoodies and t-shirts, forged a developing and definable brand identity at *MFL* events, rather like the way merchandise was used to signify ones' commitment to abstinence in the US-based movements studied by White (2009). Such engagements also communicated a form of consumerism that was equally derided by activists more broadly; the turn to the bespoke perhaps was a means of negating any association with mass production – yet this was still identifiable as a set of consumption practices. More generally in our ethnography, we encountered badges of Our Lady of Guadalupe pinned to people's clothing, as well as bracelets featuring her, and on one occasion she even featured on a shopping bag used to carry the anti-abortion materials (such as leaflets) to the clinic site (see Fig. 5).

Our Lady of Guadalupe as a material object was heavily utilised. But her imagery was squarely referenced alongside other anti-abortion material. This further consolidated the idea that the Virgin, along with God (see Chapter 4), opposed abortion, and interlaced pious religious imagery with specific material objects opposing abortion. Our Lady of Guadalupe was utilised in multiple ways:

Fig. 5.   Shopping Bag Depicting Our Lady of Guadalupe.

In the doorway, there is propped up an image of Our Lady of Guadalupe, and on the other side, a yellow sign containing graphic images. The main text says 'Abortion Hurts Women'; Dangers include: breast cancer, severe haemorrhaging, serious depression and death. It then outlines that 3D scans open a window to the womb. There are four images of such 3D images, and then the final section of the sign is divided into two – on the one hand a foetus at eight weeks and 11 weeks gestation in the womb; on the opposite site the remains of a foetus of the same age (field notes, Northern Ireland [NI]).

They take up quite a lot of room because they have a large number of signs. These include a large picture of Our Lady of Guadalupe, a slightly smaller advert for the *Good Counsel Network* (*GCN*) crisis pregnancy centre (CPC), a blown up image of an embryo and a collection of foetal dolls (field notes, Midlands).

As well as the pictures of Our Lady of Guadalupe (…) there was also a picture of Mary with aborted foetuses in her hands, falling and around her feet. A couple of graphic pictures of foetus were also present (field notes, NI).

Two men carry the big Our Lady of Guadalupe picture at the front with a monk holding a microphone just behind (...) they line up opposite the clinic next to the pavement edge. The big sign is opposite the closed pedestrian entrance. The counsellors stay on the pavement with their rosaries and leaflets (field notes, South-East).

Our Lady of Guadalupe was a frequently utilised resource by anti-abortion activists. She was invested with conservative meanings regarding essentialised motherhood, to denote not just an anti-abortion stance, but an anti-child sacrifice stance. This contributed to broader meanings invoking ultra-sacrificial motherhood – at no point did activists recognise or acknowledge the broader range of meanings invested in her by others, such as how she has also been read through the lens of lesbian iconography (De Alba, 2011). It is our assumption that such alternative readings would be deemed sacrilegious by these devotees; for them, Our Lady of Guadalupe demonstrated a strictly conservative interpretation of motherhood. The material cultures surrounding Our Lady of Guadalupe were plentiful and worth specifying in some detail. As Morgan argues, material culture is integral to religious practices, offering a mediating role 'serving to bolster one world against another, to police the boundaries of the familiar, or to suture the gaps that appear as the fabric of a world wears thin' (1998, p. 10). Our Lady of Guadalupe therefore served an important purpose in defining the boundaries of the group, and as a mechanism for signalling their opposition to abortion as a collective, thereby fostering a set of social practices that were mutually invested in (Morgan, 1998). Whilst there has been debate and controversy within Catholicism regarding the status accorded Mary, with concerns even expressed by some of the Catholic-identifying anti-abortion activists we spoke to that she is not elevated above God, the fact that images were venerated within Catholic churches as part of anti-abortion campaigns meant that endorsing the Virgin in this way obtained tacit approval from at least the localised church authority. As Morgan argues:

The material culture of religion is widely understood to sacralise space, to delineate in spatial parameters the site of point at which the holy is manifested and made to communicate to believers the crucial signifiers of their identity as believers. The sacred is therefore experienced as invested in a place – a church, altar, or devotional image, for example – as the concrete expression of a community's relationship to the divine.

(1998, p. 182)

Connecting the venerated image of Our Lady of Guadalupe within the church with the myriad objects deployed of Our Lady of Guadalupe at anti-abortion sites created a sense of sacred assurance, a tacit acknowledgement that the church approves of their activism. In the broader contestations over public space, Our Lady of Guadalupe was therefore utilised for various forms of symbolism: not only an expression of ultra-sacrificial motherhood and opposition to abortion, but also the idea that the anti-abortion activists were under God's protection, bolstered through the support of church authority. Indeed these broader spatial contestations – and the varying ways anti-abortion activists navigated the geographies surrounding clinic sites – will be the focus of the rest of this chapter.

Geographies of Activism: How Space Makes a Difference

As emphasised earlier in the chapter, being present at an abortion clinic was highly meaningful for activists. As Doan (2007) argues, being active by directly intervening is an important marker for anti-abortion activists to demonstrate commitment to their sacred work, and it also seeks to collectively reinforce their community commitment. Moreover, the emphasis on abortion as a cause of mental health issues, with assumptions of ongoing abortion regret, positions the anti-abortion activists as 'saving' women from trauma (Ehrlich & Doan, 2019; Lee, 2003). This risk calls for direct action by anti-abortionists at the site of potential harm. Similar to the motivations that Ehrlich and Doan (2019) found in the US CPC movement, the activists need to ensure they could reach women before it is too late. They argue that from the anti-abortion activist's perspective:

> Mired in crisis, a woman's decisional incompetence is implicated as a symbolic roadblock that pushes her off God's ordained path unless she is saved through the intervention of a caring counsellor who can guide her in the right direction.
> (Ehrlich & Doan, 2019, p. 79)

To displace their activism to another location (e.g. praying to end abortion at a church) was not something they accepted; for them, their presence at the clinic both highlighted public awareness regarding the abortions taking place and gave them a direct opportunity to intervene, fulfilling the sacred role they had been called to.

Importantly though, the physical location of the abortion service had a major impact on the way that they were able to connect with clinic users. In Scotland, abortions often take place in hospitals, which reduce the opportunities for targeting women. Hospitals are typically on sprawling sites, comprising numerous healthcare buildings. As hospitals are technically on private grounds, anti-abortion activists are prevented from entering, and are thus unable to stand right outside the buildings where abortions take place. This is what we observed at a hospital in Scotland:

> If you were arriving at the hospital by car, your attention would not be directed towards the activists at all, as you would be looking at turning either right or left into the road opposite them. [Regarding the hospital entrance they were stood at:] This is not the main entrance; it is however the closest entrance to the Maternity and Gynaecology building (...) We assume they chose

this position because of its proximity to Maternity and Gynaecology (field notes).

In other words, these activists were probably motivated to stand on this particular piece of public land because it was the closest they could get to the abortion service. Because this was outside of the hospital perimeter, however, their impact was significantly reduced, as those accessing the hospital by road would not have to directly engage with them. The hospital car park, taxi rank and bus stops were all in the hospital grounds, so in some instances, road users might not even notice them when travelling past. Even engagement for pedestrians was minimal, because the activists stood on the opposite side of the road, bordering a piece of fenced off derelict land, where there was little pedestrian traffic. However, whilst those entering for abortion services were less identifiable, as we have previously argued, this does not mean that the presence of anti-abortion activists does not cause distress (Lowe & Hayes, 2019). At other Scottish hospital sites, the visibility of the activists to road traffic was much more noticeable, particularly when placards were utilised, which clearly specified the purpose of their activity. This meant that drivers of a minority of the cars going past would react in some way, in terms of gestures, honking, or verbal interaction. Sometimes this engagement was hostile; at other times, it was positively endorsing the activism. On other occasions, it was hard to tell.

Meanwhile, many abortion services in England occurred in standalone abortion clinics, under the model of contracting out *National Health Service (NHS)* procedures to charities such as *BPAS (British Pregnancy Advisory Service)* and *MSI Reproductive Choices*. Often clinics were situated in affluent residential areas, where a large Victorian or Edwardian house been converted, perhaps with a clinic extension (the building may previously have been a nursing home). Whether these clinics had a car park or not mattered: some had no parking facilities at all; others only had enough room for staff parking, so all clinic users would physically need to walk to the entrance. Some clinics had enough room for taxis to enter the grounds to drop people off. This meant that clinic activists were at a much closer proximity to service users, enabling greater levels of interaction to take place:

> The clinic is a large period building on the corner (…) This is a very salubrious part of town. The activists situate themselves … outside the main entrance to the premises. The pavement is wider on this side (…) Although the perimeter space inside the grounds is not large, there is space for around 10 cars (…) This means that there is a mixture of pedestrian traffic entering through the entrance, as well as cars pulling into the driveway (field notes, North).

> …the location (…) is perfect for them. It is off the main road; they can patrol the gates in comfort, where they have a bit of space to keep an eye on who is coming along the road (…) It is a pleasant

place to be, they haven't got traffic whizzing past them every five
seconds (interview with Angela, local resident opposing anti-
abortion activism, South-East).

The pavements are about a metre wide, so walking down either
side of the road, you are quite close to the activists. The clinic
doorway is only about 1–1½ metres away from the pavement, and
people entering have to stop to ring the bell. This means that
women have to stand within touching distance of the activists
for the time it takes to be let into the clinic. There are two
pavement counsellors directly outside the entrance (field notes,
South-East).

This close proximity was also apparent when abortion services were offered
within GP surgeries and other health clinics – again, these buildings tended to be
smaller, with less opportunity to avoid engagement with anti-abortion activists.
This also raised issues regarding the multi-purpose use of the building, so that
people accessing the building for any medical service would encounter the
activists. At one site in Northern Ireland (NI), there were large graphic signs and
anti-abortion activists praying with amplification equipment outside a site that
hosted a range of services, including those used by children with autism.

Activists could also manoeuvre the space in such a way as to make encounters
with abortion service users more likely:

A blue car is parked directly outside the pedestrian entrance to the
clinic, half on the pavement; a *40DFL* poster is propped against
the front bumper plate, so that anyone approaching [the clinic]
from the main road will see it. It is difficult for a pedestrian to
squeeze past the car on the pavement; anyone leaving [the clinic]
this way will be forced either to slow down, or to walk in the street,
next to the activists. It later becomes clear that the car belongs to
one of the activists (field notes, North).

The geography of the sites had an impact regarding the levels of engagement
from activists. Passing a vigil in a car gave far less opportunity for activists to
engage, but at some sites where pavement counselling was very pronounced, every
opportunity was taken to engage with clinic users, whether they were in a car or
not. Accessing a clinic site by car was not necessarily a barrier to engagement,
especially if a car window was open:

At 9.45 a car pulls in and parks; the activists do not attempt to
engage, but it would be difficult given that the car turns in
relatively quickly and does not stop until inside the gates. At
9.50, a car is leaving the car park; it stops next to the vigil
waiting to pull out in the traffic. There is a man in the passenger
seat, a male driver and a woman in the rear. The passenger

window is open and the pavement counsellor takes a couple of paces towards the car and tries to talk to them. I can't hear the conversation, but he turns away before the car pulls away. Just after, a man walks towards the gates from the clinic entrance; he lights a cigarette as he is walking. When he gets to the gates, the pavement counsellor starts to approach him. The man replies, shaking his head and heads back into the car park. Shortly after, a car drives out of the clinic, the widows are closed and there is a break in the traffic and the pavement counsellor makes no attempt to engage them (field notes, North).

Meanwhile, when hospitals were used as abortion clinics, the complexity of public-private ownership of the land could enable much controversy regarding where anti-abortion activists stood. This was most evident at a hospital in the Midlands, where activists moved their location. Initially (2016 and 2017), activists stood, displaying signs, on the grass river bank opposite the entrance to the building were the abortion clinic was situated. This display was prominent because it was elevated on the bank. Although abortion service users did not typically need to walk directly past them, the activists were highly visible. They used this land as its ownership was ambiguous. The activists did not think they were on hospital land and did not move when security asked them to. But in 2018 the Hospital Trust decreed that they could not stand so close to the building, and instead, the activists moved to a small vehicular bridge over the river beyond ownership of the hospital. Because this was adjacent to one of the car parks, some service users would be required to walk past them, though anyone arriving by public transport or utilising another entrance to the hospital would not. Meanwhile, at a hospital in a city in the East, the anti-abortion activists outlined that the hospital did not allow them onto their land, with an administrator showing them a map on their first day of activism to explicitly explain which land they could and could not stand on. However, the activists did negotiate to use the hospital toilets.

Pavement Counselling and Leafletting

It is at this juncture that it is helpful to explore more precisely how activists tried to engage passers-by and clinic users. We have already outlined the religious practices such as prayer, which could be quite solitary or insular in nature. The behaviours described here are more intentional about directly engaging the general public. At some sites, the forms of prayer did not involve any broader engagement, as this quote indicates:

They were right in front of the railings on the high-raised cobbles which were not a part of the formal pathway. They are not in a position to hand out literature to passers-by as they are not on the main pathway (field notes, South-East).

Yet at other sites, the use of leafletting and pavement counselling was very pronounced. There was an interrelationship between leaflet engagements and pavement counselling. Pavement counselling could be buttressed through having leaflets available. Pavement counselling had the explicit intention of 'counselling' someone attending the clinic, to dissuade them from having an abortion. It was framed in therapeutic terms, and as a form of help and support. On the surface, leaflet engagements appeared to be focused on distributing leaflets rather than having any 'counselling' function, as these encounters demonstrate:

> A woman exits the clinic and Annette offers her a leaflet. She takes it and stuffs it into her bag (field notes, North).

> There is a young couple walking down the road towards the clinic. As they go past the activists, one tries to hand them a leaflet; the man seems to take it without thinking, then seconds later throws it back at them. One of the activists bends down and retrieves it from the clinic path. Slightly later, another woman approaches the clinic and ignores them (field notes South-East).

However, as the pavement counselling guide illustrated, it was important for activists to ensure that the leaflet stayed in a woman's hands. It gave instructions that:

> Some people prefer to say 'Here's a leaflet for you' so as to not give the option of declining (...) Tell her to read it carefully (...) If the woman does not stop, walk beside her briefly and hold out your hand extending the leaflet as you talk (...) Always try to get the leaflet in the woman's hand but she must accept of her own free will. If she takes off and won't listen to you but has taken a leaflet there is a chance she will read it inside the abortion centre.

Thus, the strategy of giving out leaflets could be seen as part of their attempts at pavement counselling. As the guide mentioned elsewhere, 'saves' sometimes came from women changing their minds after they had initially entered the clinic. This was inevitably always seen as an outcome of their activism, rather than non-directive discussions with abortion service staff.

As we have seen, attempts at leaflet distribution could be met with polite refusal or declining in a more overt and demonstrative way. Leafletting could be accompanied by other forms of activism such as prayer:

> The woman made some approaches to people as they entered and left the clinic, holding out what looked like the same literature, an envelope with 'Ask to See the Scan' on the outside. She was not very successful in this as her position slightly further down the road meant that by the time people were level with her, they were often already on the clinic grounds. She did this for about

20 minutes, then seemed to return to prayer. She left on her bicycle about an hour after she arrived (field notes, North).

The exact nature of the activities at a given site was dependent on the activists present at the time. Practices therefore changed hour by hour, as different people were involved:

> It makes a difference who is outside the clinic as to whether or not they are approached. A man and woman exit at 7.00 and the person outside the clinic makes no move towards them. Slightly later at 7.05, the pavement counsellor has changed to a woman wearing a quilted coat. She tries to talk to two women as they leave and when they ignore her, she walks alongside them for a couple of seconds trying to give them a leaflet (field notes, South-East).

Some activists were more motivated to speak to clinic users than others. Activists framed pavement counselling as a form of help and support, and described their activity as being benign and sympathetic:

> Richard mentioned that sometimes they were accompanied by a counsellor who would stand further up near the entrance (...) and would offer women another way, and that there are other options, such as the baby being adopted (field notes, South-East).

> We would stand outside praying silently and with leaflets offering help if mothers wanted to change their mind. We didn't have banners, we didn't have posters, and we didn't have anything to frighten or worry people. But we had, as I say, just a leaflet and a rosary and in fact usually my companion would pray and I would talk to people. You couldn't do both at exactly the same time. We never tried to stop anyone going in, but we just stood there on the pavement, we didn't block the pavement because we knew that would be wrong (Rosie, interview).

Pavement counselling encounters differed by context and geography, with particular individuals (young women) targeted more frequently, as they were understood as individuals most likely to be seeking an abortion (even if they were in the vicinity for another reason entirely):

> Two young women (early 20s) exit the building at 12.40; this is the first time the anti-abortion activists react. Audrey tries to engage them in conversation and holds out her arm with the clipboard as if offering them a leaflet. The two young women seem to ignore her and turn to walk up the street. Audrey takes a few paces after them, still trying to engage them in conversation. She is walking

slower, and so whilst they are followed briefly, she does not attempt to catch up with them (field notes, NI).

Two women, one a nun, cross over the road to stand directly outside the clinic, one on each side of the door. (...) They give leaflets out to passers-by that will take them; they seem to target mainly young women. They also try to talk to people coming in and out of the clinic, especially those having a cigarette break. Some people do engage with them, but most ignore them (field notes, South-East).

This indicates how close pavement counsellors got to the abortion clinic, given that in both of these examples, the proximity between the clinic user and pavement counsellor was very narrow. This was compounded when there was a singular pedestrian entranceway, as clinic users had no alternative but to walk past the activists. When there were multiple pedestrian entrances, pavement counsellors demonstrated persistence and ingenuity in ensuring both entrances were covered at once, even if there was only one pavement counsellor:

There are two entrances to the clinic; a footpath between the hedge and a small gravelled driveway. If there is only one person on duty, they tend to walk up and down between the path and the drive, to cover all bases (...). As soon as they hear the gravel, they are there. Juliet [pro-choice counterdemonstrator] mentions that one of the men is very quick at running between the gate and the entrance to the driveway, that he will run between the two to try to cut people off as they come out of the drive (field notes, South-East).

In more open spaces, the likelihood of whether a clinic user would be approached or not seemed to be directly related to their own body language and demeanour, and the level of confidence from the pavement counsellors and those distributing leaflets themselves. Brisk walking and a clear idea where one was heading could dissuade pavement counsellors from approaching a person:

Another woman walks briskly down the street from the right-hand side speaking on her phone. The pavement counsellor had stopped pacing, but was facing more to the left. She went round him, and up the path, but he didn't seem to want to try to engage with her (field notes, South-East).

Meanwhile any uncertainty about one's geographical surroundings, such as women consulting maps to find the clinic, or slow walking, were more likely to be targeted:

A couple have walked into the street and then stopped looking around as if uncertain as to where to go. They move on a few paces, then stop again a few metres away from the praying group (…). As she enters the clinic gate, the woman pavement counsellor attempts to engage her in conversation (field notes, South-East).

A young woman walks down the street and stops on the pavement in front of the clinic (…). She is holding her phone and focusing on the screen as if she was looking at a map/for an address. The woman pavement counsellor took a few steps towards her and was trying to engage her in conversation but she was ignoring her (field notes, South-East).

[A couple] walked slowly down the road and turned into the clinic. The pavement counsellor obviously said something as the woman turned her head towards him as she passed. They didn't stop to engage with the pavement counsellor though. I think it was the slower pace that gave the pavement counsellor time to try to engage with them. Two younger women, maybe early 20s, walk down the street and into the clinic. The pavement counsellor moves his leaflet slightly towards them, but they ignore him (field notes, South-East).

Susceptibility to being stopped was linked to levels of vulnerability. Although researcher presence meant that clinic activists were typically mindful of their behaviour, we did witness examples when women in extremely vulnerable situations were approached:

A car pulls up outside the small driveway of the clinic and a woman opens the front door quickly, leans out and is sick in the gutter. The pavement counsellor notices this and starts walking towards the car. The woman gets out of the front seat of the car and goes to take a bag out of the back, by which time the pavement counsellor is right by her. She walks alongside the woman as she approaches the clinic and goes in the gate. The pavement counsellor is talking to her, but the woman doesn't appear to reply (field notes, South-East).

Angela, a local resident of a clinic site who was part of a campaign group opposing the activists said she witnessed women experiencing unwelcome contact, and highlighted that this was exacerbated by an embedded politeness, where women felt they had to listen:

I'm afraid we Brits are too polite. You know, I have stopped and intervened with one of their conversations a few times (…) what happens for the most part is that the women didn't want the conversation, they were stopped, they didn't want the conversation and is pleased when someone rescues them. And they can turn their back on the protestor and go into the clinic (Angela, interview).

Angela intervened when she witnessed a woman who demonstrated reluctance about being approached. These observations also emphasise the gendered nature of public space encounters mentioned above; women's levels of power to manage an exchange with a stranger is governed by gendered norms and rules (Lowe & Hayes, 2019). Women in general terms are more likely to experience targeted and routine harassment from men who they do not know, what Gardner (1995, p. 4) calls 'public harassment'. Gardner explains that there are various activities comprising this harassment, including pressure to divulge personal information, explicit verbal remarks, and embodied intrusion, which can include non-verbal interactions like following someone or touching them. Meanwhile, politeness is understood as an essentialised feminine trait. Despite the potential threat surrounding the encounter, for a woman to act in a hostile manner to a stranger is deemed anathema unless she feels heightened anxiety and physical intimidation. Encountering anti-abortion activists confuse the expected norms of behaviour, especially when the activists themselves are much older. To respond in a negative manner to older people runs counter to expected feminine behaviour. As Skeggs (2005) has argued, in public places women who do not show appropriate gendered propriety are often denounced as having no moral worth.

Our observations also revealed the lengths clinic users would go to, to avoid interaction with anti-abortion activists:

> Of note are a young couple and a woman wearing a leather jacket. She comes round the corner of the clinic and clocks the activists diagonally opposite her. The couple proceed to climb over the low wall of the clinic and into the muddy garden, thereby avoiding the formal entrance ways, but meaning that there was the possibility that the activists did not spot them. Shortly afterwards a woman proceeded to remove her leather jacket and hold up her jacket against her face, hiding her face from view until she entered the clinic itself (field notes, South-West).

> A woman was seen speeding up then running into the clinic grounds. When she got on the driveway she started to walk again. Immediately in front of the clinic are some large bushes that help to screen people from the activists (field notes, South-West).

Some clinic managers told us that they were letting women leave through alternative exits so clients did not have to walk past the activists. However, the ability of clinics to assist was often limited due to geographical constraints.

Summary

This chapter has focused on how religious ideas and material objects were mobilised by activists to strategically position themselves as opposed to abortion, along with how they utilised the space outside abortion clinics to enact their campaign. Overall, this was a form of embodied lived religion, melding together religious practice with their activism. In Britain, because of the overwhelmingly Catholic belonging of the prayer vigil participants, it was Catholic objects specifically which were materially utilised to facilitate prayer. Catholic forms of identity were written through the material objects and types of prayer (e.g. the centrality of the Rosary). This even cultivated specific anti-abortion material cultures, often using imagery of Our Lady of Guadalupe, which also included the crafting of particular garments. This investment enabled bonds to be forged and religious practices to be consolidated through traditional Catholic beliefs, but it meant that they would also exclude anti-abortion activists of other religious persuasions. Whilst the prayer practices and the visuality of the rosary beads consolidated particular Catholic beliefs, it came to dominate the imagery as signifying an anti-abortion stance. This monopolisation of meanings around certain objects like rosary beads meant that objects carrying sacred significance for a broader range of Catholics, whether anti-abortion or pro-choice, came to be invested in a very narrow range of understandings, and, as we will see in the next chapter, gave pro-choice activists the justification to utilise well-worn phrases such as 'Get your rosaries off our ovaries' in their campaign.

Meanwhile, we also examined the spatial when we focused on the sites for activism, demonstrating that the geographical locations themselves made a difference regarding how impactful the activism was. Activists located at sites where abortions took place on vast hospital grounds and from which activists were excluded had a very different feel to the very intimate proximity of activists at standalone clinics. The activists typically positioned the clinic site as a space evoking evil and harm and their practices were forged around managing this, whether through particular material objects or the very specific task of approaching clinic users through their pavement counselling. This was understood as a therapeutic practice hinged around 'helping women', but this was largely seen as unwelcome by service users. Some service users demonstrably avoided the activists utilising quite drastic measures. For pro-choice activists, this situation was untenable and they sought to challenge anti-abortion activism in the public sphere. The next chapter focuses on their campaign.

Chapter 8

The Pro-Choice Response: Counterdemonstrations

Introduction

We have now outlined the motivations of anti-abortion activists, their religious practices and the way that they occupied the space outside clinics. This chapter will deepen the understanding of how space is used for activism by bringing in the perspectives, motivations and actions of counterdemonstrators. We will highlight the complex ways regarding how religion gets positioned in the debate and the way different emotions are deployed, such as anger and humour. We will emphasise that public sphere dynamics regarding anti-abortion activism relate not only to how religion is understood but also to the importance of recognising the public sphere as a *gendered* space. We begin, however, with a brief reminder of the experiences of those who encounter the anti-abortion activists in the specific space outside the clinic and the distress that their activities generate.

As Lowe and Hayes (2019) have shown, the presence of anti-abortion activists outside clinics is experienced as harassment by those seeking to access services, regardless of what specific activities are being undertaken. To understand this, we need to consider the broader context of gendered public spaces, in which women in particular are often subjected to unwanted public attention, and therefore need to be wary of being watched or approached by strangers (Lowe & Hayes, 2019). The following accounts, from a range of sources, clearly illustrate the negative impact that the anti-abortion activists have:

> Though they did not approach me, I felt harassed as I walked through the gate knowing that they watch me and they know the reason I am here.
>
> (In Lowe & Hayes, 2019)

> The moment I saw them outside I was panic and shy, they are intruding my personal decision one way or the other, I have to cover my face when next am coming here cos I don't feel safe or secure.
>
> (In Lowe & Hayes, 2019)

Anti-Abortion Activism in the UK, 141–168
Copyright © 2022 Pam Lowe and Sarah-Jane Page
Published under exclusive licence by Emerald Publishing Limited
doi:10.1108/978-1-83909-398-220221020

A man approached me and called me 'mother' on my way into the clinic. This upset me greatly. They also tried to show me a picture of a baby on the way out. This upset me so much at a time when I already felt terrible. When you go to a clinic like this you don't want anything to draw attention to you.

(*Ealing Council Consultation Report* Appendix 1 2018, p. 40)

I accompanied a friend into the clinic who had been raped and become pregnant. A woman approached her with a model foetus, saying that my friend had 'other choices apart from killing her baby'. My friend became very distressed and said she had been raped. The woman then said that this was 'very sad but it wasn't the baby's fault'.

(*Ealing Council Consultation Report* Appendix 1 2018, p. 24)

As we will see in this chapter, the accounts of anxiety, distress and fear are largely ignored, discounted or disbelieved by the anti-abortion activists who stand outside clinics. They believe their actions are compassionate and supportive and understand themselves as offering assistance to those in need (Lowe & Hayes, 2019). This position stems from their support for ultra-sacrificial motherhood. As Chapter 4 demonstrated, the rationale for these beliefs is rooted in their religious motivations for their actions.

Interventions

Pro-choice groups in different places sought to mitigate or challenge the activities of anti-abortion groups outside of clinics, with varying degrees of success. In Wales, a combination of political pressure and counterdemonstrations resulted in the police obtaining a voluntary agreement at one site that moved the anti-abortion group a short distance away from the clinic to the opposite site of a nearby junction. As the clinic is on a street full of pedestrians, it is impossible to target those seeking abortion. Observations after the move showed the anti-abortion activists mainly engaging in quiet or silent prayer, often in a huddle facing each other, rather than looking towards the clinic entrance. This was the only example we found where anti-abortion activists voluntarily de-escalated their activities and is in sharp contrast to the impact of interventions elsewhere.

In Northern Ireland (NI), the harassment of clinic users led to the adoption of clinic escorts who underwent training in issues such as conflict de-escalation and personal safety. Many of the escorts reported being assaulted by the anti-abortion activists as they physically placed themselves between the clients and the activists. One of the escorts told us that

I came out one time, with a client, who was highly distressed (...) she was squealing and crying and we got her away as quick as possible, but they were relentless. They were just coming (...) they would bump into us, they would shoulder bump you and try to get in front of you, they would be reaching over the top of you. So I was shouting that we don't want any engagement here. And we got to the [traffic] lights, and this girl, they were threatening (...) to report to the police, we are going to report this on social media, and she just lost the plot and she ran into the oncoming traffic, to just try to get away from these people. And I had to run out after her to stop the traffic. And I turned round and obviously they hadn't followed us into the traffic, but they were laughing as they walked back to the clinic doors.

The ongoing conflict outside this particular independent clinic halted when Parliament started to provide free abortions for NI residents in England, which led to the clinic no longer providing its paid-for service.

National attention on the activities of anti-abortion groups became focused on one London-based clinic site where anti-abortion activism was very intense, regular and intrusive. A new group, *Sister Supporter*, emerged, which challenged their activities. Later on, *Sister Supporter* recruited people to form similar groups in other locations where anti-abortion activism took place. They were identifiable by the pink bibs they wore and would typically display signs such as 'Do they bother you? Come and talk to us'.

Sister Supporter was formed out of a group of concerned local residents, who witnessed the various anti-abortion groups that coalesced at their local abortion clinic. Because there was a vast expanse of grass in front of this particular London-based clinic, it was a prime location for various anti-abortion groups to congregate. It required pedestrian access and had a narrow entrance way to the clinic, which enabled maximum impact for anti-abortion activists to interact with service users. The site had developed a reputation for being a focal point for anti-abortion activism, developed over many years. Indeed, in regional towns and cities, we would encounter anti-abortion activists who had travelled to this particular site to demonstrate their support; this location was therefore something of a pilgrimage for anti-abortion activists. There were many different anti-abortion groups that coalesced, encouraging an almost constant anti-abortion presence at the clinic site. It was also a location where impromptu groups emerged, such as one who recreated an altar dedicated to Our Lady of Kodeńskiej (a Polish manifestation of Mary), accompanied by a candle and a foetal doll. The various anti-abortion groups at this site did not necessarily support each other. Graphic images were a key cause for contention between anti-abortion groups at this location. For example, the activists from *Good Counsel Network* (*GCN*) would take a break when members of the *Society of Pius X*, who displayed graphic images, arrived for a couple of hours each Friday. The groups who did not use graphic images set themselves up as being fundamentally different, demonstrated through *GCN's* evidence pack to the *Ealing Council Consultation* when a bufferzone was being debated at this site. They state that they have an 'entirely different approach' (2018, p. 1834) that is 'peaceful' and 'prayerful'

(2018, p. 1837). In an interview, Maria, who prayed at abortion clinics, explained why many anti-abortion activists disapproved of graphic images:

> ...they are setting out to shock and offend and you know, their intentions may be good in the sense that they are trying to get people to stop and think about it, but (...) I think they've kind of lost sight of that a bit because they're coming across as offensive and not supportive (Maria interview).

At this particular site, anti-abortion activism had become a public spectacle, with a heightened visible presence of activists who dominated the public space, in whatever guise that activism took. Beyond the *Pius X* 'Friday group' who deployed graphic imagery, at other times, foetal dolls, religious altars and signs were used. Because of its centrality at the heart of the anti-abortion campaign, this particular clinic was frequently used by numerous anti-abortion groups, who differed in their tactics, engagement with material objects and use of space. This could also make the encounters for clinic users unpredictable – whilst some groups silently prayed, others went to great lengths to engage clinic users in conversation. Those accessing abortion services could therefore have various experiences when accessing the clinic.

Over time, the presence of *Sister Supporter* became more embedded, and they claimed space of their own through propping their signs against the railings and setting up chairs and tables with tins of cake and flasks of tea (see Fig. 6). They became central to local campaigns for bufferzones around the clinic site and local residents knew who they were and would stop to chat, asking how the campaign was going. Residents living locally were typically concerned that the anti-abortion activists were next to a public park, with parents escorting children past the distressing imagery. Indeed, a public consultation in the area revealed that of the local residents that responded to an online consultation to create a bufferzone around the clinic, 90.4% were in favour (*Ealing Council Consultation Report*, 2018). In contrast, the overwhelming majority of those opposed did not live in the local area and responded via a template message written by an anti-abortion organisation (*Ealing Council Consultation Report*, 2018).

Despite the day-to-day 'civil inattention' (Goffman, 1963) between the groups, there were various contestations. Some of this revolved around the use of space. At the centre of the grass was a mature tree, and both groups attempted to use the tree as a prop for their material objects. Whilst the anti-abortion groups typically hung religious medallions in the tree, *Sister Supporter* utilised the trunk to display various signs, such as 'Stop the harassment of women', secured with bungee cords around the tree. When graphic images were on display, *Sister Supporter* would sometimes form a line in front of the clinic, shielding anyone approaching from that imagery.

Whilst disturbances between groups were typically muted when a researcher was present, we did witness various antagonisms. This happened at a clinic in the North:

Sarah-Jane approaches [*40 Days for Life* (*40DFL*) activist]. It is clear the woman is agitated. Sarah-Jane asks if she is alright. She says not, and says she is livid about 'them'. Sarah-Jane asks what has happened. Anne [the activist] says she had gone over to two 'young ladies' who were entering the clinic to ask if they would like some information and straight away they accused her of harassment. She defended her actions by saying that we are allowed to give them information because it helps them to change their minds sometimes. Especially as some of them have been forced to come. And they called the police, which Anne says she is not bothered about because she is not doing anything wrong. But she says it's frustrating because they have been coming for years, but *Sister Supporter* have only recently started coming. And she said to call the police for that, would definitely be considered a waste of police time (…) She said that we are not protestors. But we are trying to help people. She then described *Sister Supporter* as protestors, indicated, in Anne's view, by the way they had intervened when Anne had gone to speak to the two women earlier. She said nobody had ever said that they are not allowed to approach people (…) Then she said it was all so horrible as they were killing babies, so as a diversionary tactic, they want to vilify the prayer vigil. She said that the world was upside down. She said all she was here for was to help mothers and fathers and to save babies (field notes, North).

Later we obtained the version of events from the *Sister Supporter* activists who explain that Anne was continuing to try to engage a clinic user who had asked Anne to leave her alone. They said that when they told Anne they would report this to the police, it 'didn't faze Anne one bit'. Whilst we cannot be certain that it was about this incident, later we hear that Anne has been convicted of a public order offence and given a restraining order banning her from being outside the clinic. This incident illustrates two key elements about the contested spaces. First, because the anti-abortion activists understand their activities as 'saving' women, they always see their actions as supportive (Lowe & Page, 2020). Second, although confrontations in the contested space outside rarely result in criminal convictions, it cannot be assumed that the behaviour by anti-abortion activists in the space does not result in breaches of the law.

At other locations there were local interventions by a small number of volunteers not explicitly connected with an organised group like *Sister Supporter*. Sometimes these were individual initiatives to stand with an opposing message to the anti-abortion activists. In interviews with pro-choice activists, they discussed the personal costs; if their name became associated with pro-choice activism, this could lead to online abuse and harassment. Georgia had instigated a petition in her small community opposing the anti-abortion activism and had stood on her own, with her baby in a sling, opposing the activists outside her local clinic. Her motherhood was frequently referenced by local activists, her being asked 'How can you be a mum and support abortion?' Because of the publicity generated she now regularly encountered negative messages through her Facebook and Instagram feeds, including people sending her images of dead babies. This went beyond the local context and was connected to people as far afield as the United States (US).

Meanwhile anti-abortion activists also emphasised the abuse encountered whilst participating in clinic vigils, including verbal abuse and, occasionally, physical abuse, but there were few reports of being harassed beyond the clinic vigil:

> They said they had coffee thrown over them on one occasion and a car drove very close to them and onto the verge where they were situated (field notes, South-West).

> A man regularly says how smelly they are because of the rubbish they are speaking. Someone else said they were going to hell as they were judging people (field notes, Wales).

Apart from in NI, physical violence at clinic sites was infrequent. We only directly witnessed one incident at a clinic in the South-East in 2019. A passer-by confronted an anti-abortion activist and a tussle began between the two men. The anti-abortion activist was holding on and punching the passer-by as he sought to leave the area. We heard other reports from pro-choice activists and local residents of physical aggression. A response to the *Ealing Council consultation* stated:

> I have been physically assaulted on more than one occasion by the anti-abortion protestors after picking up pictures from the ground. This including being punched, kicked and attempting to stamp on my fingers.
> (*Ealing Council Consultation Report* Appendix 1 2018, p. 42)

Particular individuals were known for their aggressive personalities, and pro-choice activists could feel intimidated:

> Juliet described an incident when she (…) saw a large group [of anti-abortion activists] under the tree and she had photographed them. One of the men had immediately come over to her and had been quite threatening, saying that she could not photograph them, and told her to delete the photo, and give them her camera. And he was then blocking her way. She had said, 'do you really want to do this?' She described him as being really intimidating (field notes, South-East).

As in the incident we witnessed above, direct abuse reported by anti-abortion activists typically emerged from passers-by rather than organised pro-choice activism, as this example typifies:

Fig. 6.   Counterdemonstration Signs.

A man came to try and physically remove the signs that we have, you know, the posters that we have. And when I asked him not to, he said that we weren't allowed to, I said, 'yes the police know we're here; they're happy with us being here' and he physically picked them up, opened my car door and threw them into my car – and threw them, he didn't just place them (...) he was kind of shouting – he was a passer-by; he wasn't at the clinic – but there was a lot of aggression and it was verbal, it wasn't physically towards me but he was being very physical with the posters, throwing them around – they're big heavy things you know – so yeah, he was one very angry man (Jacquie interview).

In this instance, the anger was displaced onto the anti-abortion objects themselves; we frequently heard reports from anti-abortion activists of passers-by interfering with the signs in some way, sometimes by attempting to physically remove them. Meanwhile, pro-choice activists were typically (though not always) women. Again, we must reflect on the gendered dynamics at play here. Beyond the gendering of participants, the pro-choice campaign strategy was often feminised – bibs that were pink, handmade signs, tins of homemade bakes. The feel of the pro-choice activism outside clinics was therefore not framed in terms of physical aggression. Although there were examples of antagonisms over the use of space and occasional verbal exchanges (as indicated above), the levels of perceived threat were muted. For example, at one clinic site, the pro-choice activists deployed pink string to mark out a potential bufferzone area. Rarely did we ever hear anti-abortion activists at clinic sites say that they felt threatened by pro-choice activists. Yet in public discourse, there was a tendency

Fig. 7.   Prayer Vigil with Line of Pink Counterdemonstrators in the
Background.

for anti-abortion activists to conflate organised pro-choice activism with acts of
physical aggression by passers-by, as this speech at *March for Life* (*MFL*)
reveals:

> She says she has a fan club in pink that follows her wherever
> she goes – where they go, they go, and gestures to the
> counterdemonstrators. She says all the volunteers have to put up
> with this kind of hate on a regular basis. And she says people tell
> her that she is so brave, sitting on Victoria Derbyshire's[1] sofa with
> two people who are against you, and she says that actually, these
> people who are out for four and five hours a day, being spat at in
> the street, having cigarette butts stabbed into their coats, having
> their pictures smashed up and coffee poured over their heads,
> etcetera, etcetera. She says that these are documented police
> reports of actual events that have happened to our counsellors
> and volunteers outside of abortion centres. Those are the people
> who are brave, so she asks that everyone puts their hands together
> for them, and the crowd obliges (field notes *MFL*).

---

[1]A British journalist who previously hosted a current affairs programme for the BBC.

Fig. 8.   'I Asked God. She's Pro-Choice'.

In this narrative, the 'fan club in pink' – meaning *Sister Supporter* – is equated with individuals who spit at and pour coffee over anti-abortion activists. Yet our extensive engagement with clinic sites reveals that these incidents emerged from angry (usually male) passers-by or those accompanying women into the clinics, rather than pro-choice activists. Indeed, explicit physical violence was connected with masculine rage and hostility. This can be understood because of the way the public sphere is gendered – public spaces have been devised and controlled with the needs of white heterosexual men in mind (Logan, 2015; Lowe & Hayes, 2019; Pain, 2001; Skeggs, 1999). Women therefore have to navigate public spaces carefully and were therefore far less likely to be the ones engaging in aggressive behaviour. As Georgia's single-woman pro-choice campaign demonstrated earlier, women on their own were actually very vulnerable for being a target; even pro-choice activists who congregated in groups did not escape masculine hostility from a minority of anti-abortion male activists. Equally, we must recognise that anti-abortion activists were also subject to these same gendered dynamics, with women anti-abortion activists also being particularly vulnerable for targeting.

Understanding Clinic Counterdemonstrations

Thus far, we have explored the specific dynamics outside clinics, including examples where there was a pro-choice presence. There were two principal aims of the pro-choice activists, which often depended on if the abortion service was open or closed. If open they aimed to offer support to clinic users accessing abortion services, though this was mediated through particular material objects deployed for activism (e.g. use of signs indicating their position and their message). If the anti-abortion activists were not *in situ*, the pro-choice activists would typically not be there either. If the abortion service was closed, the remit was more typically a counterprotest, challenging the anti-abortion position, especially their positioning directly outside of abortion services (see Fig. 7).

We now expand our remit to consider more explicit forms of activism that were specifically about opposing the anti-abortion activists, rather than supporting women accessing the clinic. Due to space, we mainly focus our analysis on activism outside clinics and hospitals, rather than public engagements more broadly, though it should be noted that anti-abortion activism occurs in other spaces too. For the duration of fieldwork, we encountered activism in town and city centre locations, near parliamentary or other government buildings, including the use of graphic images, *Society for the Protection of Unborn Children* (*SPUC*) pro-life chains, with an aim of conveying the anti-abortion message to passing traffic, as well as the annual *MFL*. All these events evoked different moods and emotions; in future publications, we will analyse this in more detail.

Here, we primarily focus on the counterdemonstrations emerging at the clinics themselves. We are making a distinction between activities, whose principal aim was to offer moral support to enable women safe passage to or from the doors of the clinic, and counterdemonstrations, whose main aim was to take a stand against the position of the anti-abortion activists. Whilst some groups focused on one activity rather than the other, others would slip between them, typically displaying pro-choice banners and messages whilst also aiming to provide a barrier between service users and anti-abortion activists. A key issue when pro-choice activists organised a counterdemonstration was reflexivity regarding the context and avoiding anything to further marginalise those accessing the clinic. Anything rowdy and disruptive was usually contained to occasions when the clinic was closed. This was often at the behest of the clinics, and some pro-choice groups liaised with the local clinic to find out days that they would not be seeing clients. However, there were occasions when large numbers of anti-abortion activists congregated outside clinics when they were open, as part of specific targeted events. Pro-choice activists therefore upped their own numbers, to enable a counter-presence.

In 2016, in the South-East, we witnessed one occasion where there was no counterdemonstration, and 25 anti-abortion activists participated in a *Helpers of God's Precious Infants* (*HOGPI*) procession from the local Catholic Church to the abortion clinic. They then remained outside the clinic to pray for several hours. The clinic itself was in a large old house, with a driveway but not enough space for clinic users to park in it. All users of the clinic therefore had to find somewhere to park on the road and go past the congregated group. This was a highly pressurised situation for clinic users to encounter, and a police officer took it upon himself to escort women up the steps to the clinic door. It was the only time we witnessed a police officer performing this function; on many other occasions when they were present, police officers typically just stood and watched. More generally, therefore, the presence of the police alongside groups of activists increased the public spectacle surrounding abortion, drawing more attention to women seeking to enter and breaching their healthcare privacy (Lowe & Hayes, 2019; Lowe & Page, 2020).

A similar procession by *HOGPI* at another clinic site (closed at the time) in the South-East was accompanied by a pro-choice counterdemonstration, comprised of 33 anti-abortion activists and 25 counterdemonstrators. The latter had been asked to wear pink by the organiser:

> Once the procession arrives at the clinic [the counterdemonstration] starts to become more vocal; they start chanting the usual pro-choice chants and one has a megaphone. You can still here the monk with a microphone but the detail of what he is saying is unclear. The anti-abortion activists have laminated prayer cards and most have visible rosaries. Many kneel on the ground the whole time whilst some of the others alternate between kneeling and standing. At times it is just the monk chanting, whereas at others the group joins in. When the anti-abortion activists get louder, [the counterdemonstration] do as well (field notes, South-East).

The dynamics therefore shift considerably compared with the previous *HOGPI* procession mentioned. The aural dimensions are important as each group tries to outdo the other in terms of vocality, with various uses of microphones and megaphones. When the anti-abortion activists start singing hymns, the counter-demonstrators start singing 'She'll be Coming Round the Mountain'. The materiality of both groups differs markedly. Whilst prayer books, rosary beads and an enormous image of Our Lady of Guadalupe typify the material objects of the anti-abortion activists (with a number of participants indicating their status as monks or nuns through their attire), the pro-choice counterdemonstration was embodied through colourful handmade signs, with various pro-choice slogans, and the explicit use of the colour pink.

Whilst the counterdemonstrators moved around, the anti-abortion activists were more stationary and many chose to kneel as they prayed. Visually, this therefore gave the upper hand to the counterdemonstrators, who laid claim to the space more extensively, with their pro-choice message being very clear and visible. Whilst one may assume that one side of the campaign was religious and the other non-religious (or even perhaps anti-religious), it was far more complex. Visually, the anti-abortion activists had laid claim to particular material objects like rosary beads which came to be associated with their campaign (see Chapter 7). As we have reflected in a previous chapter, this monopolisation of a certain religious object in anti-abortion contexts has repercussions, as it comes to embody the broader anti-abortion movement; a greater diversity of meanings are therefore challenging to enact. Any negative religious sentiment could focus on the rosary beads, and at this site, a young woman carried a cardboard sign with the felt-tipped words, 'Get your rosaries off our ovaries!', and a hand-drawn image of both a uterus and rosary beads. At the same time, alternative religious theologies were presented by the pro-choice campaign. Another young woman carried a sign with the message, 'I asked God. She's Pro Choice' (see Fig. 8). This was an explicit challenge to the hierarchical and traditional masculinist understandings of Christianity, from which traditional theologies about women's roles (and a valorisation of their identities as mothers) emerge. Invoking God as a woman – aligned with feminist theological interpretations – was therefore a means of demonstrating that the anti-abortion activists did not have the monopoly on the religious interpretations around abortion and that a pro-choice position was compatible with a Christian identity.

Georgia, the lone activist who received online abuse, equally reflected:

> I've got a few Catholic friends, and they're all really totally baffled by [anti-abortion activism], and they get quite annoyed, because I think it's in any religion. When one party of that religion do something bad, it's like the whole religion gets this bad name. So, one of my friends, she goes to church and stuff like that as a Catholic, and she's totally in support of what I'm doing. But again, she gets annoyed because everyone assumes that she would be pro-life.

Religion therefore becomes reified as oppositional to abortion, obscuring the numbers of religious individuals who abhor anti-abortion activism (Page & Lowe, 2021b). Indeed, it may equally be assumed that pro-choice counterdemonstrations would be fully secular, but the reality, as the 'I asked God. She's Pro Choice' sign indicates, was more complex. This complexity is further illustrated in the feedback to the *Ealing Council Consultation* whereby those opposed to the bufferzone indicated that it undermined religious freedom, whereas others questioned the activities:

> Peaceful prayer vigils do not constitute 'harassment'. Freedom of religion should be respected and the rights of the victimised babies in grave danger of their lives upheld.
>
> (*Ealing Council Consultation Report Appendix 1*, 2018, p. 9)

> I wish to register my support of the implementation of the PSPO [Public Spaces Protection Order]. This is in direct response to notice being given at my Parish Church (Ealing Abbey, I am a regular practising Catholic), notifying all parishioners of this consultation and asking all to contribute. It was at worst highly disingenuous, the way it was done, and at best missed the point: this is about the horrifying intimidation of highly vulnerable women. The methods used by the pro-life protestors cannot be condoned or allowed to continue.
>
> (*Ealing Council Consultation Report Appendix 1*, 2018, p. 8)

In addition to the comments by the general public, the local Church of England (CofE) and Methodist churches were supportive of the bufferzone being put in place. As we indicated in Chapter 1, the response from the Methodist Church stated that

> ...we must offer support and protection to those who are visiting the clinic and are vulnerable. If that means that as churches we need to adapt our activities to enable that protection and to prevent others using 'prayer' improperly and unethically to apply pressure or coercion then we must do so.
>
> (*Ealing Council Consultation Report,* 2018, p. 57)

We witnessed alternative theologies being invoked through counterdemonstration messages at other sites. In Scotland, a *40DFL* vigil-end event engaged a sustained counterdemonstration, with one participant holding a handmade placard saying 'No Uterus No Opinion*', accompanied by an image of Jesus surrounded by rainbow colours. The asterisk was explained in the following terms: 'Unless you're Jesus but he's cool with it' [abortion]. Sarah-Jane spoke to her:

> The woman was explaining how she was a Christian who belonged to a queer-affirming local church, but our conversation was interrupted by an anti-abortion activist who tells her that her sign is 'sacrilege' and to 'get that down'. The counterdemonstrator says very firmly, 'No'; the woman asks her why not, and she responds saying that she is not wearing the crucifix for the good of her health. The woman storms off, but later returns to say that she loves the picture of Jesus, and exclaims publicly that she thanks God for bringing that picture. Sarah-Jane asks how the counterdemonstrator interprets this about-face, and whether she saw it as a form of apology. She says she is not sure, and she is still trying to process it (field notes, Scotland).

The anti-abortion activist had interpreted the sign as being anti-Christian, blasphemous and desecrating, but then had to reconfigure her understanding when realising that the counterdemonstrator was a Christian. This prompted a change in behaviour, and something akin to an apology was given. Offering alternative Christian theologies on abortion directly challenged the anti-abortion cause and could have resulted in theological argument. But rather than focus on the message, Jesus was foregrounded as the person who they could both sacredly identify with. This diffused any further tensions over how abortion itself was interpreted through a Christian lens.

In 2017, in the Midlands, we attended the *40DFL* closing prayer vigil, which was publicly advertised as being a candle-lit vigil and therefore likely to generate a high number of participants. We arrived to find a solitary anti-abortion activist outside the clinic (it's a Sunday evening and the clinic is closed). We were not expecting any counterdemonstration, but unexpectedly, a feminist group from a nearby university arrived. As we waited for other vigil participants to attend, it became increasingly apparent that their plans had changed, and that a broader closing vigil event was not happening that evening. Whether the *40DFL* organisers had got wind of the counterdemonstration is difficult to say – our attempts at talking to vigil participants and obtaining this information (another activist arrived later to join the prayer) were unsuccessful on this occasion. The feminist group discussed what to do, and they decided to stay where they were, with one articulating that it 'wouldn't be right' to protest at the church itself. On one side of the road were 20 counterdemonstrators, with a megaphone and handmade banners. On the other side of the road were two prayer vigil participants, holding candles. Whilst they said their prayers, women from the counterdemonstration delivered impassioned speeches about how being pro-choice is a human right. Another woman revealed her story of sexual assault and how access to abortion and contraception was therefore fundamental. They also started singing older pop songs, particularly from Abba's back catalogue. On speaking with the counter-demonstrators, it was clear that a number were Christian, and later on, religion was specifically referenced in their speeches:

> The pro-choice group started to sing an Abba song (*Dancing Queen*). The lyrics are followed until the last line, where they say 'digging the pro-choice movement'. They are getting more vocal as a group, and they start verbalising comments to the anti-abortion side, such as 'God told us to love each other; to love one's neighbour and you stand here and harass women'. The other women cheer at this point. The woman continues with 'You are taking the Bible and using it against women'. And other statements such as 'God loves us, so we should be able to choose what we do with our bodies. He gave us autonomy'. And comments such as churches are open to everyone and your actions are 'turning people away' from church; and what you are doing is 'wrong'. The speaker then articulates that she does not hate the anti-abortion side, but argue that they are 'pushing ignorance' and are 'liars'. At this point another pro-choice activist shouts 'Shame on you'. The main speaker calls their actions 'shameful'. The speaker affirms that God loves her and everyone participating on this side of the road and that she is praying for those on the opposite side of the road. Another woman says something along the lines of, 'We are pro-choice', and this generates a cheer.

Similar to the 'I asked God. She's Pro Choice' sentiment, these activists had a very different articulation to what God's intentions were and demonstrated a position of faith that sat comfortably with being pro-choice. The anti-abortion activists were critiqued for using sacred texts to hurt and undermine women. This was seen as inherently wrong and a misuse of scripture.

In other encounters, there was a more antagonistic relationship generated between religion and the counterdemonstrations. For example, *Feminist Fightback's* interventions regarding concerns about the potential impact on clinic users in relation to *HOGPI* processions led them to the space of the church itself. While other counterdemonstrators refused to go to churches, *Feminist Fightback* saw this as a fitting space for activism. In 2015, we observed them taking their demonstration to the Catholic Church, which was the starting point of an anti-abortion procession. Whilst the anti-abortion activists were inside hearing the Mass which preceded their actions, *Feminist Fightback* set up a noisy protest outside, utilising kitchen implements like baking trays and frying pans.[2] They justified their amplified music and pro-choice chanting as similar to the prayers and hymns that the anti-abortion activists intended to use outside an abortion clinic. After the Mass finished, the anti-abortion group came outside and positioned themselves behind an image of Our Lady of Guadalupe. *Feminist Fightback* then prevented them from leaving the area by forming a human barricade on either side. The police were called; they attempted to negotiate between the two groups with very little effect. After nearly an hour, *HOGPI* was able to set off to the abortion clinic, with *Feminist Fightback* in noisy attendance. At about 100 metres from the clinic, *Feminist Fightback* stopped, allowing the anti-abortion group and a line of police officers to take up position directly outside. They explained that they were respecting the wishes of the clinic who did not want anyone outside.

For the anti-abortion activists themselves, the targeting of the sacred space of a church was deplorable and sacrilegious, and complaints were made about their activities being intimidating and distressing to parishioners. This response is similar to the feelings that pro-choice groups feel about the space outside of abortion clinics, where service users are targeted. Both groups have differing sacred commitments (Lynch, 2012a); the sacred space for anti-abortion activists is the church – indeed, the abortion site, as Chapter 4 emphasised, is understood in profaning terms – as a place of evil and destruction. Meanwhile, the pro-choice activists understand the abortion clinic as the space where their sacred commitment – reproductive justice – is enabled and enacted and therefore needs protection from those who seek to take this right away. Sites such as the church and the clinic therefore become moments of 'intense identification' (Lynch, 2012a, p. 134), when sacred assumptions are challenged in some way. Other pro-choice groups were more cautious about deploying religious sites as a target for their activism. Indeed, in general terms, the general public can often be deeply attached to church buildings, even if they never utilise them, emphasised at moments when they are threatened with crisis (Davie, 2007). This, coupled with the understanding that

---

[2]Using kitchen implements to signal dissent is a common global strategy, particularly around women's issues. Walker's (2018) analysis of local United Kingdom (UK) newspapers in the nineteenth century, for example, showed domestic abuse was mentioned in local newspapers as the most common reason for subjecting to 'rough music' (as it is called in UK folklore). In Argentina, cacerolazos protests were used by the Las Madres de Plaza de Mayo to protest against the disappearances of their children under the military government (Goddard, 2007).

churches are populated by older parishioners, means that church-based activism becomes a more contentious public sphere activity. Equally, the overt religious displays at clinic sites are also unwelcome by a general public who understand religion, as well as abortion, as a private matter (Aston, 2016; Knott, 2010; Lowe & Page, 2019a; Millar, 2017).

A similar event where the role of religion in the counterdemonstration messaging was more antagonistic occurred at a *40DFL* Sunday closing vigil in the Midlands just outside the entrance to a large hospital. It was very quiet, with few people entering or leaving the hospital by that entrance, and no abortions were happening that day. Six individuals were praying, along with a counterdemonstration comprised of 26 people, including many banners (home-made and professionally printed), songs and speeches. Both groups were opposite each other, on either side of the road. The last *40DFL* vigil of the season was symbolic for the counterdemonstration as they had been fundraising for an abortion charity for the duration of the 40 days as part of their protest against the presence of the anti-abortion activists. Presenting this cheque formed part of their public campaign, which drew heavily on humour. The comedic Monty Python back catalogue was utilised (*Meaning of Life* and *Life of Brian*), largely emphasising the negative role religion played in society. At the same time, the messages around religion were complex; although it was certainly the case that some individuals were very combative, others emphasised being Christian and pro-choice:

> The portable speaker system is then utilised to play Monty Python's *Every Sperm is Sacred*. A number of pro-choice activists are smiling broadly and laughing at the lyrics.[3] The pro-choice participants then organise themselves so that they are more clearly displaying their banners. These include professionally printed pro-choice posters, as well as a large number of home-made signs with messages such as 'If the fetus you saved was gay, would you still protect their rights', 'If Mary had an abortion, we wouldn't be in this mess' and 'Your Body, your Choice'. All of these signs were on cardboard with the messages painted in white. A woman starts to repeatedly shout, 'My body my choice; a woman's right to choose (…)'. She is holding a hand-made sign saying, 'A woman's right to choose'. *Every Sperm is Sacred* has now ended, and other music is played (…). The same woman starts a new slogan, taunting, 'You're going to lose in Ireland. We're going to win'. 'Abortion is going to be made legal in Ireland in May and you're going to lose, you're going to lose, you're going to lose. The eighth is going to get repealed and you're going to lose. Ha ha ha'. She is dancing about on the spot to the music. Another

---

[3]*Every Sperm is Sacred* was used in Monty Python's *The Meaning of Life* film (1983). It specifically invokes Roman Catholicism and gently mocks the sacred status given to sperm, given the papal ban on artificial forms of contraception.

sign is on white fabric and in black and magenta pink letters; it says, 'Keep your theology off my biology' (...). A woman on the pro-choice side says that she is a pro-choice Christian; not in God's name. The woman who is shouting all the slogans moves on to say, 'You know there are pro-choice Catholics? You know there are pro-choice Christians?' She also invokes the priest abuse of children scandal. 'We know what Catholic priests do to little boys' (...). The organiser reaches for a microphone connected with the portable PA speaker system and thanks everyone for coming and says that they will be revealing the cheque and the money they have raised for *Abortion Support Network*. Someone then starts reciting lines from the *Life of Brian*, 'He's not the Messiah; he's a very naughty boy!' (...). Some of the prayer practices now include kneeling. If the anti-abortion activists are saying their prayers out loud, you can't hear them. The pro-choice side have the monopoly in numbers, as well as the loudness of the message, especially with the inclusion of the sound system.

To disentangle the various dimensions of this demonstration, we must analyse it carefully. The presence of the speaker system as well as a large printed cheque gives an indication that there was a planned element to this event; the counter-demonstration clearly wanted to put forward the case that the presence of the *40DFL* activists at a hospital site was inappropriate and damaging to those seeking clinic services. Yet, at the same time, those assembled represent different interests and agendas; the counterdemonstration does not comprise a singular group with the same views and approaches to activism, although in that moment, they are united in standing together to oppose the prayer vigil. Whilst key individuals have organised the event, they do not set themselves up as being 'in charge'; they invest in a democratic approach where anyone can use the microphone to speak. This means that there is much opportunity for 'unplanned' encounters, with various messages conveyed – even those that run counter to the intention of the original organisers. Nobody is policing what slogans and signs people have made. This openness also allows certain voices to become more audible than others. The woman who explicitly taunts the anti-abortion activists and equates Catholic priesthood with paedophilia takes up more of the space, whilst the pro-choice Christian's voice – who desires to make a theological point that the approach of the anti-abortion activists is not godly – is muffled and muted. Equating all Catholic priests with paedophilia is a sweeping judgement and can be deemed anti-religious. It is sentiments like this, also conveyed in chants such as 'get your rosaries, off our ovaries', and 'If Mary had an abortion, we wouldn't be in this mess' that anti-abortion activists use to argue that *all* counterdemonstrations are anti-Catholic, amplified because the counterdemonstrations are usually understood as uniform groups. Just like, as outlined in Chapter 7, rosary beads become a symbol of an anti-abortion position, anti-religious messages by a minority of pro-choice counterdemonstrators become the lens through which all counterdemonstrations are framed and understood.

Anti-religious sentiments can also be off-putting for pro-choice Christians, who may feel displaced by a counterdemonstration that they interpret as anti-religious. For example, at another event, a Christian woman (Sandie) had brought her Bible to the counterdemonstration, on which she had stuck pink heart-shaped post-it notes, with slogans such as 'God is Love' and 'Standing alongside women who need abortion'. Yet, she later reflected the challenges of her positioning as a religious person:

> Sandie highlights an anti-abortion activist who has got a cross, the same as her, and she then sighs. She said she felt compelled to be here but had never been at a protest where somebody else of faith was so visibly on the opposing side. She said this was a totally new experience. She said her emotions were mixed about it (...) Sarah-Jane asks if she was going to go back with the main counterdemonstration group, but senses she doesn't want to (...). Sandie says that she doesn't like it when they deliberately try to taunt the other side.

At this particular campaign, the organisers were hyper-aware of religious identities and were inclusive of pro-choice individuals who were religious; ordinarily, they had a core activist who was Catholic and who spoke at the rallies. But individuals who were more antagonistic could change the tone of the event, so that for Sandie as a pro-choice religious individual, she felt somewhat uncomfortable.

Returning to the *40DFL* closing vigil, on closer examination, it was not explicitly *designed* to be *anti*-religious. Although anti-religious sentiments do emerge as events unfold, in its inception, it was a critical engagement with forms of religion that cause harm to others – individuals who are less powerful than the religious doctrine itself. The event revolves around critiquing powerful religious theologies for negatively impacting women's lives, rather than being a blanket critique of religion per se. In order to achieve this aim, they utilised satire and parody as their underlying framework. Interpretations of Monty Python have softened over the years and is now generally considered in terms of endearment in general British culture.[4] Yet the Monty Python sketches, which often parody Catholicism, have the potential to cause offence in conservative Christian circles, albeit not typically in liberal ones. The use of Monty Python is a clever move, as it situates Python humour as part and parcel of the British landscape, with the

---

[4]When *Life of Brian* was released in 1979, it was banned in several countries (Norway and Ireland) and generated claims of blasphemy, but in the twenty-first century, blasphemy is no longer illegal in England and Wales. *Life of Brian* fails to evoke similar sentiment and is now more likely to be read rather differently, even as relatively respectful of Christianity given the deep knowledge of the Christian story required to understand the humour (Almond, 2019).

assumption that everyone will 'get' the joke. This is achieved because the humour deployed is now very dated, heightening its embeddedness and social acceptability in British culture.[5] If you are offended, then you are understood as being far too sensitive. As Kuipers argues, societies operate with their own humour regimes, these being 'unwritten rules stipulating who can joke about what' (2011, p. 69). The power of religion has frequently been the object of mockery in UK society. Yet the specific gibes toward Catholic theology (e.g. the *Every Sperm is Sacred* Song) heighten the possibility of offence being caused, particularly as those participating in prayer vigils are far more likely to faithfully follow those same theologies which are being critiqued.

How can this particular counterdemonstration be understood in relation to the use of public space? Arguably, on this occasion, this display is disproportionate. Looking at it visually, on one side you have six prayer vigil activists holding signs opposing abortion. Their prayer cannot be heard, their heads are lowered; at times they kneel. Their body language is one of deference. They show no reaction to the counterdemonstration. Meanwhile on the other side, the counterdemonstration is loud and rowdy. There is a lot of noise, through sing-songs, speeches and banners. In terms of the use of space, the counterdemonstration has the upper hand and has the loudest voice. Yet the counterdemonstration was protesting against 40 days of prayer vigil presence at the hospital site. The strength of feeling opposing this activity was conveyed within the various pro-choice speeches; we feature here excerpts from a hospital worker describing the lived impact of their activism and a man discussing freedom of speech and power:

> [She] starts by saying that many people who come to work here have their own experiences of how very difficult it is having children. She talks about the very difficult choices people have to make. And she said that they didn't want to be reminded of this when they come to work every day. She said that she knows of staff members brought to tears (...). She said what upsets her the most is people coming to the hospital to access services of all sorts, to support a pregnancy, to make difficult decisions during the pregnancy, and she says she was once one of those people (...) She tells the vigil activists that what they really need to think about is that when abortion is made illegal, the abortion rates do not go down (...) She then says that 1 in 3 pregnancies end in miscarriage (...) 'That is a totally legitimate reason to be accessing hospital services to help her, and it is not right that she has to walk past you as she is accessing those services. (...) What you are doing here does not reduce abortion at all. And I hope you have a think about

---

[5]Monty Python humour has, however, been critiqued more recently for its outdated attitudes to issues such as racism and disability (Almond, 2019). Our point is that, specifically regarding the critique of religion, there is little backlash to the Monty Python canon.

that before you come back next year. I really don't want to see you here again'.

He says 'you are not just praying by standing there, because if your God is infinite, you can stand where you want (...). Why do you need signs to pray? You don't need signs to pray; God knows full well what you are doing, because he is all seeing and infinite, right? (...). The reason you are here is to have an effect on the people who are using the [clinic] facility (...). You are intimidating and you are bullying (...) When we exercise our freedom of speech we speak upwards to power. (...) Or we debate as equals. That is exercising freedom of speech. When you are speaking downwards towards vulnerability, that is not freedom of speech. That is harassment. That is intimidation. That is bullying. And that is why we oppose you'.

It was in the speeches that the core message was conveyed, and the argument for why anti-abortion activism at clinics was so problematic. For the hospital worker, despite the submissive body language, the anti-abortion activists' approach should not be mistaken for passive prayer practice. Instead, she articulated the harms being caused towards *all* those who walked past, who may have their own heart-breaking reproductive story. She argued that the anti-abortion activists fundamentally misunderstood the issue, and their approach was harmful, rather than helpful. Meanwhile, in one fell swoop, the other speaker critiqued anti-abortion activism in terms of its religious necessity, freedom of speech and power dynamics. He doubted the religious impetus to simply pray to God, as that could be enacted anywhere. Instead, he argued their practice was an abuse of power, because it targeted those who were weaker and more vulnerable and did not fit into the criteria for freedom of speech. This also helps understand why the pro-choice activists believed their use of humour to be acceptable. As Kuipers notes,

...humour and laughter often function as a social corrective (...). The unwritten rules of humour in most western societies stipulate that humour in the public sphere should be 'upward' and 'inward'.

(2011, p. 71)

By 'upward', Kuipers means those with equal or greater amounts of social power; 'inward' means the capacity to critique one's own group through humour. Whilst on the one hand, Catholics are a minority group in the UK, on the other hand, those involved in anti-abortion activism have positioned themselves against individuals at a particularly sensitive time. The humour therefore acts as a 'social corrective'. In addition, the consequences of the Catholic Church's broader approach to reproductive healthcare across the world were referenced in other speeches (e.g. Ireland and the death of Savita Halappanavar) – at this level, the Catholic Church is a powerful player in the diminishment of reproductive rights

(Miller, 2014). Furthermore, as some of the activists disclaimed a past Catholic identity (often associated with childhood upbringing), some activists could also induce the humour from an 'inward' perspective.

Overall, the underlying message conveyed by the counterdemonstration was to highlight the anti-abortion activists' position outside clinics as misguided at best and damaging to women at worst. Despite their quiet demeanour, their prayer practices had a real adverse effect, and this needed to be challenged (Page & Lowe, 2021a). This strength of feeling can illuminate why the counterdemonstration was organised and the specific tactics used. Instead of anger and overt violence, they used humour to make their point, this being understood as a more successful strategy. This was also in evidence when the cheque for *Abortion Support Network* was presented, with the organiser of the event directly addressing the anti-abortion activists:

> We have been sponsoring you for the last 40 days, to continue with your vigil. And people have been putting money forward to say well done for staying out here in the snow and the rain, over the last 40 days. And the money will be going to the *Abortion Support Network* (there is big cheer from the crowd. Two women in the background hold up a giant cheque with the sum of £563.29 displayed). If you are not aware of the work that they do, they support women who have to travel from Ireland – from both NI and the Republic of Ireland, and from the Isle of Man to access abortion – they help with things like travel and accommodation and their expenses. And because of your efforts, we have managed to raise £563.29 (a big cheer from the crowd and applause). And what we would really like to know is if anyone from over there would like to receive their cheque as we are really, really proud of your efforts (crowd members say phrases like 'go on, come on'. Someone addresses someone specifically – 'Come on Simon'). [The pro-choice organiser] responds, 'No? that's a shame'. The music starts up with The Scaffolds' *Thank U Very Much* song. Everyone participating in the counterdemonstration follows the words on A4 sheets of paper to start singing: 'Thank you very much for the abortion dosh, thank you very much, thank you very, very, very much. Thank you very much for the abortion dosh, thank you very, very, very much'.

Irony is deployed – the anti-abortion activists standing to oppose abortion day after day is directly connected to raising funds for an abortion charity. Subverting the lyrics of *Thank U Very Much* also lightens the tone – there is nothing here that suggests anger, although a clear political point is being made about the plight of women who have to travel to seek abortion services. Overall, humour was the intended lens through which this counterdemonstration operated, and it was not designed to be anti-religious, but rather to critique powerful theologies that have negative consequences for women's lives.

Help or Harassment? Interpreting the Impact of Anti-Abortion Activists

Anti-abortion activists and pro-choice counterdemonstrators are diametrically opposed in how they understand clinic activism. As previous chapters have demonstrated, anti-abortion activists viewed abortion as damaging to women; their presence at clinic sites was a means of helping women. Meanwhile, pro-choice activists understand those very same actions as causing harm to service users and saw their presence at clinic sites as necessary to counteract the activities of anti-abortion groups.

When it was posed to anti-abortion activists that their presence may cause distress, this was usually rebuked, as these quotes demonstrate:

> Clive said they can be the first people to offer help and support. This might feel overwhelming which is why some women might get upset. He does not accept that some women may find the demonstrations at clinics as threatening or harassment, or that being prayed for is unwelcome. He claimed that if people are feeling traumatised when faced with a 'benign' situation, then this suggests the trauma is within them and nothing to do with the external event. [In other words they are fearful because they are conflicted about the abortion rather than because of the demonstration] (field notes, Midlands).

> Jennifer says that for someone who is in distress and wants support, we have help and resources, and she again reaffirmed that it was about loving the woman as well as the child, to which Margaret wholeheartedly agreed and said that we try to support the woman in this situation. She said that they were not about confrontation and instead they were there to try to support women (field notes, Scotland).

> Lloyd said that they didn't want to frighten or intimidate people. He said they were there to help. Mike said it was prayerful. It was about praying for the aborted babies and praying for the mothers, and that their position was that they were caring, loving and thoughtful and not judgemental or hurtful, and with no malice whatsoever (field notes, Scotland).

Their actions are therefore presented fully in terms of offering compassion and support; they felt that any negative feelings towards them were not about their activism per se, but attributed to the inner turmoil over seeking out an abortion. Many assumptions are made here about motherhood and abortion causing distress, as we have outlined in previous chapters. It was typical for anti-abortion activists to fully align their actions with help and support. However, in some conversations, it became apparent that causing women who were accessing services discomfort was deemed a just aim, although it was conceded that this should not spill over to harassment, as this interview with Toby, Derek and George reveals:

(Toby):   We are there as a prayerful witness. We are not there to chant anything or to harass anybody.

          (...)

(George): And it is a silent witness as well, as Toby says, there is no sort of chanting, or kind of placards in our hands or anything like that. It is just a presence, a witness.

          (...)

(Toby):   [S]omeone might just be uncomfortable with the fact that you are there (...) it is a grey area to talk about what, where the actual boundary is (...) if someone says I don't want a leaflet, or whatever it is, then I wouldn't keep going (...) harassment would be when I think, you are being vocal and you are invading that person's space and you are making them uncomfortable and you continue it. But we don't do anything near that.

(George): The freedom that we have got in this country is that we can stand outside an abortion clinic, with placards and we could chant (...) we purposely don't do that, because it is too much (...) [Last year] a pro-abortion group came to *40DFL* at the same time as we were there, and they did have placards, and saying 'It's your choice' and 'go ahead' (...) It was crazy to see actually, because if someone is going through abortion, they don't need that vocal kind of shouting down, shouting to encourage it. That doesn't speak to me of compassion... (...) but I would be very conscious of being compassionate, calm (...) but there is going to be a level of uncomfort, because we believe that it is wrong, and that umm, the child in the womb has a, has a right as well (...). But we love the women as well, you know (...) we try not to go near harassment, but there is going to be a level of uncomfort.

Toby and George reflected on what action would constitute harassment, with the idea that anything that was quiet and respected bodily boundaries was acceptable. Shouting and waving banners was seen as harassment, with George arguing that pro-choice activists were more problematic in their behaviour than their quiet prayer vigil. They therefore made fundamental distinctions between the kinds of behaviour deployed at a clinic site, rather than the underling messages underpinning that activism.

Yet behind the public displays was a fundamentally different orientation to the women they encountered. Whilst the pro-choice activists advocated for bodily autonomy, with the decision-making resting firmly with the woman, George and Toby conceded that they prioritised the life of the foetus, and this meant that women may well experience discomfort at their presence. Whilst they professed 'love' for the woman, this was secondary to their belief that a baby was being killed. George was keen to reference compassion, but ultimately recognised his presence caused distress. Typically speaking, anti-abortion activists did not develop this level of reflexivity, seeing their presence only in positive terms, and not understanding why they did not generate broader support for their activities from their religious communities. George was unusual in displaying such self-scrutiny and recognising that – however unassuming and 'peaceful' their demeanour – their activism caused distress.

It was more common for us to encounter individuals who had not even contemplated that their behaviour might be deemed problematic in any way:

> When he was asked about the distress it causes some women, he seemed to be genuinely thinking through this idea, and Pam felt it had never occurred to him that his 'compassionate' approach could be experienced differently. He didn't address why they should be imposing their beliefs on others (field notes, North).

Meanwhile when Maria was asked whether this was trying to change the minds of people in a vulnerable position, and who were in a less powerful position, she responded:

> No. I would never have seen it like that. It's interesting that you capture it like that, 'cause I just see it as we're people and they're people' and it's kind of as simple as that really (Maria interview).

Again, there was a lack of reflexivity regarding how intimidating it would be to encounter any sort of anti-abortion activism outside a clinic, especially if one was in a position of vulnerability. Maria did not recognise any power differentials between her and those seeking clinic services and instead understood as her having an equal footing with them. This belies the way public space is experienced by women, as a space where women have far less power, as they navigate unwelcome attention (Lowe & Hayes, 2019). Research demonstrates that women do find any form of activism – whether it is noisy, quiet, premised on banner-waving or underpinned by prayer – intimidating (Lowe & Hayes, 2019).

Meanwhile, groups like *Feminist Fightback* and *Sister Supporter* demonstrated greater reflexivity regarding the impact on those seeking services. Their key goal was to ensure women could access the clinic and to counter the negativity and distress caused to women in accessing those services. Women's needs and concerns were central to their aims. Yet Emma-Louise reflected on whether the additional presence of *Sister Supporter* helped or hindered their goals:

> She explained that the anti-abortion activism here is about the message and women being subtly undermined, and an intrusion into women's private lives. It is not aggressive in a masculine way, which means it's harder to police, and means that the authorities do not want to intervene unless it is actively violent (…). She says they have a good relationship with the clinic and occasionally they bring them a cup of tea. They also try to explain to clients why there are people outside, and explaining that the people in the pink vests are there to ensure that they are alright. But one woman coming to the clinic said to her one time that she wasn't helping either. She was cross and irritated about the presence of the anti-abortion group but felt the presence of a counter group drew further attention to it. Emma-Louise explained to the woman that they didn't want to be here either. But there are other people who need someone to help them get out the car and it's hard to know whether you are making it better or worse because each situation is different and what each individual needs is going to be something different. Most people don't want to talk to anyone or have attention drawing to it, and it's hard to know whether you are helping if Irene (the main anti-abortion activist) is there and just standing or pacing, and not being outwardly obnoxious to individuals. Some women do need physical assistance to reach the clinic, due to the anti-abortion activism.

The visual display of pink bibs versus a 'pacing' anti-abortion activist who may or may not approach clinic users, and where there was little to indicate their anti-abortion sentiment, made it a challenging call for Emma-Louise to make and raises interesting questions regarding whether abortion as a public spectacle was magnified by the presence of groups like *Sister Supporter*. At the same time, they wrestled with the reality that there were some women who felt paralysed by the activists outside and who would therefore not keep their appointment at the clinic. Meanwhile groups like *GCN* (Ealing Council Consultation, 2018) argued that there was a lack of clarity regarding who clinic users found intimidating and challenged the idea that it was solely the anti-abortion activists, arguing that clinic users were more intimidated by *Sister Supporter*.

Anti-abortion activists were motivated by the numbers of women they deterred from having an abortion and were keen to reference the women they had helped, rather than reflect on how their behaviour might be perceived by the majority of those accessing the clinic:

> Janet said that she heard in England, someone had chosen not to go ahead and have the abortion, and they went up to the people involved in the vigil to say it was because of them standing there praying (field notes, Scotland).

Clinic 'saves' were noteworthy, to such an extent that the news travelled far and wide. Indeed, at public events like *MFL*, a woman who had continued with the pregnancy usually featured on the billing (see Lowe & Page, 2020). On some occasions, the same woman's story featured for consecutive years. This in and of itself demonstrates how infrequent the 'saves' actually were, if a clinic vigil in Scotland had to use the story from 300 miles away to validate the idea that they were helping women.

Meanwhile, on interviewing an abortion provider regarding how women experienced the clinic vigils, it was clear that even silent activism was experienced negatively and could have serious implications for women who did not want to walk past the activists:

> ...we always get the sense that *CBR* (*Centre for Bioethical Reform UK*) are considered beyond the pale, and *40DFL* and *GCN* are somewhere in the middle, but as I said that is not necessarily women's perception of the difference between the two (...) [the result of the vigils] was not that women were not having abortions, but they were presenting later. So they were coming for appointments, too intimidated or upset to come into the clinic, but they would come back later (...). This is so intimidating for women that it could have a knock on for their health, because (...) once you have made your decision, it is safer the earlier your abortion takes place (...) We had a case this week where the woman was so upset that she cancelled her appointment, and I'm sure that what those groups would say is that is good, because what their presence is doing is making women think twice, but we think it is fine if women want to think twice, and they should discuss their decision as much as they want to (...) [But] in what other area would we accept that the best way to help someone make a massive life decision is by them being approached by strangers in the street?

Angela, who was part of a residents' campaign against anti-abortion activism at her local clinic, likened the experience of going past the anti-abortion activists as 'walking the gang plank' and that it was 'the women that are on their own that I think are vulnerable', hence her support for groups like *Sister Supporter*.

It is clear that activism around abortion has become a public spectacle at the clinic sites themselves, which begs a more broader question about the appropriateness for any activism to take place at a site for healthcare and rationalises the need for bufferzones around all clinics. As a private medical decision, it seems disproportionate for women and pregnant people to have to encounter strangers assessing what is in their best interests, with no knowledge of the circumstances of their life. However well-meaning they feel their intentions are, anti-abortion activism at clinic sites is inappropriate. Groups like *Sister Supporter* will typically only be present for as long as the anti-abortion activists are outside clinics. But in asking anti-abortion activists to reflect on their presence and whether their actions can be justified results in a defensive position; their fundamental belief is that they need to be at the clinic in order to dissuade women from seeking an abortion, seeing it as the last possible opportunity to do so. Why do anti-abortion activists feel they have the right to take such a stance? If anti-abortion activists abhor abortion, then a clear response would be to not personally have one; there is no need to impose that belief on others. However, this is to comprehend the issue in individualising terms and as a personal choice. As we have demonstrated throughout the course of this book, anti-abortion activists do not share that worldview. Their activism stems from their devotion to ultra-sacrificial motherhood in which the pregnancy is a gift from God. As Luker argues, 'Because these views are thought to be located in the natural order of things, the church argues that they are applicable to everyone, Catholic or not' (1984, p. 60). Their zeal to be present at the clinic site is therefore firmly rooted in their faith beliefs, indicating why legislation is necessary, as they are unlikely to give up activism outside clinics voluntarily.

Summary

This chapter has focused on the contested space of the abortion clinic, with a much more explicit consideration of the activities and tactics of pro-choice counterdemonstrations. Space is continually negotiated; the parameters of the spaces in which activists engage in the abortion debate are not fixed, but are mediated through everyday practices, material objects and emotions, as both groups stake a claim to, and explicitly demonstrate, their sacred commitments. Previous chapters have explicitly outlined how anti-abortion activists convey their deeply held sacred commitments relating to an anti-abortion stance, premised on ultra-sacrificial motherhood. This chapter has investigated what happens when this sacred commitment comes up against the sacred commitment of the pro-choice activists, that of reproductive justice. The flavours of the campaigns differ enormously, in terms of the colours, noises, embodied practices, clothing worn and narratives conveyed. Many of the feminist-driven pro-choice campaigns feminise their message, through the use of bright pinks, home-made signs and utilising domestic objects like frying pans to orchestrate a protesting din. Meanwhile the anti-abortion activists demonstrate their commitment to traditional church teaching, through intense public and communal prayer displays, where heads are bowed and, in some cases, embodied through kneeling. Attempts are made to claim spaces, such as the case at one clinic site where anti-abortion and pro-choice activists utilise a particular tree to display their material objects, whether that be fixing to the trunk a 'Stop the harassment of women' sign or the hanging of religious medallions. Yet, spatial parameters follow particular dominant norms; power is negotiated in very specific ways relating to how both religion and gender are constituted in the public sphere (Reilly & Scriver, 2014).

Anti-abortion activism impacts clinic users and staff members working at clinics the most, especially when the geography of the clinic is such that they are forced to pass the vigils on foot, and in situations where pavement counsellors are present. But beyond this, the activism is also impactful on the general public.

Given that public displays of intense and conservative religiosity are generally unwelcome by the public, along with the fact that abortion is an issue that is not typically openly discussed, anti-abortion activism generates much discomfort for the general public. In places where public consultations have occurred about anti-abortion activism, residents have overwhelmingly supported the implementation of a bufferzone.

Despite being a routine medical practice that many women and pregnant people will experience in their lifetime, abortion is an issue that is publicly silenced (Bloomer, O'Dowd, & Macleod, 2017; Hoggart, 2017; Millar, 2017). Meanwhile religion in the public sphere is acceptable so long as it is tempered and softened, such as being 'made safe' through tourism (Knott, 2010). Overt displays of conservative religion are not welcome and viewed with deep suspicion. Because of the ways the discourses around abortion and conservative religion are navigated in the public sphere in the UK, it is understandable that in this environment, bufferzones are seen as the most appropriate solution.

Chapter 9

Abortion Cultures

Introduction

This chapter will develop further some of the ideas introduced earlier about the ways in which the anti-abortion groups understand and explain public acceptance of abortion. We will focus on how they understand themselves, their actions and why abortion has come to be a prominent part of their religious practice. Whilst anti-abortion activists often posit that there is a 'truth' about abortion, historical evidence illustrates that there have been different Christian interpretations of abortion over time. The chapter starts with examining the idea of a 'culture of life' and a 'culture of death' developed within Catholicism and how this understanding aligns with the position taken by some evangelical Christians. It illustrates the ways in which abortion is a foundational issue for constructing a battle between good and evil, and, by taking an active role against abortion, the anti-abortion activists are aligning themselves with goodness and godliness. This spiritual battle is constructed emotionally as both a religious belief and a social movement. The differentiation between those who support or oppose abortion creates boundaries and hierarchies within religious communities, setting up anti-abortion people as the 'true believers' and denigrating those within their faith position who do not hold the same views as lacking religious authenticity. It also aligns those who support access to abortion as on the 'wrong side' of a divinely inspired battle.

The chapter will illustrate how abortion is situated as both a cause and symbol of broader moral decline. The rise of individualism and consumerism is seen as introducing the ability to 'pick and choose' moral divisions, rather than following the 'natural order' of things decreed by God. For some, these fears overlap with far-right nationalism; concerns over abortion are articulated as part of the idea of 'replacement theory' – the racist notion that white people will be out-birthed by other ethnicities. Overall, this chapter will extend our argument by illustrating the ways in which religious understandings help construct the anti-abortion activists' sacred commitments and how they form the bedrock of their motivations and actions. This will explain why we need to understand their actions as a highly specific and lived religious practice.

Anti-Abortion Activism in the UK, 169–187
Copyright © 2022 Pam Lowe and Sarah-Jane Page
Published under exclusive licence by Emerald Publishing Limited
doi:10.1108/978-1-83909-398-220221022

'Culture of Death' and the 'Culture of Life'

As Sjørup (1999) points out, there is no explicit reference to abortion in either the Old or New Testament, and thus Catholic Church doctrine about the 'wrongfulness' of abortion is premised on internal church teaching, rooted in natural law (an understanding that there is a divinely devised 'natural' order to the world that can be used for making moral judgements). Moreover, because the Catholic Church views many methods of contraception as abortion, the two issues are heavily intertwined. Until 1869, the church penalties for abortion differed depending on whether the foetus was assumed to be ensouled or not, so early abortion was punished less harshly. Pope Pius IX removed this ensouled/ unensouled distinction, thereby generating uncertainty regarding the point of ensoulment and encouraging the idea that ensoulment *could* occur at conception (Kamitsuka, 2019; Sjørup, 1999; Tauer, 1988). This illustrates the variations over time on the teaching of abortion, an issue that many of those in the Catholic Church choose to overlook (Miller, 2014). Sjørup (1999) emphasises how, in the twentieth century, contraception also became a key element upon which papal authority was built. It could be argued that there were two key moments for this. The rejection of any relaxation on the prohibition against contraception in *Humanae Vitae*, published by Pope Paul VI in 1968, and the papal encyclical *Evangelium Vitae*, published in 1995 by Pope John Paul II. The latter set out an understanding of the 'contraception mentality' and a 'pro-abortion culture'. The Catholic anti-abortion activists we encountered often based their understanding of abortion on the 'culture of death' idea set out by Pope John Paul II in *Evangelium Vitae*, and references to him were more common than to other more recent popes.

At the time of *Humanae Vitae*'s (1968) publication, it had been widely expected that the Catholic Church would support at least some methods of contraception in line with the recommendations of the *Papal Birth Control Commission* set up a few years previously (Sjørup, 1999). Despite a careful consultation process, Pope Paul VI rejected their modest reforms and reaffirmed in *Humanae Vitae* (1968) that contraception (other than periodic abstinence) was 'intrinsically wrong' (S14). He argued that every 'marital act' reaffirms the 'intrinsic relationship to the procreation of human life' (S11). In other words, (hetero)sex should always carry the possibility of conception; reproduction, rather than pleasure, was its primary purpose. Although predominately about contraception, abortion was also condemned:

> We are obliged once more to declare that the direct interruption of the generative process already begun and, above all, all direct abortion, even for therapeutic reasons, are to be absolutely excluded as lawful means of regulating the number of children.
>
> (S14)

Harris (2020) has shown how, in Britain, the publication of *Humanae Vitae* was contested, with debates in the mainstream media as well as large scale meetings, marches and cathedral 'sit-ins'. Her research demonstrates that many of those who supported the position taken in *Humanae Vitae* had concerns about wider changes in society, such as growing secularism, sexual permissiveness and degeneracy amongst young people. She argues that the British Catholics who welcomed the continued conservative position saw *Humanae Vitae* as 'an antidote to societal drifts towards seeming religious and moral decline and a reiterated clarity in church teaching' (Harris, 2020, p. 423). As we will outline shortly, these concerns are still articulated by many anti-abortion activists today. The conservative Catholics were not alone at the time in their alarm about changes in social life. As Weeks (1989) states, in the 1960s, many of those who were against shifts in attitudes and behaviour in relation to sexuality and gender coalesced around decrying the emerging 'permissive society', and a range of individuals and groups emerged to challenge the changes, although these were largely unsuccessful. Importantly, anti-abortion activists still denounce many of the progressive changes made since the 1960s (such acceptance of cohabitation and same-sex marriage), whereas the vast majority of people in the United Kingdom (UK) support them.

After the publication of *Humanae Vitae*, other teachings of the Catholic Church also reaffirmed the absolutist position against abortion. In 1974, the *Sacred Congregation of the Doctrine of the Faith* published a *Declaration on Procured Abortion* which set out that a fertilised egg has a right to life as a new human person (Sjørup, 1999). Almost all of the anti-abortion activists we encountered endorsed this position; 'From conception, no exception' was a common sign displayed or slogan shouted at anti-abortion marches, and as noted in Chapter 7, this phrase was utilised on the wristbands for a number of *March for Life (MFL)* events. However, it was the publication of *Evangelium Vitae* that developed these ideas more fully and argued strongly that abortion was unacceptable as pregnancy was deemed a divine gift and therefore sacred. Moreover, abortion was positioned as both the cause and *symptom* of moral decline and therefore of singular importance. Pope John Paul II stated that:

> …we are facing an enormous and dramatic clash between good and evil, death and life, the 'culture of death' and the 'culture of life'. We find ourselves not only 'faced with' but necessarily 'in the midst of' this conflict: we are all involved and we all share in it, with the inescapable responsibility of choosing to be unconditionally pro-life.
>
> (1995, p. S28)

As Vaggione (2020) argues, this encyclical goes beyond just a denouncement of issues such as abortion, contraception and euthanasia. It set out a framework which linked these acts to broader changes in society which, the Pope argued, led to a denial of what should be the unchanging 'moral' codes that should remain incorporated into legal systems, regardless of whether or not people were advocating for democratic change (Vaggione, 2020). Later on, the term 'gender ideology' was developed in Vatican discourse to incorporate many of the issues contained within the idea of the 'culture of death', with Cardinal Ratzinger, the future Pope Benedict XVI, playing a central role in the development of this concept (Vaggione, 2020). Whilst in different contexts 'gender ideology' can have a different emphasis, it includes broad concerns about feminism, sexual freedom, lesbian, gay and trans acceptance, the decline of marriage, rising numbers of divorces, sexual education in schools and a decline in parental authority, as well as increased access to abortion and contraception. As Vaggione argues, gender ideology is considered as anti-life, anti-family and 'destructive of nations' (2020, p. 256).

Although the terms 'culture of death' and 'gender ideology' were rarely mentioned specifically by most of the anti-abortion activists we encountered, many of their concerns were aligned with these ideas. As we have already described, abortion was usually associated with young unmarried women and linked to a rise in emasculated men who no longer took responsibility for pregnant 'girlfriends'. A blog post on the *MFL UK* website states:

> With the commercialisation of sex, men can avoid the responsibility of fatherhood and this contributes to a 'perpetual adolescence'. Men live for their Xbox, live in constant narrative of comedy, who take little interest in studying the deeper questions of life and objectify women as a means of their recreation.
>
> (Donaghue, 2019, *sic.*)

The assumption that it is necessary in society for women to be dependent on men is a common theme in the writings of right-wing commentators and often evoked in critiques of teenage motherhood (Arai, 2009). The belief in gendered roles, and an assumption that abortion emasculates men, also occurs in the United States (US) (Arey, 2020; Ehrlich & Doan, 2019). As we will explain later, the immorality and general degradation in society, which is associated with abortion, were often seen not just as a moral wrong, but part of a bigger sacred battle against evil. As Doan (2007) argues, morality movements, like anti-abortion organisations, encourage dualistic narratives such as 'good' and 'evil' as it fosters a simplistic rather than nuanced understanding of the issues. It is particularly worth noting that, in their opposition to the 'culture of death', they are situating themselves with the 'culture of life', which as Sanger (2006) argues, aligns them with idea of goodness as well as godliness. This is fundamental to their sacred commitment, positioning their attitudes and beliefs in wholly positive terms.

Unlike hierarchal Catholicism with its papal pronouncements, for evangelical Christians, there is no single doctrinal pronouncement. Rather, scripture becomes the overriding basis for their theology. However, as Kamitsuka (2019) points out, the Bible is largely silent on abortion so there is no direct prohibition that can be used. She suggests that because of the absence of clear prohibitions, those that seek biblical sources often extrapolate from verses not specifically about abortion, such as the prenatal description of prophets or claims about God's will. Kamitsuka argues that:

...the biblical basis is weak and entails highly questionable notions that God's will is coterminous with the biological event of the fertilization of an ovum (...) pro-life proponents have not come close to making a convincing case for predestined fetal personhood that would justify overrunning a woman's exercise of moral discernment in deciding what she will do regarding an unwanted pregnancy.

(2019, p. 68)

Indeed, in the US context, Lewis (2017) argues rather than being scripture-based, some of the Catholic understandings of abortion were adopted by evangelical Christian leaders in the 1970s in order to persuade others to oppose it. Williams (2015) agrees with this assessment, adding that rather than being guided by the Bible, the fight against abortion became the symbol of trying to resist what they considered to be a decline in the moral order more generally. What is clear is that abortion became a litmus test for a broad range of concerns about changes in society, and the evangelicals became a major force within the US Religious Right (Flowers, 2019; Mason, 2002). In Britain, conservative evangelical Christians lack the same political position. Meanwhile, as mentioned earlier, this is not the case in the politico-religious context of Northern Ireland (NI), demonstrated, in particular, through the interrelationship between the *Democratic Unionist Party (DUP)* and the Free Presbyterian Church.

Although the evangelical anti-abortion activists drew on other religious arguments, there were parallels to the Catholic understanding of abortion as a 'culture of death'. There was a fair degree of consistency amongst how the evangelical Christians we encountered viewed abortion. Like their Catholic counterparts, they often argued that life should be protected from conception and raised concerns about the decline in moral values in society. Although they had similar views to Catholic activists on ultra-sacrificial motherhood as 'natural' and saw abortion as harmful to women, many of the evangelical anti-abortion activists had a stronger focus on the foetus as a 'victim', especially in their public messages, for example, the comparison to slavery. As we explained earlier, it was much more common for evangelical Christians to use graphic images. This division is likely to be partly because, as we outlined in Chapter 2, the Catholic opposition to abortion has always contained an emphasis on motherhood.

Lewis (2017) in the US has emphasised that broader concerns about issues such as religious rights in schools brought evangelical activists into the abortion debate, which enabled their broader concerns to be channelled. The context is different in the UK, where there is not the same public debate on this issue. Lewis emphasises the centrality of the construction of victims in their discourse, evidenced through demonstrating the 'reality' of abortion through 'war pictures' – graphic images of abortion (Eades, 2019; Ginsburg, 1989). This focus on 'victims' also means that evangelicals were more likely than Catholic anti-abortion activists to talk publicly of abortion in terms of 'murder' or 'baby genocide' (see Chapter 6). For example, a card given out in a Midlands clinic in

2019 by evangelical Christians had the words 'You shall not Murder (Exodus 21:13)' printed on one side, and on the other, the text started with the phrase 'Abortion is the sin of murder' before setting out a series of biblical references about sin, the need to repent, seek salvation and follow the will of God. In their internal messages, the *Centre for Bioethical Reform UK (CBR)* also claimed in 2016 that Satan is responsible for abortions and that it is a form of child sacrifice:

> [It is] important to identify abortion as 'child sacrifice' in the church as it is to identify abortion as 'genocide' in the secular culture. Child sacrifice is not just another form of sin. It is an especially egregious form of sin which demands an especially vigorous response from people of faith.

This statement illustrates clearly the ways in which the framing of abortion often varies between internal and external audiences. The internal messages assume a specific religious position and a universal belief that abortion is sinful. Meanwhile, the external framing is aligned to the secular and invokes alignment with arguments about human rights. They are therefore tapping into different sacred forms (Lynch, 2012a), depending on their audience. As we have described elsewhere, the rights-based claims made by anti-abortion activists are largely unsuccessful (Lowe & Page, 2019b). In Britain, there is widespread cultural understanding that opposition to abortion is religiously based, aided by the religiously coded material objects we described earlier. This means that regardless of the framing, the public at large reads anti-abortion activism as religious. Alongside the emphasis on sacrifice and sin, *CBR* also has internal statements linking abortion to the work of Pagans, who are assumed to be aligned with the devil. Here again we can see similarities between the Catholic and evangelical positions. Although most of the Catholic anti-abortion activists we encountered did not directly refer to child sacrifice, there was widespread use of the image of Our Lady of Guadalupe which, as we previously explained, symbolised the triumph of Christian values over non-Christians, including an ending of child destruction rituals. Thus although using different theological routes, both Catholic and evangelical Christians used similar symbolism in constructing their sacred battle as a religious mission, and this was a central element in the emotions embedded in their activism.

'Spiritual Warfare' against 'The Evil Enemy'

In their study of the US, Baker, Molle, and Bader (2020) found that those who were against abortion and other 'gender ideology' issues were more likely to have strong beliefs in religious evil. Their research found participants' beliefs about religious evil are central to explaining the conservative views they held. They argue that:

Thinking that powerful, evil forces influence the material world means framing moral debates not simply as differences of opinion, but as manifestations of Satan's power and ongoing battles in a spiritual war.

(2020, pp. 13–14)

The anti-abortion activists firmly positioned themselves in a battle of good versus evil; Satan versus God; heaven versus hell. Anti-abortion activists understood themselves on the side of the righteous – of the good, godly and doing works that would help secure their own salvation (see Chapter 4). Activities outside clinics were therefore twofold: a spiritual mission that would potentially 'save' those seeking clinic services, as well as enhancing their own chances of being saved (Lowe & Page, 2020). The most frequent way that this was achieved was by casting abortion as a profane activity – something which they deemed a 'moral indignation' (Lynch, 2012b, p. 6). Meanwhile, the presence of Satan and his demons were directly referenced less frequently. Overall, this discursively situated their accounts in terms of a form of spiritual warfare. As Marshall (2016) argues, spiritual warfare is deemed to be the only salvation for a decadent society suffering from moral decline.

The anti-abortion activists therefore made clear distinctions between the sacred and profane. On the one hand, abortion, abortion clinics and counterdemonstrators were deemed profaning manifestations which perpetuated harm, sinfulness and even evil. In contrast, they understood themselves and their activities in sacred terms and as a means of portraying their sacred commitments to traditional understandings of church teaching, gender roles and the valorisation of motherhood – what we have called ultra-sacrificial motherhood. Because their activities aligned with traditional religious practices such as praying and utilising religious objects which are embedded with devotional meanings, it meant that they were able to utilise these established meanings to imply that their actions were godly and sacredly inscribed. For example, prayer is generally socially understood in benign and harmless terms (Page & Lowe, 2021a). And some groups were keen to reject activities they deemed problematic, such as the divide that emerged between groups who used graphic images and those who did not. This also enabled the various groups to put boundary markers around their activities, to demonstrate their own sacred claims (Lynch, 2012a). They were also able to benefit from the assumption that the sacred and the religious are one and the same – and the idea that as their ideals were rooted religiously, this generated forms of transcendental approval. However, this is problematic and ignores the sacred commitments of other religious groups who take a pro-choice view, as well as secular groups who demonstrate their own sacred commitments aligned with a pro-choice position (e.g. the idea of reproductive justice – see Chapter 8). Here, we delve more deeply into how anti-abortion activists constructed abortion in profaning terms and how this existed on a continuum, moving from harm, to sin, to evoking evil.

The continuum of the 'wrongfulness' of abortion was sometimes expressed in terms of it being morally wrong or harmful. As we have outlined in earlier chapters, the exact expression of this varied depending on the activist, organisation or specific materials. It was often expressed as a factual designation that, if abortion was explained properly to people, then those who supported abortion would simply change their minds. Put simply, it came back to the broad idea that the 'reality' of abortion was hidden or misunderstood. This position that there should only be one understanding of abortion, conveying surprise when others do not feel the same, is similar to that identified by Ginsburg (1989). More recently, it can be seen in the insistence by anti-abortion activists that foetal-centric grief and regret is a universal response to abortion (Ehrlich & Doan, 2019; Millar, 2017). Although within this framing, often the anti-abortion activists themselves frequently stated that the 'wrongfulness' was about human rights rather than religion, as we have argued elsewhere, it was clear that their religious beliefs about abortion being profane underpinned their position (Lowe & Page, 2019a, 2019b).

The next stage along the continuum was to describe abortion in terms of sinfulness. This was less frequently referenced, which corresponds with a general turn away from discussing sin in contemporary society. As Turner (2008) outlines, historically, the professionalisation of areas like medicine moved understandings of deviance away from sin towards concepts such as disease and crime. In addition, as we summarised earlier, the shift to risk as a governing framework has led to both family policy and moral regulation movements to move towards extending governance through ideas about harm prevention (Hunt, 1999; Lee, 2014; Macvarish, Lee, & Lowe, 2015). As Hunt states:

> ...while in Christian and other moral codes adultery is inherently sinful, with the rise of secular currents and religious heterogeneity, moralising discourses increasingly linked immorality to utilitarian claims about the personal or social harm associated with the wrong.
>
> (1999, 7)

When sin was specifically mentioned by anti-abortion activists, it could be as a generalised description of abortion, rather than directed to a specific individual act:

> Paula commented that she believed that Hilary Clinton had said that abortion should be made available to full term without regard for what method was used, including dismemberment.[1] At this point Janice makes a noise of disgust and said 'good Lord', she says you do wonder what is happening within society now. Paula said that the biggest sin against God is to deny life (field notes, South-East).

---

[1] As Ludlow (2008) outlines, the rhetoric of 'dismemberment abortion' as an anti-abortion description of the Dilation and Extraction procedure is complex and rooted in their political strategy of positioning abortion as gruesome. This overlooks the clinical reasons that this procedure may be needed.

As noted in Chapter 5, activists were careful in their outward messages regarding sin, so as not to position women seeking abortion as being sinful, ameliorated through the idea that everyone was in a sinful state.

The final way the profane was evoked along the continuum was in terms of evil. Compared with wrongfulness and sin, this was the least referenced form, but some of the anti-abortion activists clearly understood abortion in more apocalyptic ways, situating their actions as part of the battle between good and evil. For example, as mentioned earlier, the leaflet explaining why Birmingham was chosen for the site of *MFL* in 2016 claimed that abortion service providers 'helped spread evil through our nation'. Thus, Birmingham then became labelled as an especially sinful place which is ripe for targeting by anti-abortion activists.[2] This links with Kirby's (2017) idea that spiritual warfare can be spatialised and connected to a specific location. The embodied practices of marching through the city literally lays claim to that space, situating their campaign as 'good' triumphing over 'evil'.

Like the example of this leaflet, we found that the positioning of abortion as evil was more common in internal communications and actions than the information directed to an external audience. This was not unexpected as social movements often utilise different messages depending on whether they intend to recruit and build internal support, or be directed externally to try to enact broader change (Rohlinger, 2002). This can be evidenced in the claims made by the Catholic nun about the dangers of being outside of an abortion clinic and the broader risks from non-Christian people and practices that we outlined in Chapter 6.

During the course of fieldwork, we occasionally spotted bottles of holy water that anti-abortion activists had brought with them, although we did not directly witness them in use (see Fig. 4). Other actions included the suggestion that anti-abortion activists could undertake a 'Jericho Walk' around an abortion clinic when they were prevented from standing outside praying due to COVID-19 restrictions, but were permitted daily exercise. The 'Jericho Walk', a prayerful circling of a building seven times, is a symbolic ritual based on a biblical story calling for particular divine intercedence. Moreover, as we mentioned earlier, in 2016, a group of about 35 anti-abortion activists gathered with a large wooden cross and processed with it around the local streets circling the Midlands clinic, stopping along the route to perform the Stations of the Cross. Both this and Jericho Walks would seem to be a way of utilising public space to both mark and contain the 'evil' of the abortion clinic alongside holding a theological significance of calling for God to intercede and close the clinic. Moreover, although those that spoke directly of issues such as evil or Satan were in a minority, the sense of righteousness that came from feeling that they were on the side of 'good' against a 'wrong' was an emotion that united and motivated the vast majority of the

---

[2]Interestingly, not only is our University situated in Birmingham, but at least one member of staff was involved in setting up the original clinic that was the cause of this apparent evil. The implications of this for how anti-abortion activists read our work were unclear.

anti-abortion activists we encountered. Their sacred commitment was therefore fuelled through the generation of positive emotions within the group.

Hope and Despair: The Use of Emotions

As Jasper (2011) outlines, emotions are always present in social movements and are a necessary component of mobilising or motivating participants, as well as shaping frames and goals. The range of emotions will vary, and the collective emotions in a large crowd will be different, from the emotional highs and lows of individual and small groups, to the gains, losses or day-to-day actions that activists are carrying out. Jasper (2018) argues that the long-term emotional attachment that individuals have as activists with a particular social movement is best understood as an affective commitment. He describes this as relatively stable feelings towards others, which can create internal bonds and loyalties, as well as engendering negative emotions towards the 'opposition'. In a similar way, Riis and Woodhead (2012) point out that all religions aim to shape the emotions of their believers, although the extent to which this takes place will vary. Both Jasper (2011) and Riis and Woodhead (2012) draw from understandings of emotion as arising by and through the social context and social relationships rather than being inherent internal properties. This is the approach that we are taking and, following Lupton (1998), we are not so much interested in what the emotions are, but we want to examine the role they play.

As Lupton (1998) points out, emotions are often associated with positive understandings of spirituality and soulfulness. Her interviewees were not necessarily associating this with religion, but an inner self that was beyond conscious control. Moreover, she argues that having the 'right' emotions is an indicator of positive moral value, for example, feeling sadness or empathy due to the difficulties experienced by others, even if not directly impacted. Moreover, it is important to be clear at this point that the way that activists describe and interpret their own emotions, or the emotions of the side they are aligned with, may be interpreted differently by those with opposing views. Generally speaking, it was common for each side to describe themselves in terms of positive emotions (e.g. love, care, joy) and describe those opposed to them in terms of negative emotions (e.g. fear, anger, hate). As we explained in Chapter 5, understanding pro-choice supporters as having negative emotions or being emotionally damaged was understood by anti-abortion activists through an assumption that they had not recovered from previous abortion experiences. This furthered the sacred commitments of the anti-abortion activists, by situating abortion as inherently opposed to ultra-sacrificial motherhood.

In her study in the US, Stein argues that amongst the Christian conservative activists she interviewed, their activism was a 'reparative act' (2001, p. 116). This study showed that the activism becomes critical to their sense of identity, and both the emotional and cognitive elements combine to allow the activists to see themselves as a positive force in the world, but this stemmed from a persistent narrative of shame. Whilst all of the anti-abortion activists we encountered saw themselves as a force for good, it was rare to encounter a narrative of shame or an understanding of their actions as reparation. Where this did take place, notably it was when a few men described their motivations for anti-abortion activism, by expressing shame and regret over their previous sexual behaviour. They specifically linked their current involvement as a penance for previous actual or imagined abortions. For example, Jeoffrey stated that he was there because he had had a 'dissolute' life, and it was a personal penance, because his actions may have led to women needing abortions, although he was not aware that any of his previous sexual partners had obtained one (see Chapter 4). We did not encounter any of the abortion regret narratives described by Ehrlich and Doan (2019) of men being 'deprived' of fatherhood. Instead, most of the other accounts about masculinity were focused on an actual or potential loss of 'natural' responsibility and wrong or sinful behaviour.

However, it was much more common for prior abortions to be described as a regret that had, or could be, forgiven by God. This aligned more broadly with the general sense that the movement was on the side of the righteous by positively doing God's work (Doan, 2007; Lowe & Page, 2020). This was frequently the position of women who mentioned that they had previously had an abortion. One activist specifically mentioned a priest telling her to take up 'life work' during her confession at an anti-abortion run 'recovery' event. Whilst it is not clear how many of the anti-abortion activists we spoke to had themselves had an abortion, this type of narrative corresponds with those who promoted post-abortion recovery groups run by anti-abortion organisations (Husain & Kelly, 2017). Husain and Kelly's (2017) study revealed a structured process in which those who had abortions were encouraged to accept their deviance, internalise abortion regret and transform these emotions into a testimony of God's love and forgiveness. They are saved and can then save others. This narrative for anti-abortion activists allows them to maintain the position of abortion as harmful whilst simultaneously aligning themselves with the positive emotions that the movement claimed for itself. Importantly, whilst the testimonies of women whose abortions caused them regret and despair, at least initially, were accepted without question, positive abortion testimonies advocated by the pro-choice movement were dismissed outright. As we outlined earlier, the idea that women who support abortion are 'hardened' or in denial explains their assumption that such testimonies are not valid. This aligns with their sacred commitment to ultra-sacrificial motherhood.

The idea that the anti-abortion activists were involved in the movement out of 'love' was a common position, particularly held by those standing outside of abortion clinics. As an emotion, 'love' has a particular cultural position as a positive emotion. As Jasper (2018) argues, positive emotions such as love engender collective solidarity and loyalty, and they reinforce bonding and boundaries through discourses and symbols. Indeed, Ahmed (2004) has shown how the need to be seen positively has even led to fascist groups declaring themselves to be 'organisations of love' (2004, p. 44). This transformation allows the fascists to position themselves as the 'true victims' of an aberrance in society whilst also ensuring that those within the group can align with the positive emotion of love, rather than the hatred that they feel towards others. The positive affected commitment of a social movement produces the collective sense of the group, inspiring members and creating confidence and 'a sense that history is on your side' (Jasper, 2018, p. 106) and enables their sacred commitments to be affirmed through particular emotional registers. The focus on 'love' also aligned the activists with their religious understandings of 'divine love' and the call on Christians to 'love thy neighbour'. These ideas are often a core element to golden rule Christianity in which there is an emphasis on caring for others as a key tenet of religious practice (Ammerman, 2014) and inscribed with positive meanings. Yet, in the case of anti-abortion activism, whilst anti-abortion activists might align themselves with golden rule Christianity, the effect it had was distinctly harmful. As Lynch (2012a) notes, sacred commitments can engender highly negative outcomes.

As we have previously described, by positioning themselves as exhibiting love and care, the anti-abortion activists rarely recognised that their actions outside of abortion clinics caused distress. The positive emotions they expressed about themselves and their actions motivated, bonded and sustained them as activists as well as aligned them with the goodness and godliness of the 'culture of life'. This endorsed their sacred commitments to traditional church teaching and essential-ised motherhood. Meanwhile, the alignment of abortion with negative emotions reinforced its symbolic position with the 'culture of death', affirming their belief that abortion was a profaning 'moral indignation' (Lynch, 2012b, p. 6). This often re-surfaced in the narratives of the anti-abortion activists who described abortion clinics as emanating negative emotions. Anti-abortion activists described them as uncaring and cold places and positioned themselves as the loving and caring antidote for those seeking abortions. The anti-abortion activists therefore con-structed the space of the abortion clinic in negative terms, with their communally generated positive emotions framed as the corrective. This spatialised their sacred and profane commitments, contrasting the 'evil' clinic with their 'good' and 'godly' intentions, embodied through their emotional positioning.

For the anti-abortion activists, their actions in opposing abortion was an integral part of the way in which they practised their faith, and they drew strength and resolve from knowing that they were embodying the will of God. As Aune (2015) points out, ritualised practice emerging from social interaction is central to understanding the meaning of religion in everyday lives. Whilst it was more explicit during prayer vigils than in some of their other actions, we would nevertheless argue that sustained involvement in the anti-abortion movement was a central ritualised practice to anti-abortion activists, and their response to and within the movement was shaped by the emotional positioning of abortion within their own religious interpretation. In particular, a sense of belonging and believing (consolidated through events like *MFL*) shaped group identities and boundaries, giving an emotionally charged sense of purpose, mission and certainty to many of the activists and groups involved. It also positioned the anti-abortion activists themselves as the 'true believers' in terms of their faith.

Being an anti-abortion activist gave the activists themselves a positive feeling of status within their faith practice. They perceived themselves as the 'true' representatives of their religion. They gained emotional strength from this position which is based on an understanding of static religious 'truth' and overlooked the historical changes that have already taken place, or that religious positions may change in the future. Those within their faith tradition who adopted a pro-choice positioning were deemed as misguided; for them, all Christians should be united in their opposition to abortion. Their collective ideas about abortion could be seen as a form of totalising ideology. Anthony, Robbins, and Barrie-Anthony (2002) describe the division of people and ideas by tight-knit religious sects into dual categories – good/evil, saved/dammed – as a core element within a totalising ideology, and it is fundamental to both the call on adherents to confront the 'other' as well as developing a positive view of the self as a 'true believer'. This as a lived practice of faith allows the anti-abortion activists to challenge the pro-choice opposition, but also deny the 'true believer' status to others within their faith who do not hold the same views or even actively campaign for abortion. In particular, for the Catholic activists, the lack of engagement by priests in actively opposing abortion (detailed in Chapter 4) was seen as a particular problem, and, as they could not deny them 'true believer' status, they needed to explain their absence in other ways, such as the pressure of their work.

Religious Advocates against Moral Decline

One of most striking claims that were repeatedly made by the anti-abortion activists was that they do not see or believe themselves to be protesters or activists at all. This was particularly the case outside of abortion clinics when they foregrounded their activities as 'just praying' (Page & Lowe, 2021a). As we have outlined earlier, their activities very much focused around religious displays and ritual constituting a specific religious practice. Yet at the same time, they denied that religion was 'really' their main reason for being present and emphasised ideas about science and human rights instead, particularly in their public-facing campaigns (Lowe & Page, 2019b). This demonstrates the complexity regarding how sacred commitments are publicly articulated; anti-abortion activists attempt to situate their own sacred forms alongside far more prominent and visible sacred commitments at the societal level. In a context where scientific discourse is given much prestige, incorporating science-like ideas into their campaign was an attempt to make their ideas more palatable to the general public. This is similar to the ways in which ideas around gender equality is integrated into their message, such as their belief that abortion harmed women and must be stopped to prevent gender discrimination. Unlike Munson's (2002) study of anti-abortion activists in the US, we found little appetite for political mobilisation, demonstrating the very different contexts in which anti-abortion activism operates. Although concerns about abortion were seen as having a political element, and the activists we spoke to would sign petitions and write to MPs about abortion when asked, political change was not necessarily seen as the answer for many of the activists we encountered. Instead, they wanted to enact a moral change – to make abortion 'unthinkable' at the level of society. For example, one of the activists we interviewed stated:

> I would like to see abortion not regarded as a necessity, I would like that to be a process over time. I would like it [to be] immediate, but that's not how society works. I would like it when no one thinks abortion is an answer. That it was no longer necessary, there was no demand. That we address the personal and social situations that give rise to it. (...) I don't think you can make a legislative change and it is all done. It doesn't work that way. I am horrified by some of the stuff from the US who think you can just criminalise people. That is unrealistic and inhumane.
>
> (Amanda)

Positioning themselves as moral advocates rather than as protestors or activists is in line with the anti-abortion movement as primarily about moral regulation. In his study of moral regulation movements, Hunt (1999) has shown that alongside targeting the behaviour in need of reform by others, they often have a self-governing impact on their own members. They seek to adopt a strategy of retraditionalisation and command governance through individual responsibility. This, as Hunt (1999) argues, allows the adoption of fluid notions of harm that have moved from 'vice' and 'sin' to concerns about health. Central to the concerns of moral regulation movements are social anxieties about particular aspects of social life. Elsewhere, we have shown how this conceptualisation was adopted in the UK to raise objections to the decriminalisation of abortion by evoking risk-based narratives that create 'harms' and victims' (Lowe, 2019). Yet as their argument failed to detach itself from the moral beliefs of the movement which are not shared more broadly in society, it is unlikely to be a successful political strategy.

Nevertheless, the understanding of anti-abortion activism as predominantly concerned with a need for retraditionalisation draws attention to the ways in which abortion was seen as a symbol for the broader moral decline that they objected to. This was a cluster of ideas hedged around the problems that they considered arising from a decline in religious values, changes to sexuality, alongside rising commercialisation and individualisation. This collectively was considered to be an 'abortion culture' which allowed the 'abortion industry' to flourish (Lowe & Page, 2020) and aligns with the idea of a harmful 'gender ideology' (Vaggione, 2016). For the activists themselves, 'abortion culture' was both a description of the general acceptability of abortion in the UK and an understanding of the societal changes which led to abortion. This was often viewed in opposition to the sacred understanding of life that they believed that their traditional moral values represented. Similar to some of the accounts found by Haugeberg (2017) in the US, abortion represented the ascendance of secular humanism which was deemed to be the antithesis of what they deemed to be the divinely ordered. The development of the 'abortion industry' descriptor alludes to a profit-driven practice in which care is compromised which, in particular, fails to recognise that abortion in the UK is funded through the *National Health Service (NHS)* (Lee, 2003; Lowe, 2019).

As we have outlined earlier, religiously informed ideas about motherhood being 'natural' for women were frequently mentioned by anti-abortion activists. As we have argued elsewhere, their ideas of motherhood as women's supreme role arose from and reinforced the norms of gender roles they strongly believed in:

> ...anti-abortion participants draw on conservative religious teaching, to reaffirm gender complementarity and women's essential role as mothers. These conservative narratives, espoused by various popes, emphasise women's 'inherent' sacrificial nature, and willingness to put the needs of others before their own.
>
> (Lowe & Page, 2019a, p. 177)

This ultra-sacrificial form of motherhood positions women's bodies as central to their understanding of abortion and above their other societal concerns over ungoverned sexuality. Thus, although it was clear that ideally it would be within marriage, continuing with the pregnancy was advocated in all circumstances. Moreover, anti-abortion activists often connected abortion with young, unmarried women, although when asked, they acknowledged that older and/or married women also sought abortions. Indeed, the stereotype of the young, unmarried mother underpinned the argument regarding the availability of abortions being detrimental to men's natural role in taking responsibility for pregnancy. As we outlined in Chapter 2, the association of abortion with, as they saw it, illicit sex has a long history. Consequently, it is unsurprising that the widespread acceptance of sex outside of marriage was seen as a marker and source of the moral decline they objected to.

Alongside this concern about a decline in family values was a more generalised anxiety about changes in societal values in which individual pleasure and consumption are prioritised. The idea that individualism and consumerism were having a negative impact on social relationships partly seemed to stem from the position that traditional understandings of sexuality and marriage were in decline. There was concern that increased emphasis on individual personal desire encouraged sex outside of marriage and divorce and meant that people could make their own moral choices rather than following a divinely ordained plan. Outside a clinic in the South-West, an activist expressed concern about families valuing iPhone and leisure activities over family life and argued that it was never the case that people might choose abortion for financial reasons. She stated that:

> We say that we would prefer people to go back to chastity, and waiting before they dive headlong into a relationship, so you can trust that person, come what may. 'This is true love, and I will be with you through thick and thin' (...) 'I don't think money is the answer; we ought to be a more caring society'.
>
> (Miriam, South-West)

On a previous encounter with Miriam and her companion Beatrice, we had asked their opinion on the welfare cap which currently restricts the number of children that are supported through government benefits. From its introduction, concerns were raised that the welfare cap impacted on abortion decisions as well as increased child poverty, and this proved to be the case (*BPAS*, 2020; Campbell, 2021). Neither Miriam nor Beatrice had been aware of the policy change prior to our conversation, and at the time, seemed concerned about the issue when we informed them. However, in a later encounter, this initial concern about the link between welfare provision and abortion was largely dismissed by Miriam and Beatrice as an outcome of the rejection of traditional family values. More widely across the UK, the majority of those actively criticising or campaigning against the welfare cap during the period of fieldwork were organisations that are largely supportive of abortion (including abortion service providers themselves), rather than anti-abortion activists. However, we would argue that rather than just seeing this an indicator that anti-abortion activists are not concerned about the lives of children after birth, as some pro-choice people have argued, it is an outcome of their focus on abortion as the *foundational* cause of societal ills from which other issues stem.

The belief that abortion was both a foundational cause and an outcome of broader moral decline emerged from their religiously informed framework that this was a battle between good and evil. This meant that future abolition would have both symbolic and wide-ranging practical outcomes that would go beyond abortion itself. As Miriam outlined to us, there were many difficult issues that needed to be tackled in the world but 'if we start somewhere, it has got to be here'. In other words, it was not that the anti-abortion activists were unconcerned about issues such as child poverty, but that they believed that these *arose from* the changes that the passing of the *1967 Abortion Act* had introduced. For them, ending abortion would put the country back on a moral path which would inevitably lead to other changes for the better. Moreover, the rise of individualism and the decline in respect for traditional family values was not the only change that some of the anti-abortionist had concerns with. For a minority, abortion was considered to also be a threat to the nation itself.

Abortion as an Attack on the Nation

In a minority of cases, anti-abortion activists in Britain raised issues that reflected white nationalist concerns. The societal understanding of women as bearers of the nation (Yuval-Davis, 1997) means that abortion has long been a focus of those who wish to assert or maintain a specific nationalist identity. There are some documented links between UK white nationalist and anti-abortion organisations, for example, one of the founding members of the far-right organisation *Britain First* was an evangelical Christian also involved with anti-abortion groups (Allen, 2014). This meant that, in contrast to other far-right organisations, there was a much stronger emphasis on Christianity within the ethos of *Britain First*, with a particular focus on anti-Islam campaigns (Allen, 2014). Although we did not encounter the particular hatred purported by far-right groups against Muslims, it was noticeable that anti-abortion activists specifically mentioned Muslim women as welcoming their Christian intervention outside clinics. The notion that Muslim women are oppressed by their religion and patriarchal South-Asian culture is a common discourse which re-purposes neo-colonial state ideologies to police the behaviour of individual women (Allen, 2015; Mahmood, 2011). Moreover, the emphasis that the activists placed on 'saving' Muslim babies often seemed to have echoes of the missionary work of Britain's colonial past. Racism in the UK is intertwined with the history of colonialism (Solomos, 2003), within which white missionary women had a particular responsibility for the 'education' and 'reform' of women in colonised countries (Dutta, 2017). Moreover, the cultural association of Muslim women with religious piety meant that a hijab-wearing pro-choice activist was singled out as being on the 'wrong' side by anti-abortion activists when she participated in counter-activism at an abortion clinic in a city in the North.

Although infrequent, the most common form of racism that we encountered during fieldwork was expressed through anti-immigration sentiment. Some anti-abortion activists explained that the *1967 Abortion Act* was the reason that Britain had a 'problem' with immigration. If we had more babies, we were told, then we would not have needed so many people to migrate here. For example, one of the activists stated:

> So many children are being aborted, that the population is far below replacement level, native European, which is why half of Africa and Asia are trying to get here.
>
> (Walter, South-West)

In another example, there was a direct comparison made between the number of abortions annually and the number of migrants entering the country. During the period of fieldwork, anti-immigration sentiment was widespread due to the debate about the UK leaving the European Union (Franklin & Ginsburg, 2019), yet Brexit was not a factor that was directly mentioned by the activists when discussing immigration. It is important to note that ideas about white nationalism are often embedded in the discourses about the number of abortions (Baird, 2006; Millar, 2015). In white majority nations, the imagined abortion-seeker is discursively constructed as a white woman, and thus access to abortion can be seen as a threat to the (white) nation (Baird, 2006; Brookes, 1988; Millar, 2015). The notion that white people are being 'replaced' is a central organising concern in many far-right movements (Wilson, 2020). Thus, although those who articulated disquiet to us about the loss of (white) babies and the changing composition of nationhood through migration may not have been active supporters of nationalist movements, the global connections between nationalist and anti-abortion movements is likely to have formed part of the framing of their opinions.

The most concrete examples we found of white nationalism in the British anti-abortion movement were at *MFL*. We observed a number of far-right flags and symbols being displayed by a small number of individuals attending many of the marches. However, our observations suggested that the individuals displaying them were not attending as a block representing organised far-right groups. Importantly too, there was no evidence that the *MFL* organisers had directly promoted the event to white nationalists. Yet, there were instances when nationalist ideas were endorsed. In 2017, one of the speakers representing *CBR* drew on the English nationalist symbolism of St George as a warrior and argued for a need to harness national pride to defeat abortion:

> I looked to God and I was like, God, what am I supposed to say? And he said remind England of her identity. And I looked to the English flag, the symbol that sets us apart from every other nation. I thought about that story behind that flag. The dragon terrorised the kingdom, the people driven by fear who sacrificed their children to appease it and the hero, St George, who risked his life to save others, and slayed this beast. This is what the flag of England represents, this is the story of England's identity, the cross of St George. Victory over a dragon that demands sacrifice. And victory over death. For fifty years we have sacrificed our children to abortion, and it is time for George to arise (field notes).

The specific evocation of English nationalism is significant here; culturally, it is positioned as a 'white' identity, in contrast to 'Britishness' which tends to be more inclusive of other ethnicities (Hussain & Miller, 2004). This narration clearly draws on the symbolism of child sacrifice and positions Christians as heroic in standing against evil. Similar narratives are deployed by British far-right groups in their Islamophobic assertions around (white) Christians saving children from sexual exploitation by 'non-white' people (Allen, 2014). This speech also drew on similar apocalyptic narratives to those found in the US (Mason, 2002). As *CBR* is a UK offshoot of the North American organisation, this is not that surprising.

American narratives on abortion were more frequent at successive *MFL* events than our other encounters with anti-abortion groups because they often invited US speakers to participate. In 2020, the event was moved online due to the COVID-19 pandemic and one of those participating was Fr. Frank Pavone from *Priests for Life*. Notably, a picture of Donald Trump was displayed on the wall behind him as the interview was being livestreamed. Pavone has been sanctioned for his open endorsement of Trump on more than one occasion, and this was found to be a breach of his clerical position (Catholic World Report, 2020). There are clear connections between far-right ideology and anti-abortion groups in the US, which combine in their active support of Trump (Mason, 2021). However, it is important to point out that whilst there are clear traces of far-right thinking present in the British anti-abortion movement, we have not found it to be well-developed nor have there been any attempts at organised violence for decades. Although we did encounter populist and racist narratives, these were not wide-spread, and there was no sign that they were increasing during the course of our fieldwork.

In NI, the different legal history of abortion and history of ethno-political conflict provided a different context to the display of nationalism. In particular, the claims that people on the Island of Ireland rejected abortion were a common refrain, even amongst those who claimed a UK rather than an Irish identity. Notably, despite the rejection of this position in the Irish referendum in 2018, it was not uncommon for this position to be restated. In 2019, the *March for their Lives* in NI drew support from groups across the Island of Ireland and, just like marches in Britain, there were a few signs and symbols of far-right groups on display. For example, a few individuals carried signs supporting the *Irish Freedom Party*, who support unification across Ireland; their anti-immigration rhetoric includes alluding to 'replacement theory'. Others present included members of the DUP, who despite their unwavering support for NI to remain in the UK, nevertheless positioned Westminster as dishonourably imposing abortion on NI against what they claim is the wishes of the people (Sheldon, O'Neill, Parker, & Davis, 2020). This overlooks the cross-community support for abortion (Pierson & Bloomer, 2017; Sheldon et al., 2020).

Summary

Whilst the nationalist claims asserted in different parts of the UK amongst those who oppose abortion are important to document, overwhelmingly it is religious beliefs and practices that shape the anti-abortion movement in the UK. Their lived religious practice of anti-abortion activism is dominated by conservative religious views not shared by the majority within their religion, nor in wider society. The understanding of their actions as sacred work aligns them with goodness and godliness, allowing them to dismiss any accusations that they could possibly cause harm to others. They assert a clear divide between sacred and profane from which they gain emotional strength to build and sustain themselves as a religious moral reform movement. This both secures their position in their own minds as good Christians and dismisses others in their faith as lacking religious authenticity and those outside of their faith as aligned with the profane. Moreover, their understanding of abortion as a *foundational* cause of moral decline and societal problems allows them to focus exclusively on abortion, rather than being concerned about broader social issues. Abortion is literally positioned as the root of evil, and thus, many of the activists seem to assume that ending abortion will bring about a re-traditionalised society and end many of the other transformations that they object to.

Chapter 10

Conclusion

Bringing together the fields of the sociology of reproductive health and the sociology of religion, the aim of this book has been to understand the motivations and practices of anti-abortion activists who utilise public spaces to promote their activism. Whilst there is a globalising trend within anti-abortion groups, the local and national context is an important element within the discursive framings. It is only by examining closely the specific contexts that we can fully understand the complexity of anti-abortion activism. We have argued that to understand the motivations and actions of United Kingdom (UK) anti-abortion activism, we need to consider the interrelationship between lived religion, gendered ideologies and the societal context of religion and public views on abortion (Reilly & Scriver, 2014). Indeed, because of the differing way religion is situated, the UK positioning of anti-abortion activism is different from the activism encountered in other locations such as the United States (US). This concluding chapter considers the main conceptual points our sociological project offers:

- How the worldviews of the anti-abortion activists are translated into a moral regulation movement that builds on specific understandings of ultra-sacrificial motherhood;
- What the embodied and spatial commitments of anti-abortion activists tells us about religion in the public sphere in the UK;
- The opposing sacred commitments of the anti-abortion and pro-choice groups, giving us a more complex understanding of UK culture in relation to the sacred, profane, secular and religious;
- We make recommendations regarding obtaining the balance of rights and freedoms between the right to freedom of religion and the freedom to healthcare privacy.

Worldviews of a Moral Regulation Movement

The opposition to abortion emerges from and is reinforced through the religious beliefs of anti-abortion activists. Anti-abortion activist worldviews are deeply held and understood as sacredly ordained by God. Their fundamental belief is that life begins at conception, with no exception, and that a woman has no right to change God's will and make autonomous decisions about her body. Any counter-argument

Anti-Abortion Activism in the UK, 189–198
Copyright © 2022 Pam Lowe and Sarah-Jane Page
Published under exclusive licence by Emerald Publishing Limited
doi:10.1108/978-1-83909-398-220221024

questioning their theology regarding God's will and purpose is rebutted. Fundamentally, they believe that God opposes abortion. A pregnant woman, for them, is already two separate persons, and a woman has no right to interfere with the status of the foetus. Even in the 'hard cases' of pregnancy due to sexual violence, foetal anomaly and a woman's life being in danger, anti-abortion activists still prioritise foetal rights. Their belief is also that a woman should adhere to their worldview, because of their valorisation of ultra-sacrificial motherhood. This is an extreme form of sacrificial motherhood and literally implies that a woman puts her perceived motherhood responsibilities before everything else, even putting her life on the line if required.

These beliefs mean that anti-abortion activism is a specific religious practice for the activists. Involvement in the movement enables activists to see themselves as both good and godly people. Moreover, for the anti-abortion activists, abortion is a *foundational issue*, the cause of other problems in society. For them, 'abortion culture', with its alignment with the 'culture of death', is a pivotal part of their complaints about 'gender ideology', a collection of progressive changes which include secularisation, challenges to traditional gender roles and rights accorded sexual minorities. The harm introduced by 'abortion culture', through its individualised and consumer-orientated emphasis on making choices rather than accepting the divine plan, is thus wider than abortion itself. Therefore, ending abortion becomes the first step to deal with all other social issues, from poverty to immigration.

These beliefs are rooted in the religious position of the anti-abortion activists. Despite claims to the contrary, those active in opposing abortion in public spaces who articulate a non-religious position are few and far between. Yet anti-abortion activists are keen to present their campaign as one that appeals to both religious and non-religious demographics. This is achieved through linking their arguments to discourses that are endorsed and esteemed in broader culture – namely, scientific discourse, human rights discourse and gender equality discourse. Scientists themselves rarely make claims about issues such as when life begins or when personhood is achieved, but anti-abortion activists extrapolate their own 'scientific' conclusions. They have attempted to make their claims more robust by directly citing scientific research. But they make erroneous claims in their campaigning, such as the idea of a correlation between abortion and mental health issues. Meanwhile the discourse of human rights and gender equality is utilised to convey the idea that abortion is bad for women, as it inevitably results in harm to them, and it revokes the rights of the foetus, who is understood as having full rights to personhood from conception. Claims are made that foetuses should have protected human rights and be included as a protected characteristic in the *Equality Act*, despite the position of the United Nations being that it is *access to abortion* that is understood as the human right, thereby protecting the human rights of women and pregnant people rather than foetuses. Furthermore, anti-abortion activists make claims that abortion is an 'industry' out to make a profit and is therefore against women's real interests. Yet this claim makes little sense in a country where the majority of abortions are funded by the *National Health Service* (*NHS*). Meanwhile disingenuous claims are made about the superior healthcare available to women in places where accessing abortion is highly challenging. Despite promoting the idea that an anti-abortion approach will result in better outcomes for women, in this worldview, the rights of women themselves are clearly curtailed, given the strong expectation for women to always continue with a pregnancy and the follow-on endorsement of ultra-sacrificial motherhood.

This positions the anti-abortion campaign as a moral regulation movement. As Hunt (1999) outlines, moral regulation requires the deployment of a moralised discourse which seeks to reform an issue deemed to be immoral through the mechanism of a moralised subject. In this case, the anti-abortion activists primarily target women (the moralised subject) to end the 'evil' of abortion. As we have shown, the moralised discourse they adopt, whilst still rooted in their beliefs about 'sin', has shifted to a focus on harm and health. This is in line with other moralising campaigns (Hunt, 1999). Moreover, by positioning themselves as the 'saviours' of women and 'babies', they could claim their actions were performed out of 'love'. As Jasper (2018) argues, positive emotions have the effect of strengthening the bonds between the activists themselves and cementing their commitment to the movement. Whilst this is the case in all social movements, for the anti-abortion activists, the claims of 'love' aligned with the Christian under-standing of 'divine love' and the mission to 'love thy neighbour'. Whilst for the activists this reinforced their position as exercising the goodness of golden rule Christianity (Ammerman, 2014), the effect it had on those seeking abortion was distinctly harmful (Lowe & Hayes, 2019).

Embodied and Spatial Orientations: Religion in the Public Sphere

Anti-abortion activists deliberately bring conservative forms of religious belief into the public sphere, where they make a public statement regarding their opposition to abortion. This is buttressed through particular religious practices, such as prayer, and religious objects such as rosary beads, prayer cards, holy water, crosses and images of Our Lady. These embodied practices contribute to the cultivation of a pious body that is understood as fulfilling God's command-ments. In this way, anti-abortion activists are enabling a particular kind of lived religion, consolidated through particular clothing choices, the use of objects with deep religious resonance (such as rosary beads obtained on a religious pilgrimage) and prayers that are interpreted as having an anti-abortion meaning. Material objects in particular are deemed significant and we have spent some time detailing these materialised and embodied practices. Because these religious objects are invested with particular meanings in the course of their public campaign, and because certain religious objects such as rosary beads are dominantly associated with Catholicism, this results in a situation where the objects themselves come to be understood as representative of the anti-abortion campaign in the vicinity of the abortion clinic. The anti-abortion activists frequently make reference to the idea that their beliefs around abortion are divinely ordained, claiming a monopoly regarding what God apparently thinks about abortion; this is a type of sacred claimsmaking and does not actually mean that they *do* have the sacred monopoly, even if they believe this to be the case.

Indeed, it is powerful to align oneself with a sacred other-worldly authority and to stake a claim that you 'know' that your beliefs and practices are aligned with that other-worldly force. This can be consolidated through the use of material objects which are appropriated to display this alignment, buttressed through their traditional and historic associations. Because of the broader investment in objects such as rosary beads with this sacred power, it can therefore be an effective way to monopolise the sacred claimsmaking. But even in religious terms, this is not the only sacred claimsmaking in town. Indeed, those belonging to the same religious faith express concern at the sacred symbols such as rosary beads having been appropriated – objects that they interpret very differently. Meanwhile, anti-abortion activists are perturbed by Christians who do not share their commitments.

Whilst the Catholic Church hierarchy has been vocal in its opposition to abortion, statistics demonstrate that Catholics in general, whilst more likely to be conservative, are very close to the general population in their attitudes (Clements, 2014; Woodhead, 2013). In the course of our research, we discovered that anti-abortion activists did not necessarily generate support from other church members. This highlights that their anti-abortion activism is not representative of the membership of their faith traditions, but is instead a lived practice. Lived religion perspectives emphasise the 'active and reflexive role' that religious practitioners play 'in shaping, negotiating and changing their own religious convictions and practices' (Nyhagen, 2017, p. 496). This is but one example of lived religiosity; whilst anti-abortion activists understood their approach as the only valid way of living out their Christianity, many critiqued their particular brand of lived religion (McGuire, 2008).

The UK has been described as being a religious and secular society concurrently (Woodhead, 2012). Despite the status of state churches like the Church of Scotland, and the established Church of England (CofE) with 26 of their bishops sitting in the House of Lords, increasing numbers of people are identifying as non-religious (Curtice, Clery, Perry, Phillips, & Rahim, 2019). The non-religious category is now on the verge of taking over the category of Christianity; indeed, in some surveys, such as the representative *British Social Attitudes*, it already has (Curtice et al., 2019). As Woodhead (2013) explains, fewer than 10% of the religious population in Britain are aligned with conservative religious forms, described as a 'moral minority'. In this environment, accepted displays of religiosity in the public sphere are tempered; overt displays of religiosity, particularly of the conservative kind, generate levels of discomfort amongst the general public. This was demonstrated in 1998 at the Lambeth Conference, a decennial gathering of Anglican bishops, held at the University of Kent. Brown and Woodhead (2016) recall events where, outside the sports hall, two bishops held a banner for the church to be inclusive. Nearby, a bishop from a more conservative country, Bible in hand, started shouting that God condemns homosexuals and reminding his audience that in the Old Testament, stoning to death would be the punishment. He then attempted to exorcise a homosexual demon from the secretary of the Lesbian and Gay Christian Movement. The gathered audience – shocked and bemused – started to laugh. The pronouncements of this highly conservative bishop were diffused by humour.

Like these assertions regarding homosexuality, the claims made by anti-abortion activists are similarly highly conservative and controversial in the context of the UK. We also noted the role that humour can play in the navigation of religion in the public sphere, with humour sometimes having a key role in counterdemonstrations, as a means of challenging the anti-abortion message. This indicates the complexity of the public sphere in the UK context and the status of religion within it. There are strong expectations for religion to be a private matter and for individuals to not bring contentious religious debates into the public debate. As mentioned earlier, this was also brought into focus when in 2017, Jacob Rees-Mogg, a Member of Parliament, publicly said he was 'completely opposed' to abortion. His views were deemed extreme and roundly condemned.

This book has primarily focused on the activism that is enacted outside sites where abortions take place or where advice about abortion is given. Many activists prioritise the space outside the abortion clinic as the last opportunity to dissuade a woman from seeking an abortion. Refrains telling anti-abortion activists to relocate their prayer to home or the church therefore do not work, because persuading women against abortion is seen as doing God's work. Even if they are unsuccessful in generating 'saves', this activism 'proves' their religious commitment and is understood as contributing to the individual salvation of the anti-abortion activist. The space at the clinic is therefore invested with particular meanings through the types of bodily deportment on display (head bowed in prayer, for example) or the types of objects utilised. This is replete with emotion – the abortion clinic itself is understood as a bleak and sinister place where death occurs. Anti-abortion activists present themselves as offering hope, love and support, and struggle to understand why their actions are deemed objectionable by others.

These contestations occur in the public space. Given the general societal reticence towards abortion, its broader stigmatisation and the general feeling that abortion should be hidden away from public view (Hoggart, 2017; Purcell, Maxwell, Bloomer, Rowlands, & Hoggart, 2020), this spectacle generation causes enormous discomfort to the general public. Furthermore, religious displays in the public sphere are seen with concern, given a general understanding that religious beliefs should be privatised, and when publicised, should be in a particularly mediated and controlled form. Public toleration of outward displays of religious activism is low. Therefore, these antagonisms also reveal pertinent detail regarding how the sacred and profane is situated and understood in a secular public sphere, particularly those spaces where healthcare is offered.

Opposing Sacred Commitments: Ultra-Sacrificial Motherhood versus Reproductive Justice

The previous section emphasised the importance of the spatial in anti-abortion activism. Specific sites are chosen to enact one's activism, with powerful meanings invested in being at the site where abortion takes place. Holy water and rosary beads are deemed necessary to mitigate the deep negativity associated with the space. Throughout the book, we have given much detail to the religiously rooted sacred commitments of anti-abortion activists. A key sacred commitment for them is ultra-sacrificial motherhood. Whilst maternal sacrifice can be located in society in general terms, ultra-sacrificial motherhood takes on additional dimensions that go above and beyond the typical understandings associated with sacrificial motherhood. Maternal sacrifice is understood by Lowe (2016) as a means of regulating women's reproductive choices, in a context where having a child is deemed the ultimate desire of every woman. Such examples include the control of pregnancy and the idea that women should regulate what they eat and drink when pregnant and do everything possible to cultivate an ambient and positive environment for their future child (Lowe, 2016).

Contrasts are made between 'good' and 'bad' mothers, with 'bad' mothers positioned as those who make the 'wrong' choices, such as having a child at a time of financial stress. Therefore, abortion can play a role in the regulation of maternal sacrifice. In addition, the care of children is often child-focused, what Hays (1996) calls 'intensive motherhood'. Mothers are expected to foreground their child's needs above all others and ensure they raise productive and good citizens. Sacrificial and intensive motherhood also takes religious forms (Llewellyn, 2016; Page, 2016), especially in belief systems like Christianity where having children is often encouraged. And key tropes of sacrificial motherhood are endorsed through figures such as the Virgin Mary (Forna, 1998; Warner, 1978). Sacrificial and intensive motherhood has therefore utilised religious resources in their justification.

Meanwhile, the anti-abortion activists engage in a more demanding version of this, what we call *ultra-sacrificial motherhood*. Ultra-sacrificial motherhood draws upon more traditional and conservative interpretations of family life. More general sacrificial motherhood expectations have loosened regarding family life, so long as the child remains foregrounded. This means that separated families, single-parent families and same-sex families are expected to participate in and endorse sacrificial motherhood, with abortion also playing a potential role in demonstrating good motherhood (delaying motherhood to benefit future potential children, for instance). Meanwhile, opposition to abortion is a key factor in understanding ultra-sacrificial motherhood, but it is more than this. We define ultra-sacrificial motherhood as having the following features:

- Holding a firm belief in traditional family formations, two-parent heterosexual families, where parents are married. This is underscored by a gender division of labour where women are expected to fully invest their identities in vocational motherhood and men in breadwinning fatherhood. Furthermore, Catholic

adherents of ultra-sacrificial motherhood are strongly opposed to artificial forms of contraception, which are seen as encouraging, rather than preventing, abortion, because of their view that it encourages permissive sexual behaviour;
- An essentialised version of motherhood, which women should not only see as a desirable goal (as per sacrificial motherhood), but one in which they orient their whole selves around their mothering identity;
- That the harms of abortion are wide-reaching and centre not only on the physical and mental harm caused, but also spiritual harm;
- That there are no positive attributes to abortion; abortion is always bad for women and to progress with a pregnancy is the best course of action in every situation;
- Abortion in cases of rape and foetal anomaly are deemed not necessary. Abortion due to the woman's life in danger are downplayed; views about a woman's life in danger are discursively managed through ideas such as double effect. Ultimately it is suggested that women should sacrifice themselves (their lives) for the foetus;
- Rather than being child-centric (as per sacrificial and intensive motherhood), ultra-intensive motherhood is foetal-centric, where the needs and priorities of the foetus are foregrounded from conception, but with little emphasis on children once born. The care after birth is assumed through women 'naturally' performing their divine role as mothers.

A key feature of ultra-sacrificial motherhood we would like to emphasise is this last point – its foetal-centric components. Intensive motherhood prioritises the born child, with mothering expectations crafted around the child and requiring vast amounts of concentrated time and energy (Hays, 1996). Whilst there are many expectations – once one has decided to proceed with the pregnancy – to amend behaviours to prioritise the needs of the foetus, such as by avoiding certain foods and drinks – intensive and sacrificial forms of motherhood do not demand that women put their lives on the line. But with ultra-sacrificial motherhood, that sacrifice is embedded and expected, because far greater weight and rights are accorded to the foetus. Ultra-sacrificial motherhood becomes the sacred commitment of the anti-abortion activists (Lynch, 2012a, 2012b). Moreover, any rejection of these sacred commitments is understood to lead to foetal-centric grief and abortion regret (Ehrlich & Doan, 2019; Millar, 2017).

The presence of anti-abortion activists at clinic sites provokes a counter-reaction from those who see access to abortion as an inalienable right. Contestations emerge when pro-choice counterdemonstrators encounter this discourse, because they problematise these understandings and have an opposing sacred commitment – that of bodily autonomy and reproductive justice. The sacred/profane commitments of both groups are rooted in particular spaces. Both groups demonstrate their sacred beliefs through particular practices outside of clinics. Spatial claims are made and constituted differently. For pro-choice activists, the abortion clinic is to be protected as a sacred site, in particular, from the interference of the anti-abortion activists. Meanwhile for anti-abortion activists, the abortion clinic is a site of evil and a deathly location where lives are taken. Their sacred aim is to stop women from entering this sinful and corrupt place. Space outside the clinic becomes contested terrain, and where the broader beliefs of each respective group are enacted. Sacred commitments exist whether one is religious or not; the sacred should not exclusively be located with religiously oriented dispositions (Lynch, 2012a).

Rights, Freedoms and the Contested Notion of Harm

We have demonstrated that the faith positioning of anti-abortion activists is absolutely fundamental to their claimsmaking, as it is rooted in their understanding of what God wants them to do. Making sacred claims about what God believes is a powerful strategy and inevitably means that the anti-abortion activists are judging women entering the clinic, simply by having the worldview that God believes abortion to be wrong. Anti-abortion activists themselves do not always like language such as being judged, as for them, only God can judge. But given they have already decided what God desires, this becomes a circular argument. Because the language of being judged is so strong, they ameliorate their message through the idea that women seeking an abortion either do not know what they do or are being pressured or coerced either directly by partners, friends or family or indirectly by the 'abortion culture'. They unknowingly enter the clinic to 'kill' their 'baby'. But this then castigates women as feeble and ignorant. This sacred claimsmaking about God's own beliefs is why their presence is so hurtful for women seeking services; their argument is that a sacred power condemns their actions. This is profound stuff. For some religious women having an abortion, this leads to high levels of distress, given that alternative viewpoints – that God is fine with abortion – are largely absent. Meanwhile for non-religious women, it becomes presumptive to assume that what God thinks matters. Questions are therefore raised about why anti-abortion activists believe they have the right to convey their conservative theology in the public sphere at all. What is the balance of rights here, and to what extent should religious freedom interfere with the right to healthcare privacy?

Recent court hearings have considered these questions, in relation to the implementation of a Public Spaces Protection Order (PSPO), or to introduce a 'bufferzone' around a clinic in Ealing, West London. In *Dulgheriu and Orthova v. London Borough of Ealing*, anti-abortion activists took the council to court for implementing the PSPO. The question was raised whether this PSPO complied with Articles 9, 10 and 11 of the European Convention on Human Rights. These Articles relate, respectively, to freedom of thought, conscience and religion; freedom of expression; and freedom of assembly and association. All these articles related to the activists at the clinic site. In addition, the court judgement discussed Article 8 – the right to respect for private and family life – in relation to those seeking abortion services. It was ruled that as abortion decision-making is a private affair, it was 'an invasion of privacy' (2018, para 61) to have anti-abortion activists present when women accessed the clinic. Therefore, the court ruling upheld Article 8 in relation to the PSPO on behalf of clinic users. Because of the gravity of this right, the judge ruled that this meant that it was proportionate to interfere with the rights pertaining to Articles 9, 10 and 11 on behalf of the anti-abortion activists. The PSPO was therefore upheld. The judgement clarified that whilst Article 9 details that one has a right to *hold* a particular belief system, the practice and *manifestation* of that belief is qualified, especially in cases where it is determined (like this case) that it interferes with the rights of others. This therefore endorsed the view that in the specific healthcare setting of the abortion clinic, one retained their freedom of religion, but not the freedom to impose on the privacy of those accessing healthcare services. The balance of rights was judged in favour of the person seeking an abortion.

Bufferzones are therefore a proportionate response in not derailing freedom of speech or freedom of belief, but allowing women access to legitimate healthcare services without fear of judgement. Because their worldview is embedded as a sacred commitment, they are unlikely to be dissuaded from it, rather like the way pro-choice activists are committed to their sacred commitment to reproductive justice. Furthermore, as Article 9 of the European Convention on Human Rights articulates, anti-abortion activists have an inalienable right to their beliefs. Indeed, as this project has demonstrated, these are deeply held values that would be challenging to dislodge. The aim of pro-choice campaigns should be focused not on attempts to change the anti-abortion worldview, but moving it away from the point at which a woman seeks an abortion. Whilst anti-abortion activists are entitled to their views, however, they should not be allowed to influence or limit public provision of abortion services.

A Final Word

In a culture where public space is refracted through secularity (i.e. where belief is assumed to be acceptable only if it takes place in the private sphere), religious actors making conservative religious claims, like the anti-abortion activists, can take centre stage, with their voices dominating. Religious perspectives become reified through conservative meanings for the broader public; some counterdemonstrations also convey anti-religious sentiment, and this means that abortion debates in public spaces come to be perceived as a battle between the 'religious' and the 'secular'. This study has demonstrated that it is far more complex than this, not only in terms of the religious practitioners who condemn the actions of the anti-abortion activists, as indicated by the quote from the Methodist minister conveyed at this book's opening, but also in terms of the pro-choice activists who join the counterdemonstrations to articulate a pro-choice religious viewpoint. Furthermore, across the board, there is great diversity in perspectives on abortion – that even the Catholic Church – whilst claiming to have an uninterrupted and unaltered view on abortion – has historically shown much diversity, and where many of its own members take a divergent view to the current church hierarchy.

In the UK context, public understandings which situate abortion as fully compatible with religious conviction are muted. As both religion and abortion are seen as private matters, this is not really that surprising. In a British culture where feminism itself has often been associated with secularity and where religious perspectives within mainstream feminism have been side-lined (Aune, 2015; Llewellyn & Trzebiatowska, 2013; Nyhagen, 2017), religious factions expressing support for abortion have been downplayed. This study has demonstrated the multiple voices of feminist-oriented pro-choice activism, including religious voices – voices which challenge the sacred claim that God opposes abortion and instead articulates a different sacred claim – that of reproductive justice. Reproductive justice centres not only on the human right to have a child but also to be able to choose not to have children; those raising a child should be able to do so in a 'safe and dignified context' based on sexual and gender equality (Ross & Solinger, 2017, p. 9). Coerced reproduction, including abortion restrictions, is therefore fundamentally at odds with reproductive justice. This situates abortion as a morally exercised right, and for religious practitioners endorsing reproductive justice, abortion is understood as bringing no negative consequences for one's religious life (Turtle, 2021). For example, Tom Davis (2004), who we introduced in Chapter 3 and who was part of a clerical network assisting women in obtaining abortion before *Roe v. Wade*, does not view abortion in profaning terms, but argues that reproductive justice is a sacred good.

Challenging the debate at the level of the sacred is important for two reasons: firstly, it needs to be recognised that sacred claimsmaking (Lynch, 2012a, 2012b) is occurring on both sides of the debate. Religious conservatives do not have the sacred monopoly; expanding the view of the sacred to include secular-identifying feminists – and recognising that their commitments are sacredly held too – counters any claims to God-given moral authority. Secondly, recognising the role of religious pro-choice activists in the campaign is important at the level of inclusion and diversity (Nyhagen, 2017), bringing in feminist religious resources that support a pro-choice position expands the tools with which abortion rights can be secured. This is especially important given the challenges faced by those in worshipping contexts where abortion is not discussed or understood in wholly negative terms. Further work is needed to allow and enable women to speak about the realities of their reproductive lives in religious contexts, without stigma. Working together with an expanded array of feminist tools can help establish abortion as an ordinary, everyday event, resituating women as the moral arbiter of their own bodies.

Appendix 1

The Research Journey

This section of the book describes the journey through the longitudinal ethnography on which this book is based, a project which began in 2015. From the outset, it sought to follow some of the 'classic' features of ethnography (Hammersley & Atkinson, 2007). This meant we situate ourselves in the field, and relied predominately on observations and informal conversations as main data sources, supplemented with other relevant materials. We took an organic approach to questions and data sources, developing them over time as our qualitative analysis and understanding grew. Here we outline methods and give insights regarding the fieldwork, as well as set out our reflections and decision-making during the fieldwork. We also outline the ethical challenges of undertaking research with those with views we oppose, and the reactions that we received from the anti-abortion activists we encountered. We will also describe the ways in which the research changed as it adapted to both developments in the field and the relationships we had with the anti-abortion groups themselves. We will begin by outlining the entry that we had to the field and describing how two academic specialisms came together to be able to analyse and theorise the data that we gathered.

Pam has a long-standing academic research interest in issues around reproductive and sexual health and this has been combined with activist work in the pro-choice movement. Her combination of the two emerges from a feminist position which historically challenged the separation between the academy and activism. Her previous work meant that she had long-standing contacts with pro-choice groups and activists, so access to them was unlikely to be a barrier. However, her public profile meant that anti-abortion activists would be aware that she had publicly advocated for abortion and this could be a barrier in terms of research access. Initially, the research was planned with our colleague Dr Graeme Hayes, an expert in social movement research, and he assisted with some of the initial fieldwork. At this stage, it became clear that in order to fully comprehend the motivations and actions of the anti-abortion activists, we needed more understanding about the sociology of religion. Sarah-Jane then joined the project, bringing with her detailed knowledge about lived religion, particularly in relation to gender and sexuality.

In the United Kingdom (UK), there are several main organisations involved in coordinating anti-abortion activities outside of abortion service providers or pregnancy advisory services, but in the majority of places, it is run by local

Anti-Abortion Activism in the UK, 199–206
Copyright © 2022 Pam Lowe and Sarah-Jane Page
Published under exclusive licence by Emerald Publishing Limited
doi:10.1108/978-1-83909-398-220221025

grassroots groups. The main organisations include the *Good Counsel Network (GCN)*, *Helpers of God's Precious Infants (HOGPI)* and *Precious Life* based in Northern Ireland (NI). The *GCN* run a crisis pregnancy centre (CPC) in London and at the start of the project, organised three clinic 'vigils'. Rather than relying solely on volunteers, which happens in most places, some activists at *GCN* sites are employees (details of this are available in the public domain). Two sites that they had frequented had bufferzones imposed during the course of the project. Meanwhile, *HOGPI* (a UK offshoot of a United States [US]-based organisation) are involved outside of clinics in two ways. Monthly, they would arrange a Mass, religious procession and prayers outside an abortion clinic. This activity mainly happened in London and the South-East. They also supported local grassroots groups to set up and maintain vigils in their own areas. They had a particular prayer book that seemed to be in widespread use across Britain. In NI, *Precious Life* targeted abortion service providers when they were operating, but also *Informing Choices NI* (formally FPA) a non-directive pregnancy advisory service. These three organisations are mainly run by Catholic volunteers, although *Precious Life* relied much less on religious displays than the other two.

At the beginning of the fieldwork period, the *Centre for Bioethical Reform UK* (CBR – linked to a similar US organisation and also previously known in the UK as *Abort 67*) was also involved in activities outside of abortion clinics, although in the latter half of the fieldwork, they had moved to mainly focusing on other public spaces such as city centres. *CBR* rarely publicly display any religious messages but are mainly composed of evangelicals. Also occurring was the *40 Days for Life (40DFL)* campaign. This is an American bi-annual prayer campaign that encourages individuals to target an abortion clinic in their area. To be recognised and receive support, each individual or group that wants to take part pays a fee and is expected to conform to the principles of the campaign. Consequently, it is best thought of as an anti-abortion franchise. Although we were predominately focused on activism in public places, we also monitored what was being said by other organisations. These include *Christian Concern, Both Lives Matter* and the *Society for the Protection of Unborn Children (SPUC)* who were all engaged with debates about street-based anti-abortion campaigns even though they were only infrequently directly involved.

The ethnography encompassed a range of methods, and this was approved by the University Ethics Committee. The main methods used were observation, informal and formal interviews, and documentary analysis. Most of the observations were in public spaces, frequently outside of abortion clinics where anti-abortion activists stood attempting to change the minds of those who sought abortions. When we arrived on site, we would normally stand some distance away from the clinic and observe what was taking place for a period of time before approaching and asking the anti-abortion activists, and if present, any pro-choice counterdemonstrators, if they would be willing to talk to us. We took photographs of the sites, taking care to ensure that there were no clinic users in the vicinity at the time. Most of the photos were focused on the signs and symbols that were being displayed. We counted the number of people present and made field notes about their activities such as if they were chatting or praying. We would also ask for copies of leaflets or any other materials that they were giving out. The activities of most groups outside of abortion clinics were highly dependent on who happened to be present at the time. Many of the anti-abortion activists brought signs and religious materials from home and took them away when they left. In most places, whether or not they approached people directly also seemed to be an individual decision. This meant that what took place at any given moment was highly unpredictable, leaving abortion service providers unable to reliably inform service users in advance.

For the first two years, we focused on England and Wales, but expanded to Scotland and NI in 2017. Overall, we undertook fieldwork outside 30 abortion service providers, visiting the majority on multiple occasions and usually staying for 1–2 hours. However, it was not infrequent that when we arrived, no one was there. Whilst this was obviously better for the service users and clinic staff, it was also frustrating in terms of the research project. It is, however, a reminder that anti-abortion activism outside clinics is not widely supported, and new sites would spring up then disappear as their continuance was often dependant on a few key activists. For example, the *40DFL* campaign asks organisers to be present outside a clinic for 12 hours a day over 40 consecutive days. This only seemed to happen at a few sites, with the majority doing far less. Most would either do fewer days a week, fewer hours a day or both. Some abortion service providers only had anti-abortion activists outside during a 40 days campaign, whereas at others with year-round presence, activity would increase over this period.

At 10 of the sites we visited, there were pro-choice groups organising some form of counteractions. These were again mainly organised through local grass-roots organisations. The activities that took place varied, with some acting as clinic escorts and ushering service users past the anti-abortion activists. Others would be mainly focused on counter-demonstrations; they would also display signs and banners. At most sites, the pro-choice activists were in regular conversations with the abortion service provider and liaised over when they should be present and what action to take. Some abortion service providers actively discouraged the attendance of pro-choice groups or asked them to only come when the clinic was closed, as they felt it would add to the difficulties faced by service users. When we began fieldwork, the links between the pro-choice groups were often patchy, but after their role in getting the first legally backed bufferzone in place in Ealing, London, *Sister Supporter* developed resources to share their experience in order to assist others to use the same legal framework.

Alongside the fieldwork at abortion clinics, we also undertook observations at other public events. Decisions about which events to include have been made to reflect the different activities nationally, as well as being driven by significant events that have taken place during the course of fieldwork. They included public meetings of both anti-abortion and pro-choice activists, debates in local and national government about the impact of anti-abortion activism outside clinics, and court hearings related to the first legally imposed bufferzone. We also attended the annual *March for Life* (*MFL*) in Britain, which was held initially in Birmingham (2015–2017) before moving to London (2018–2019) and their live-streamed replacement event in 2020. We attended similar mass gatherings in NI and Scotland. We took photographs of the events and fieldwork notes of the activities and speeches. We also used tally counters to calculate numbers attending, taking more than one count where possible, to form the best possible estimate. In 2015, we also had permission to undertake a short survey of those attending *MFL*, although when we asked to repeat this in 2016, we did not get a response.

Alongside the field notes, photographs and materials such as leaflets gathered outside abortion clinics and at public events, we also collected other public documents and statements. These included data on the websites of anti-abortion organisations and documents relating to court cases about the activities of anti-abortion activists or bufferzones. We were granted access to a pre-existing data set of comments made by service users to an abortion service provider about the encounters with anti-abortion activists as they entered the clinic. We also undertook a small number of in-depth interviews with activists from both sides. When formal interviews took place, when permission was given, we audio-recorded and transcribed them or took detailed notes when it was not. We have also consistently used pseudonyms and removed other identifying data. As the numbers of people who take part in activities outside abortion clinics are quite small, we have not included any demographic data as we feel this could make them identifiable. For the same reason, we have also not named individual clinic sites, and rely on larger geographic areas as descriptors. All the data (fieldwork notes, photographs, interview transcripts, documents) were analysed thematically through a system of close reading, coding and comparison (Braun & Clarke, 2006) and NVIVO was used to manage the dataset.

For both of us, this has been the most challenging and complex research project that we have ever been engaged in, and it raised a number of ethical questions. Both Pam and Sarah-Jane are pro-choice, and Pam's previous work meant that we had 'insider' status with pro-choice campaigners but were likely to be viewed with distrust by anti-abortion activists. Moreover, as others have pointed out, it can be difficult to spend time with individuals and groups whose views you feel opposed to (Blee, 2007; Pilkington, 2016). There is a huge emphasis on developing rapport as a way to develop detailed researched datasets, and this raises questions about data collection where rapport is unlikely or impossible (Smyth & Mitchell, 2008). As Smyth and Mitchell argue 'sometimes we are simply not able to put ourselves in their shoes' (2008, p. 450) and we need to draw on other forms of reflection to understand those that we disagree with. Throughout the research we have tried to ensure that we report how the activists see themselves and make it clear where we present our analysis of the situation, particularly if this challenges what they have said. In this book, we have given much space to detailing the narratives, beliefs and practices of anti-abortion activists, taking great care to accurately describe their activism. As Avishai, Gerber, and Randles (2013) have argued, feminist research has long supported that we privilege the voices of those we study, and this can also be applied to research with groups that reject the feminist positions that we take.

From the outset, we decided that we would be open with those we encountered about our position on abortion, and were willing to be questioned about our views. We expected to be questioned frequently about this by anti-abortion activists. At the outset, we had not anticipated as much probing about our faith position (we both identify as non-religious). Interestingly, on some occasions, our professed lack of faith seemed to provoke more consternation than our pro-choice views, with one particular Catholic anti-abortion activist showing visceral horror when the lack of baptism was mentioned (Box A). At times, it could be difficult not to display a revealing emotional reaction to some of the points being made. For example, astonishment that anyone would take seriously the idea that watching Star Trek leads to child possession. As we spent more time in the field, the relationships changed with some of the anti-abortion activists we encountered. Some of them declined to talk to us any further, but others began to greet our appearance almost as acquaintances. Whilst, as Pilkington (2016) suggests, being accepted by those whose views you oppose is often 'accompanied more often by a sense of guilt than of professional achievement' (2016, p. 17), it nevertheless enabled us, in some cases, to contest some of the views they held in order to gain a more in-depth account. The extent of engagement could also be influenced by any press reporting on their activities; for example, if a negative newspaper report had recently been released, activists could be more wary and it was common in the first instance to assume that we were journalists. We always wore our university IDs on lanyards whilst *in situ* at fieldwork sites, and some often questioned us intently about our professional credentials.

Sometimes, even if the anti-abortion activists had agreed to talk to us, it was difficult to engage with them in the areas that we wanted to focus our fieldwork on. Some anti-abortion activists saw the conversations as an opportunity for them to 'educate' us about abortion and it felt like they were attempting to bring about a 'conversion' (Box A). Whilst we always answered their questions about our

---

Box A: Fieldwork Notes, English Midlands

They started digging into Sarah-Jane's identity and whether she was religious, given her academic interest in religion, and she said she wasn't but said she was raised religiously and had family members who held anti-abortion views. She was asked whether she was baptised, and when she said she wasn't (she explained her parents' religious tradition endorsed adult baptism rather than infant baptism) there was an intake of breath from Judith and she deemed this to be a very perilous situation and urged Sarah-Jane to get baptised, especially in the Catholic faith (but there was also the inference that any branch of Christianity would do). Later on, when we ended the conversation, Judith again implored Sarah-Jane to seek out baptism (she did not implore Pam in the same way), despite Pam having already made it clear she wasn't a Christian either. This was definitely a proselytising opportunity for Judith, which was deployed with Sarah-Jane but not Pam. Instead of being asked about our views on abortion, we were asked about our religious belonging. This was the first time activists have tried to do a religious conversion rather than a conversion away from a pro-choice stance.

support for abortion and our (lack of) faith position, we tried to do this as briefly as possible and steer the conversation back towards their individual ideas, motivations and underlying beliefs rather than what sometimes felt like 'textbook' responses. Questions about their faith practices sometimes were met with blank looks. For example, some presumed that praying the Rosary is experienced in the same way for everyone, and they would express bewilderment when their specific prayer practices were probed. It was helpful in these cases, to ask about the material objects they had with them, as often a question about if their rosary beads were particularly special elicited the data that a direct question about prayer could not. As Lynch (2012a) points out, researching sacred commitments is hard because they are absolute and unwavering, thus it is unsurprising that it was hard to unpack the nuance in the anti-abortion position. Moreover, as researchers, we also have our own sacred commitment to abortion rights and bodily autonomy. This meant we needed to be reflexive both in the field and in our analysis to engage and represent the anti-abortion activists accurately, as well as ensuring that we critically engaged with our 'insider' knowledge when ana-lysing the accounts of pro-choice activists and actions.

At sites where both anti-abortion and pro-choice activists were present, this created both opportunities and dilemmas in terms of fieldwork. Such conflicts often drew sharp attention to specific aspects of contestation, but larger groups are also harder and very tiring to observe, especially if the activities take place over a few hours and get heated. On occasions, some of the pro-choice activists clearly expected us to 'take-sides', especially after the research had begun to be used publicly in the campaign for both local and national bufferzones. Negoti-ating this on the ground involved reminding the pro-choice people that we were there as researchers. If the police were also present, we explained our presence to them. This was partly to ensure that our access to both 'sides' would remain open if they sought to keep the groups apart, but also, if they were happy to discuss this, to gain their views on the action that they were policing. They also sometimes helped in providing estimates of numbers to corroborate the counts we had undertaken.

We had begun writing both academic and non-academic articles from the beginning and we also made numerous media appearances discussing the research. Some of the anti-abortion activists sought to discredit us publicly. Often these claimed that our research was biased or that we were not professionally qualified (Box B). One organisation constantly publicly claimed that we had declined to take up their offer to arrange interviews with women that they had 'saved' from abortion. Yet, in private when we tried to arrange this, they declined to take our calls. A couple of participants asked to withdraw their interviews and we removed these from the dataset. There were also attempts to both end the project and have us disciplined by making formal complaints about us to the Vice Chancellor and the Chair of the Research Ethics Committee of our University. Thankfully, these attempts failed, as we had always adhered to the strict professional ethical standards expected of us. These types of events meant we needed to increase the steps we took in the field to protect ourselves from malicious accusations. These types of professional risks are not uncommon when researching those with extremist views (Blee, 2007; Sanders-McDonagh, 2014; Smyth & Mitchell, 2008). However, unlike other researchers who undertake close proximity fieldwork with difficult or distasteful groups, we did not encounter any occasions where we were really threatened. Moreover, the risks that we encountered in the UK from anti-abortion activists were always very unlikely to be anything more than mild in comparison to other places such as the US where aggressive, hostile and criminal behaviour towards abortion service providers and their supporters is common (Cohen & Connon, 2016).

Ironically, one of the things that the anti-abortion activists seemed to object to the most was that we would watch and approach them outside of abortion clinics. On the few occasions that activists complained about us to the University, they deemed our research to be harassment. The fact that they were undertaking this very behaviour themselves to the pregnant people seeking to access abortion services seems to have slipped their attention. As we have discussed in the book, this is due to their assumptions about prayer always being a benign activity (Page & Lowe, 2021a). Indeed, whilst undertaking fieldwork, we tried to be really careful to time our approaches to not interrupt their prayers, even though we recognised this activity as causing distress to those seeking abortion (Box C).

Box B: Fieldwork Notes, North

As we started to introduce ourselves, Ian said that he knew about us, turned to Pam and said 'I know who you are' and said that she was dishonest. At this point he was stood close, leaning over Pam in an overbearing body position, although his tone was more accusatory than outright verbally abusive. He seemed to be claiming that Pam did not make it clear that she supports abortion rights. He also called her unprofessional, that he had heard this 'on good authority' and had researched Pam's work, although when asked about what he had read of her work, he did not appear to have read any of it, and instead he referred to the debate in Parliament. Over the next 20 minutes or so, the conversation was about the research and Pam in particular. Yet although the main target of his accusations was Pam, he spent more time talking to Graeme. Often whilst he would look at Pam when she was speaking, he would direct his replies to Graeme. Graeme and Pam explained how the research is separate to individual positions of abortion, although they both are supporters of abortion rights. Ian accepted this explanation and stated that he was sorry if he had got off on the wrong foot at the beginning of the conversation. A more general discussion about Ian's journey to participating in vigils took place. Over the course of the entire encounter with Ian his sexist attitude did diminish, although to the end it was clear that he was treating Graeme with more respect.

Box C: Fieldwork Notes – Scotland

Jennifer then says thanks to Sarah-Jane, but it was said in a manner which was obviously a means of trying to get rid of her in the politest way possible. Sarah-Jane says thanks for talking to me (...) Diane asks whether Sarah-Jane was one of the people 'loitering' on the other side of the road. Sarah-Jane said that she was over there for a little while as she did not want to interrupt or disturb the prayers. They all nodded and seemed satisfied by this response, which was a very polite thing to do (despite being deemed a 'loiterer' in the process). Sarah-Jane said she wanted to wait until they had finished, and they thanked her for this. Frank then said that the Rosary is very robust so you could have interrupted. Sarah-Jane laughed and said she still would feel it was a bit impolite.

Fieldwork Notes – North

We approached the activists in between prayers, but they dismissed us straightaway. One stated that 'We're not here to talk; we're just here to pray. If you want any questions to be answered you can go to the 40 days website and get in touch with the organisers'.

In comparison to other places, anti-abortion activism in the UK has received very little attention. Although small in number, they nevertheless represent an ongoing challenge to ensuring abortion access. In our experience, researching groups that hold views that are 'distasteful' and/or that you are opposed to encourages an increased level of research reflexivity to ensure that we are fair in our representation, and we would encourage others to also shine a light on the activities of anti-abortion groups.

Bibliography

Abortion Act. (1967). Retrieved from https://www.legislation.gov.uk/ukpga/1967/87/section/1

Ahmed, S. (2004). *The cultural politics of emotion*. Edinburgh: Edinburgh University Press.

Aiken, A., Padron, E., Broussard, K., & Johnson, D. (2019). The impact of Northern Ireland's abortion laws on women's abortion decision-making and experiences. *BMJ Sexual & Reproductive Health, 45*(1), 3–9.

Allanson, S. (2006). *Murder on his mind*. Melbourne: Wilkinson Publishing.

Allen, L. (2005). *Sexual subjects: Young people, sexuality and education*. Basingstoke: Palgrave Macmillan.

Allen, C. (2014). Britain first: The 'frontline resistance' to the Islamification of Britain. *The Political Quarterly, 85*(3), 354–361.

Allen, C. (2015). 'People hate you because of the way you dress' understanding the invisible experiences of veiled British Muslim women victims of Islamophobia. *International Review of Victimology, 21*(3), 287–301.

Almond, P. C. (2019). Life of Brian at 40: An assertion of individual freedom that still resonates. *The Conversation*. Retrieved from https://theconversation.com/life-of-brian-at-40-an-assertion-of-individual-freedom-that-still-resonates-114743

Amery, F. (2015). Solving the 'woman problem' in British abortion politics: A contextualised account. *The British Journal of Politics & International Relations, 17*(4), 551–567.

Amery, F. (2020). *Beyond pro-life and pro-choice: The changing politics of abortion in Britain*. Bristol: Bristol University Press.

Ammerman, N. (2014). *Sacred stories, spiritual tribes: Finding religion in everyday life*. Oxford: Oxford University Press.

Anitha, S., & Gill, A. K. (2018). Making politics visible: Discourses on gender and race in the problematisation of sex-selective abortion. *Feminist Review, 120*(1), 1–19.

Anthony, D., Robbins, T., & Barrie-Anthony, S. (2002). Cult and anticult totalism: Reciprocal escalation and violence. *Terrorism and Political Violence, 14*(1), 211–240.

Antonnen, V. (2000). Sacred. In W. Braun & R. T. McCutcheon (Eds.), *Guide to the study of religion* (pp. 271–282). London: Continuum.

Arai, L. (2009). *Teenage pregnancy: The making and unmaking of a problem*. Bristol: Policy Press.

Arey, W. (2020). Real men love babies: Protest speech and masculinity at abortion clinics in the Southern United States. *NORMA, 15*(3–4), 205–220.

Aston, K. (2016). United Kingdom: All publicity is good publicity, probably. In S. Tomlins & S. C. Bullivant (Eds.), *The atheist bus campaign: Global manifestations and responses* (pp. 334–368). Leiden: Brill.

Aune, K. (2015). Feminist spirituality as lived religion: How UK feminists forge religio-spiritual lives. *Gender & Society, 29*(1), 122–145.

Avishai, O., Gerber, L., & Randles, J. (2013). The feminist ethnographer's dilemma: Reconciling progressive research agendas with fieldwork realities. *Journal of Contemporary Ethnography, 42*(4), 394–426.

Bacon, H., Dossett, W., & Knowles, S. (2017). Introduction. In H. Bacon, W. Dossett, & S. Knowles (Eds.), *Alternative salvations: Engaging the sacred and the secular* (pp. 1–7). London: Bloomsbury.

Baird, B. (2006). Maternity, whiteness and national identity. *Australian Feminist Studies, 21*(50), 197–221.

Baird, B. (2018). Abortion and the limits of the personal becoming political. *Australian Feminist Studies, 33*(95), 129–146.

Baird, B., & Millar, E. (2019). More than stigma: Interrogating counter narratives of abortion. *Sexualities, 22*(7–8), 1110–1126.

Baker, J. O., Molle, A., & Bader, C. D. (2020). The flesh and the devil: Belief in religious evil and views of sexual morality. *Review of Religious Research, 62*(1), 133–151.

Beaumont, C. (2007). Moral dilemmas and women's rights: The attitude of the Mothers' Union and Catholic Women's League to divorce, birth control and abortion in England, 1928–1939. *Women's History Review, 16*(4), 463–485.

Bebbington, D. (1989). *Evangelicalism in modern Britain.* London: Unwin Hyman.

Berer, M. (2013). Termination of pregnancy as emergency obstetric care: The interpretation of Catholic health policy and the consequences for pregnant women: An analysis of the death of Savita Halappanavar in Ireland and similar cases. *Reproductive Health Matters, 21*(41), 9–17. Retrieved from https://www.40daysforlife.com/en/resources-faq.aspx

Beynon-Jones, S. (2017). Untroubling abortion: A discourse analysis of women's accounts. *Feminism & Psychology, 27*(2), 225–242.

Birchard, K. (1999). Pickets force pregnancy-advice centre to close. *The Lancet, 354*(9179), 658.

Blackwell, B. A. (2019). Towards a popular queer Mariology: Rediscovering the virgin through popular religiosity. *Theology and Sexuality, 25*(1–2), 131–145.

Blake, D. J. (2008). *Chicana sexuality and gender: Cultural refiguring in literature, oral history and art.* Durham, NC: Duke University Press.

Blee, K. M. (2007). Ethnographies of the far right. *Journal of Contemporary Ethnography, 36*(2), 119–128.

Bloomer, F., McNeilly, K., & Pierson, C. (2020). Abortion in Northern Ireland: First year review of the Northern Ireland (executive formation etc.) Act 2019. Retrieved from https://pure.ulster.ac.uk/en/publications/abortion-in-northern-ireland-first-year-review-of-the-northern-ir

Bloomer, F., & O'Dowd, K. (2014). Restricted access to abortion in the Republic of Ireland and Northern Ireland: Exploring abortion tourism and barriers to legal reform. *Culture, Health and Sexuality, 16*(4), 366–380.

Bloomer, F., O'Dowd, K., & Macleod, C. (2017). Breaking the silence on abortion: The role of adult community abortion education in fostering resistance to norms. *Culture, Health and Sexuality, 19*(7), 709–722.

Bourdieu, P. (1984). *Distinction: A social critique of the judgment of taste.* London: Routledge.

Bowman, M. (2017). From production to performance: Candles, creativity and connectivity. In T. Hutchings & J. McKenzie (Eds.), *Materiality and the study of religion: The stuff of the sacred* (pp. 35–51). London: Routledge.

BPAS. (2020). *Forced into a corner: The two-child limit and pregnancy decision making during the pandemic*. London: BPAS.

Braid, M. (1993, March 31). Abortion clinics under guard after clashes. *The Independent*, 3.

Braun, V., & Clarke, V. (2006). Using thematic analysis in psychology. *Qualitative Research in Psychology*, *3*(2), 77–101.

Brooke, S. (2001). 'A new world for women'? Abortion law reform in Britain during the 1930s. *The American Historical Review*, *106*(2), 431–459.

Brookes, B. (1988). *Abortion in England 1900–1967*. London: Croom Helm.

Brown, A., & Woodhead, L. (2016). *That was the church that was*. London: Bloomsbury.

Bullivant, S. (2019). *Mass exodus: Catholic disaffiliation in Britain and America since Vatican II*. Oxford: Oxford University Press.

Campbell, M. (2021). Capping motherhood: Equality-based analysis of the UK benefit cap cases. In M. Davis, M. Kjaerum, & A. Lyons (Eds.), *Research handbook on human rights and poverty* (pp. 156–170). Cheltenham: Edward Elgar Publishing.

Campo-Engelstein, L. (2012). Competing social norms: Why women are responsible for, but not trusted with, contraception. *International Journal of Applied Philosophy*, *26*(1), 67–84.

Cannold, L. (2002). Understanding and responding to anti-choice women-centred strategies. *Reproductive Health Matters*, *10*(9), 171–179.

Caruso, E. (2020). Abortion in Italy: 40 years on. *Feminist Legal Studies*, *28*, 87–96.

Casamitjana Costa v The League Against Cruel Sports. (2020). ET (case No 3331129/ 2018) [33]-[39].

Catholic World Report. (2020). Priests for Life Fr. Frank Pavone resigns from Trump campaign roles. Retrieved from https://www.catholicworldreport.com/2020/07/24/priests-for-life-fr-frank-pavone-resigns-from-trump-campaign-roles/

Chesler, P. (2005). *Women and madness*. Chicago, IL: Lawrence Hill Books.

Church of England. (2017). Abortion: Church of England statements. Retrieved from https://www.churchofengland.org/sites/default/files/2017-11/Abortion%20Church%20of%20England%20Statements.pdf

Clements, B. (2014). Religion and the sources of public opposition to abortion in Britain: The role of 'belonging', 'behaving' and 'believing'. *Sociology*, *48*(2), 369–386.

Cliff, M. (2019). *To what extent is there a silence in regards to the issue of abortion within the contemporary evangelical church in the UK?* MA thesis, University of Middlesex, Middlesex

Cohen, N. (1993, April 4). US Militants fight British abortion. *The Independent*, 2.

Cohen, D., & Connon, K. (2016). *Living in the crosshairs: The untold stories of anti-abortion terrorism*. Oxford: Oxford University Press.

Cohen, P., Mayhew, J., Gishen, F., Potts, H. W., Lohr, P. A., & Kavanagh, J. (2021). What should medical students be taught about abortion? An evaluation of student attitudes towards their abortion teaching and their future involvement in abortion care. *BMC Medical Education, 21*(1), 1–7.

Committee on Oversight and Reform. (n.d.). Planned Parenthood fact v fiction, US House of Representatives. Retrieved from https://oversight.house.gov/planned-parenthood-fact-v-fiction

Cook, H. (2004). *The long sexual revolution: English women, sex & contraception 1800–1975*. Oxford: Oxford University Press.

Copelon, R., Zampas, C., Brusie, E., & deVore, J. (2005). Human rights begin at birth: International law and the claim of fetal rights. *Reproductive Health Matters, 13*(26), 120–129.

Curran, C. (1988). Public dissent in the church. In P. B. Jung & T. A. Shannon (Eds.), *Abortion and Catholicism: The American debate* (pp. 301–319). New York, NY: Crossroad.

Curtice, J., Clery, E., Perry, J., Phillips, M., & Rahim, N. (2019). *British Social Attitudes: The 36th report*. London: The National Centre for Social Research.

Davidson, R., & Davis, G. (2014). *The sexual state: Sexuality and Scottish governance, 1950–80*. Edinburgh: Edinburgh University Press.

Davie, G. (2007). *The sociology of religion*. London: Sage.

Davis, T. (2004). *Sacred work: Planned Parenthood and its clergy alliances*. New Brunswick, NJ: Rutgers University Press.

Davis, G., & Davidson, R. (2006). 'A fifth freedom' or 'hideous atheistic expediency'? The medical community and abortion law reform in Scotland, c.1960–1975. *Medical History, 50*(1), 29–48.

De Alba, A. G. (2011). Our Lady of controversy: A subject that needs no introduction. In A. G. de Alba & A. López (Eds.), *Our Lady of controversy: Alma López's irreverent apparition* (pp. 1–12). Austin, TX: University of Texas Press.

Dee, O. (2020). *The anti-abortion campaign in England, 1966–1989*. London: Routledge.

Demerath, N. J., III. (2007). Secularization and sacralization deconstructed and reconstructed. In J. A. Beckford & N. J. Demerath III (Eds.), *The SAGE handbook of the sociology of religion*. London: Sage.

Dept. of Health and Social Care. (2020). *Abortion statistics, England and Wales: 2019*.

Doan, A. (2007). *Opposition and intimidation: The abortion wars and strategies of political harassment*. Ann Arbor, MI: University of Michigan Press.

Donaghue, D. (2019). Every mans call to fatherhood. Retrieved from https://www.marchforlife.co.uk/2019/06/15/every-mans-call-to-fatherhood/

Dulgheriu & Orthova vs London Borough of Ealing. (2018). EWHC 1667 (admin).

Durkheim, E. (1915). *The elementary forms of the religious life*. London: Allen & Unwin.

Dutch, R. (2020). The globalisation of punitive abortion laws: The colonial legacy of the Offences against the Person Act 1861. *Disrupted, 4*, 74–81.

Dutta, S. (2017). *British women missionaries in Bengal, 1793–1861*. London: Anthem Press.

Eades, L. (2019). Social realities, biological realities: The 24-week foetus in contemporary English abortion activism. *Women's Studies International Forum, 74*, 20–26.

Ealing Council Consultation Report. (2018). *Consultation documents 10/04/18.*

Ehrlich, J., & Doan, A. (2019). *Abortion regret: The new attack on reproductive freedom.* Santa Barbara, CA: Praeger.

Elsdon-Baker, F., & Mason-Wilkes, W. (2019). The sociological study of science and religion in context. In S. H. Jones, T. Kaden, & R. Catto (Eds.), *Science, belief and society: International perspectives on religion, non-religion and the public understanding of science* (pp. 3–24). Bristol: Bristol University Press.

Entwistle, J. (2000). *The fashioned body: Fashion, dress and modern social theory.* Cambridge: Polity Press.

Evangelical Alliance. (2006). Faith and nation: Report of a commission of inquiry to the UK Evangelical Alliance. Retrieved from https://www.eauk.org/current-affairs/publications/faith-and-nation.cfm

Evangelical Alliance. (2011). *21st century evangelicals.* Retrieved from https://www.eauk.org/church/resources/snapshot/21st-century-evangelicals.cfm

Evangelical Alliance. (2021a). Respond to the government's consultation on early medical abortion. Retrieved from https://www.eauk.org/news-and-views/respond-to-the-governments-consultation-on-early-medical-abortion

Evangelical Alliance. (2021b). Both lives matter: Valuing every woman and her unborn child. Retrieved from https://www.eauk.org/about-us/how-we-work/coalitions/both-lives-matter

Fisher, K. (1998). Women's experience of abortion before the 1967 Abortion Act: A study of South Wales c. 1930–1950. In *Abortion law and politics today* (pp. 27–42). Basingstoke: Palgrave.

Flowers, P. (2019). *The right-to-life movement, the Reagan administration, and the politics of abortion.* Basingstoke: Palgrave Macmillan.

Forna, A. (1998). *Mother of all myths.* London: HarperCollins.

Foster, D. (2020). *The turnaway study: Ten years, a thousand women, and the consequences of having-or being denied-an abortion.* London: Scribner.

Foubert, J. D., Angela, W., Brosi, M., & Fuqua, D. (2012). Explaining the wind: How self-identified born again Christians define what born again means to them. *Journal of Psychology and Christianity, 31*(3), 215–227.

Foucault, M. (1976). *The history of sexuality I: The will to knowledge.* London: Penguin.

Fox, M., & Horgan, G. (2020). The effects of decriminalisation in Northern Ireland. In S. Sheldon & K. Wellings (Eds.), *Decriminalising abortion in the UK: What would it mean?* (pp. 77–98). Bristol: Policy Press.

Francome, C. (1986). *Abortion practice in Britain and the US.* London: Allen & Unwin.

Francome, C. (2004). *Abortion in the USA and in the UK.* Aldershot: Ashgate Publishing.

Francome, C., & Freeman, E. (2000). British general practitioners' attitudes toward abortion. *Family Planning Perspectives, 32*(4), 189–191.

Franklin, S., & Ginsburg, F. (2019). Reproductive politics in the age of Trump and Brexit. *Cultural Anthropology, 34*(1), 3–9.

Furlong, M. (1991). *A dangerous delight: Women and power in the church*. London: SPCK (Society for Promoting Christian Knowledge).

Gale, R. (2009). The multicultural city and the politics of religious architecture: Urban planning, mosques and meaning-making in Birmingham. In P. Hopkins & R. Gale (Eds.), *Muslims in Britain: Race, place and identities* (pp. 113–131). Edinburgh: Edinburgh University Press.

Ganzevoort, R. R., & Sremac, S. (Eds.). (2017). *Lived religion and the politics of (in) tolerance*. Cham: Palgrave MacMillan.

Gardner, C. (1995). *Passing by: Gender and public harassment*. Berkeley, CA: University of California Press.

Gavigan, S. (1984). The criminal sanction as it relates to human reproduction: The genesis of the statutory prohibition of abortion. *The Journal of Legal History*, 5(1), 20–43.

Geiringer, D. (2019). *The Pope and the pill*. Manchester: Manchester University Press.

Genova, C. (2015). Prayer as practice: An interpretative proposal. In G. Giordan & L. Woodhead (Eds.), *A sociology of prayer* (pp. 9–23). Farnham: Ashgate.

Ginsburg, F. (1989). *Contested lives: The abortion debate in an American community*. London: University of California Press.

Giordan, G. (2015). Introduction: You never know. Prayer as enchantment. In G. Giordan & L. Woodhead (Eds.), *A sociology of prayer* (pp. 1–8). Farnham: Ashgate.

Goddard, V. A. (2007). Demonstrating resistance: Politics and participation in the Marches of the Mothers of Plaza de Mayo. *Focaal*, 50, 81–101.

Goffman, E. (1963). *Behaviour in public places: Notes on the social organisation of gatherings*. New York, NY: The Free Press.

Good Morning Britain. (2017). Jacob Rees-Mogg says that he opposes abortion and same-sex marriage. *ITV*. Retrieved from https://www.youtube.com/watch?v=WE6WC_BVZ4Q

Grady, D. (2019, February 26). 'Executing babies': Here are the facts behind Trump's misleading abortion tweet. *New York Times*. Retrieved from https://www.nytimes.com/2019/02/26/health/abortion-bill-trump.html

Gray, A. (2017). *Attitudes to abortion in Northern Ireland*. Belfast: ARK Research Update.

Gray, A. M., & Wellings, K. (2020). Is public opinion in support of decriminalisation? In S. Sheldon & K. Wellings (Eds.), *Decriminalising abortion in the UK: What would it mean?* (pp. 17–35). Bristol: Policy Press.

Greenwood, V., & Young, J. (1976). *Abortion in demand*. London: Pluto Press.

Guenther, L. (2012). The most dangerous place: Pro-life politics and the rhetoric of slavery. *Postmodern Culture*, 22(2). Retrieved from https://www.muse.jhu.edu/article/494803

Guest, M. (2007). In search of spiritual capital: The spiritual as a cultural resource. In K. Flanagan & P. Jupp (Eds.), *A sociology of spirituality* (pp. 181–200). Aldershot: Ashgate.

Guest, M., Olson, E., & Wolffe, J. (2012). Christianity: Loss of monopoly. In L. Woodhead & R. Catto (Eds.), *Religion and change in modern Britain* (pp. 57–78). London: Routledge.

Halfmann, D. (2011). *Doctors and demonstrators: How political institutions shape abortion law in the United States, Britain, and Canada*. London: University of Chicago Press.

Halfmann, D., & Young, M. (2010). War pictures: The grotesque as a mobilizing tactic. *Mobilization: An International Quarterly*, *15*(1), 1–24.

Hall, C. (2000). *White, male and middle class: Explorations in feminism and history*. Cambridge: Policy Press.

Hammersley, M., & Atkinson, P. (2007). *Ethnography: Principles in practice* (3rd ed.). London: Routledge.

Harris, A. (2013). *Faith in the family: A lived religious history of English Catholicism, 1945–1982*. Manchester: Manchester University Press.

Harris, A. (2020). A Magna Carta for marriage: Love, Catholic Masculinities and the Humanae Vitae contraception crisis in 1968 Britain. *Cultural and Social History*, *17*(3), 407–429.

Haugeberg, K. (2017). *Women against abortion*. Chicago, IL: University of Illinois Press.

Hay, K. (2020). 'More than a defence against bills': Feminism and national identity in the Scottish abortion campaign, c. 1975–1990. *Women's History Review*. doi: 10.1080/09612025.2020.1791405

Hayes, B. C., & McKinnon, A. (2018). Belonging without believing: Religion and attitudes towards gay marriage and abortion rights in Northern Ireland. *Religion, State and Society*, *46*(4), 351–366.

Hays, S. (1996). *The cultural contradictions of motherhood*. New Haven, CT: Yale University Press.

Heelas, P., & Woodhead, L. (2005). *The spiritual revolution: Why religion is giving way to spirituality*. Oxford: Blackwell Publishing.

Himmelweit, S. (1988). More than 'a woman's right to choose'? *Feminist Review*, *29*, 38–56.

Hindell, K., & Simms, M. (1971). *Abortion law reformed*. London: Peter Owen.

Hoggart, L. (2000). Socialist feminism, reproductive rights and political action. *Capital & Class*, *24*(1), 95–125.

Hoggart, L. (2015). Abortion counselling in Britain: Understanding the controversy. *Sociology Compass*, *9*(5), 365–378.

Hoggart, L. (2017). Internalised abortion stigma: Young women's strategies of resistance and rejection. *Feminism & Psychology*, *27*(2), 186–202.

Hoggart, L., Newton, V., & Bury, L. (2017). 'Repeat abortion', a phrase to be avoided? Qualitative insights into labelling and stigma. *Journal of Family Planning and Reproductive Health Care*, *43*(1), 26–30.

Hohmeyer, A. (2005). The National Abortion Campaign – Changing the law and fighting for a real choice. In G. Griffin (Ed.), *Feminist activism in the 1990s* (pp. 41–48). London: Taylor & Francis.

Hornsby-Smith, M. P. (1991). *Roman Catholic beliefs in England*. Cambridge: Cambridge University Press.

Hunt, A. (1999). *Governing morals: A social history of moral regulation*. Cambridge: Cambridge University Press.

Husain, J., & Kelly, K. (2017). Stigma rituals as pathways to activism: Stigma convergence in a post abortion recovery group. *Deviant Behavior*, *38*(5), 575–592.

Hussain, A. M., & Miller, W. L. (2004). How and why Islamophobia is tied to English nationalism but not to Scottish nationalism. *Ethnic Studies Review, 27*(1), 78–101.

Hutchings, T., & McKenzie, J. (2017). Introduction: The body of St Cuthbert. In T. Hutchings & J. McKenzie (Eds.), *Materiality and the study of religion: The stuff of the sacred* (pp. 1–13). London: Routledge.

International Theological Commission. (2002). Communion and stewardship: Human persons created in the image of God. Retrieved from https://www.vatican.va/roman_curia/congregations/cfaith/cti_documents/rc_con_cfaith_doc_20040723_communion-stewardship_en.html

Isaac, J. (1994). The politics of morality in the UK. *Parliamentary Affairs, 47*(2), 175–190.

Jantzen, G. M. (1998). *Becoming divine*. Manchester: Manchester University Press.

Jasper, J. M. (2011). Emotions and social movements: Twenty years of theory and research. *Annual Review of Sociology, 37*, 285–303.

Jasper, J. M. (2018). *The emotions of protest*. London: University of Chicago Press.

Jenkins, A. (1960). *Law for the rich: A plea for the reform of the abortion law*. London: Victor Gollancz.

Johnson, E. A. (1989). Mary and the female face of God. *Theological Studies, 50*(3), 500–526.

Jones, E. L. (2011). Attitudes to abortion in the era of reform: Evidence from the Abortion Law Reform Association correspondence. *Women's History Review, 20*(2), 283–298.

Joppke, C. (2009). *Veil: Mirror of identity*. Cambridge: Polity Press.

Jordan, M. D. (2000). *Homosexuality in modern Catholicism: The silence of Sodom*. Chicago, IL: The University of Chicago Press.

Kamitsuka, M. D. (2019). *Abortion and the Christian tradition: A pro-choice theological ethic*. Louisville, KY: Westminster John Knox Press.

Keane, H. (2009). Foetal personhood and representations of the absent child in pregnancy loss memorialization. *Feminist Theory, 10*(2), 153–171.

Kendell, R. E. (1991). Suicide in pregnancy and the Puerperium. *British Medical Journal, 302*(6769), 126–127.

Keown, J. (1988). *Abortion, doctors and the law: Some aspects of the legal regulation of abortion in England from 1803 to 1982*. Cambridge: Cambridge University Press.

Kim, C. J. (2011). Moral extensionism or racist exploitation? The use of Holocaust and slavery analogies in the animal liberation movement. *New Political Science, 33*(3), 311–333.

Kirby, B. (2017). Occupying the global city: Spatial politics and spiritual warfare among African Pentecostals in Hong Kong. In D. Garbin & A. Strhan (Eds.), *Religion and the global city* (pp. 62–77). London: Bloomsbury.

Knott, K. (2010). Cutting through the postsecular city: A spatial interrogation. In A. Molendijk, J. Beaumont, & C. Jedan (Eds.), *Exploring the postsecular: The religious, the political and the urban* (pp. 19–38). Leiden: Brill.

Kuipers, G. (2011). The politics of humour in the public sphere: Cartoons, power and modernity in the first transnational humour scandal. *European Journal of Cultural Studies, 14*(1), 63–80.

Kumar, A., Hessini, L., & Mitchell, E. M. H. (2009). Conceptualising abortion stigma. *Culture, Health and Sexuality, 11*(6), 625–639.

Lalor, J., Begley, C. M., & Galavan, E. (2009). Recasting hope: A process of adaptation following fetal anomaly diagnosis. *Social Science & Medicine*, *68*(3), 462–472.

Lane Committee. (1974). *Report of the committee on the working of the Abortion Act*. London: H.M. Stationery Office.

Lee, E. (2003). *Abortion, motherhood, and mental health: Medicalizing reproduction in the United States and Great Britain*. New York, NY: Aldine Transaction.

Lee, E. (2014). Introduction. In E. Lee, J. Bristow, C. Faircloth, & J. Macvarish (Eds.), *Parenting culture studies* (pp. 1–24). Basingstoke: Palgrave Macmillan.

Lee, L. (2015). *Recognizing the non-religious: Reimagining the secular*. Oxford: Oxford University Press.

Lee, E. (2017). Constructing abortion as a social problem: 'Sex selection' and the British abortion debate. *Feminism & Psychology*, *27*(1), 15–33.

Lee, E., Sheldon, S., & Macvarish, J. (2018). The 1967 Abortion Act fifty years on: Abortion, medical authority and the law revisited. *Social Science & Medicine*, *212*, 18–35.

Lewis, A. R. (2017). *The rights turn in conservative Christian politics: How abortion transformed the culture wars*. Cambridge: Cambridge University Press.

Litchfield, M., & Kentish, S. (1974). *Babies for burning: The abortion business in Britain*. London: Serpentine Press.

Llewellyn, D. (2016). Maternal silences: Motherhood and voluntary childlessness in contemporary Christianity. *Religion and Gender*, *6*(1), 64–79.

Llewellyn, D., & Trzebiatowska, M. (2013). Secular and religious feminisms: A future of disconnection? *Feminist Theology*, *21*(3), 244–258.

Lloyd, G. (1993). *The man of reason* (2nd ed.). London: Routledge.

Logan, L. (2015). Street harassment: Current and promising avenues for researchers and activists. *Sociology Compass*, *9*(3), 196–211.

Lord, J., Regan, L., Kasliwal, A., Massey, L., & Cameron, C. (2018). Early medical abortion: Best practice now lawful in Scotland and Wales but not available to women in England. *BMJ Sexual & Reproductive Health*, *44*, 155–158.

Lowe, P. (2016). *Reproductive health and maternal sacrifice: Women, choice and responsibility*. Basingstoke: Palgrave Macmillan.

Lowe, P. (2019). (Re)imagining the 'backstreet': Anti-abortion campaigning against decriminalisation in the UK. *Sociological Research Online*, *24*(2), 203–218.

Lowe, P., & Hayes, G. (2019). Anti-abortion clinic activism, civil inattention and the problem of gendered harassment. *Sociology*, *53*(2), 330–346.

Lowe, P., & Page, S.-J. (2019a). 'On the wet side of the womb': The construction of mothers in anti-abortion activism in England and Wales. *European Journal of Women's Studies*, *26*(2), 165–180.

Lowe, P., & Page, S.-J. (2019b). Rights-based claims made by UK anti-abortion activists. *Health and Human Rights*, *21*(2), 133–144.

Lowe, P., & Page, S. J. (2020). Sophie's choice: Narratives of 'saving' in British public debates on abortion. *Women's Studies International Forum*, *79*. doi:10.1016/j.wsif.2020.102332

Lozano, G. V., & River, C. (2016). *The Virgin of Guadalupe*. London: Charles River Editors.

Ludlow, J. (2008). Sometimes, it's a child and a choice: Toward an embodied abortion praxis. *NWSA Journal*, *20*(1), 26–50.

Luker, K. (1984). *Abortion and the politics of motherhood*. Berkeley, CA: University of California Press.

Luna, Z. (2018). "Black children are an endangered species": Examining racial framing in social movements. *Sociological Focus*, *51*(3), 238–251.

Lupton, D. (1998). *The emotional self*. London: Sage.

Lupton, D. (2013). *The social worlds of the unborn*. Basingstoke: Palgrave.

Lynch, G. (2010). Object theory: Toward an intersubjective, mediated, and dynamic theory of religion. In D. Morgan (Ed.), *Religion and material culture* (pp. 40–54). London: Routledge.

Lynch, G. (2012a). *The sacred in the modern world: A cultural sociological approach*. Oxford: Oxford University Press.

Lynch, G. (2012b). *On the sacred*. Durham: Acumen Publishing Limited.

Macvarish, J., Lee, E., & Lowe, P. (2015). Neuroscience and family policy: What becomes of the parent? *Critical Social Policy*, *35*(2), 248–269.

Madge, N., Hemming, P. J., & Stenson, K. (2014). *Youth on religion: The development, negotiation and impact of faith and non-faith identity*. London: Routledge.

Maguire, M. R. (1988). Personhood, covenant, and abortion. In P. B. Jung & T. A. Shannon (Eds.), *Abortion and Catholicism: The American debate* (pp. 100–120). New York, NY: Crossroad.

Mahmood, S. (2005). *Politics of piety: The Islamic revival and the feminist subject*. Princeton, NJ: Princeton University Press.

Mahmood, S. (2011). Religion, feminism, and empire: The new ambassadors of Islamophobia. In L. M. Alcoff & J. D. Caputo (Eds.), *Feminism, sexuality, and the return of religion* (pp. 77–102). Bloomington, IN: Indiana University Press.

Malvern, C., & Macleod, C. (2018). Cultural de-colonization versus liberal approaches to abortion in Africa: The politics of representation and voice. *African Journal of Reproductive Health*, *22*(2), 49–59.

Marcotte, J. (2016). The agnotology of abortion: A history of ignorance about women's knowledge of fertility control. *Outskirts: Feminisms Along the Edge*, *34*, 1–21.

Marshall, R. (2016). Destroying arguments and captivating thoughts: Spiritual warfare prayer as global praxis. *Journal of Religious and Political Practice*, *2*(1), 92–113.

Marsh, D., & Chambers, J. (1981). *Abortion politics*. London: Junction Books.

Mason, C. (2002). *Killing for life: The apocalyptic narrative of pro-life politics*. London: Cornell University Press.

Mason, C. (2019). Opposing abortion to protect women: Transnational strategy since the 1990s. *Signs: Journal of Women in Culture and Society*, *44*(3), 665–692.

Mason, C. (2021). How Trumpism fostered anti-choice violence. Retrieved from https://msmagazine.com/2021/02/09/trump-capitol-riots-women-abortion-anti-choice-violence-anti-abortion-extremists-propaganda/

Maunder, C. (2016). *Our Lady of the Nations: Apparitions of Mary in 20th century Catholic Europe*. Oxford: Oxford University Press.

McBride Stetson, D. (2001). Women's movements' defence of legal abortion in great Britain. In D. McBride Stetson (Ed.), *Abortion politics, women's movements and the democratic state: A comparative study of state feminism* (pp. 135–156). Oxford: Oxford University Press.

McCormick, L. (2015). 'No sense of wrongdoing': Abortion in Belfast 1917–1967. *Journal of Social History, 49*(1), 125–148.

McGuinness, S. (2013). Law, reproduction, and disability: Fatally 'handicapped'? *Medical Law Review, 21,* 213–242.

McGuinness, S. (2015). A guerrilla strategy for a pro-life England. *Law, Innovation and Technology, 7*(2), 283–314.

McGuire, M. (2008). *Lived religion: Faith and practice in everyday life.* Oxford: Oxford University Press.

McIntosh, T. (2000). 'An abortionist city': Maternal mortality, abortion, and birth control in Sheffield, 1920–1940. *Medical History, 44*(1), 75–96.

McLaren, A. (1990). *A history of contraception: From antiquity to the present day.* Oxford: Blackwell.

McLeod, H. (2007). *The religious crisis of the 1960s.* Oxford: Oxford University Press.

Medoff, M. H. (2012). State abortion politics and TRAP abortion laws. *Journal of Women, Politics & Policy, 33*(3), 239–262.

Millar, E. (2015). 'Too many' anxious white nationalism and the biopolitics of abortion. *Australian Feminist Studies, 30*(83), 82–98.

Millar, E. (2017). *Happy abortions: Our bodies in the era of choice.* London: Zed Books.

Miller, P. (2014). *Good Catholics: The battle over abortion in the Catholic Church.* Berkeley, CA: University of California Press.

Mitchell, C. (2004). Is Northern Ireland abnormal? An extension of the sociological debate on religion in Modern Britain. *Sociology, 38*(2), 237–254.

Mitchell, C. (2006). *Religion, identity and politics in Northern Ireland: Boundaries of belonging and belief.* Aldershot: Ashgate.

Mitchell, N. (2009). *The history of the rosary: Marian devotion and the reinvention of Catholicism.* New York, NY: New York University Press.

Morgan, D. (1998). *Visual piety: A history and theory of popular religious images.* London: University of California Press.

Morgan, D. (2010). Introduction: The matter of belief. In D. Morgan (Ed.), *Religion and material culture: The matter of belief* (pp. 1–17). London: Routledge.

Munson, Z. (2002). *The making of pro-life activists.* London: The University of Chicago Press.

National Abortion Federation. (2019). 2018 violence and disruption statistics. Retrieved from https://prochoice.org/naf-releases-2018-violence-disruption-statistics/

Nelson, L. P. (2006). Introduction. In L. P. Nelson (Ed.), *American sanctuary: Understanding sacred spaces.* Bloomington, IN: Indiana University Press.

Ngwena, C. (2014). Reforming African abortion laws and practice: The place of transpaency. In R. Cook, J. Erdman, & B. Dicken (Eds.), *Abortion law in transnational perspective: Cases and controversies* (pp. 166–187). Philadelphia, PA: University of Pennsylvania Press.

Northern Ireland Life and Times Survey (NILT). (2019). Retrieved from https://www.ark.ac.uk/nilt/2019/Background

Nyhagen, L. (2017). The lived religion approach in the sociology of religion and its implications for secular feminist analyses of religion. *Social Compass, 64*(4), 495–511.

O'Connor, J. (1999, August 6). Protestors close down abortion help centre, *Belfast News Letter*, 4.

Orr, J. (2017). *Abortion wars: The fight for reproductive rights*. Bristol: Policy Press.

Orsi, R. (2007). *Between heaven and earth: The religious worlds people make and the scholars who study them*. Princeton, NJ: Princeton University Press.

Page, S.-J. (2011). Negotiating sacred roles: A sociological exploration of priests who are mothers. *Feminist Review, 97*(1), 92–109.

Page, S.-J. (2016). Altruism and sacrifice: Anglican priests managing 'intensive' priesthood and motherhood. *Religion and Gender, 6*(1), 47–63.

Page, S.-J. (2017). Anglican clergy husbands securing middle-class gendered privilege through religion. *Sociological Research Online, 22*(1), 187–199.

Page, S.-J., & Lowe, P. (2021a). Contested embodiment: The use of prayer in public displays of anti-abortion activism. In S.-J. Page & K. Pilcher (Eds.), *Embodying religion, gender and sexuality* (pp. 21–38). Abingdon: Routledge.

Page, S.-J., & Lowe, P. (2021b). A qualitative investigation into British Catholic abortion attitudes: Lived religion, nuance and complexity. *Lived Catholicism(s) Conference*. Durham University, 15–16 November.

Pain, R. (2001). Gender, race, age and fear in the city. *Urban Studies, 38*(5–6), 899–913.

Paton v. United Kingdom App. No. 8416/78, 3 Eur. H.R. Rep. 408, 1980.

Paul, J., II (1995). *Evangelium Vitae*. Retrieved from http://w2.vatican.va/content/john-paul-ii/en/encyclicals/documents/hf_jp-ii_enc_25031995_evangelium-vitae.html

Paul, J., VI (1968). *Humanae Vitae*. Retrieved from http://www.vatican.va/content/paul-vi/en/encyclicals/documents/hf_p-vi_enc_25071968_humanae-vitae.html

Peters, R. T. (2018). *Trust women: A progressive Christian argument for reproductive justice*. Boston, MA: Beacon Press.

Pierson, C. (2018). Rights versus rites? Catholic women and abortion access in Northern Ireland. In T. P. Burgess (Ed.), *The contested identities of Ulster Catholics* (pp. 38–55). Cham: Palgrave MacMillan.

Pierson, C., & Bloomer, F. (2017). Macro-and micro-political vernaculizations of rights: Human rights and abortion discourses in Northern Ireland. *Health and Human Rights, 19*(1), 173–185.

Pierson, C., & Bloomer, F. (2018). Anti-abortion myths in political discourse. In C. MacQuarrie, F. Bloomer, C. Pierson, & S. Stettner (Eds.), *Crossing troubled waters: Abortion in Ireland, Northern Ireland and Prince Edward Island* (pp. 184–203). Chalottetown: Island Studies Press.

Pilkington, H. (2016). *Loud and proud: Passion and politics in the English Defence League*. Manchester: Manchester University Press.

Public Health Scotland. (2020). Termination of pregnancy: Year ending December 2019.

Purcell, C., Hilton, S., & McDaid, L. (2014). The stigmatisation of abortion: A qualitative analysis of print media in Great Britain in 2010. *Culture, Health and Sexuality, 16*(9), 1141–1155.

Purcell, C., Maxwell, K., Bloomer, F., Rowlands, S., & Hoggart, L. (2020). Toward normalising abortion: Findings from a qualitative secondary analysis study. *Culture, Health and Sexuality, 22*(12), 1349–1364.

Reilly, N., & Scriver, S. (2014). Introduction: Religion, gender and the public sphere: Mapping the terrain. In N. Reilly & S. Scriver (Eds.), *Religion, gender and the public sphere* (pp. 1–17). London: Routledge.

Riis, O., & Woodhead, L. (2012). *A sociology of religious emotion*. Oxford: Oxford University Press.

Rohlinger, D. A. (2002). Framing the abortion debate: Organizational resources, media strategies, and movement-countermovement dynamics. *The Sociological Quarterly, 43*(4), 479–507.

Ross, E. (2016). Locating the foetal subject: Uncertain entities and foetal viability in accounts of first-time pregnancy. *Women's Studies International Forum, 58*, 58–67.

Ross, L., & Solinger, R. (2017). *Reproductive justice: An introduction*. Oakland, CA: Univerity of California Press.

Rubin, M. (2009). *Mother of God: A history of the Virgin Mary*. London: Allen Lane.

Ruether, R. R. (1990). Women's body and blood: The sacred and the impure. In A. Joseph (Ed.), *Through the devil's gateway: Women, religion and taboo* (pp. 7–21). London: SPCK.

Sanders-McDonagh, E. (2014). Conducting 'dirty research' with extreme groups: Understanding academia as a dirty work site. *Qualitative Research in Organizations and Management: An International Journal, 9*(3), 241–253.

Sanger, C. (2006). Infant safe haven laws: Legislating in the culture of life. *Columbia Law Review, 106*(4), 753–829.

Saurette, P., & Gordon, K. (2015). *The changing voice of the anti-abortion movement: The rise of 'pro-woman' rhetoric in Canada and the United States*. Toronto, ON: University of Toronto Press.

Savage, W. D., & Francome, C. (2017). Gynaecologists' attitude to abortion provision in 2015. *Journal of Obstetrics and Gynaecology, 37*(3), 406–408.

Schmied, V., & Lupton, D. (2001). The externality of the inside: Body images of pregnancy. *Nursing Inquiry, 8*(1), 32–40.

Scott, J. (1998). Generational changes in attitudes to abortion: A cross-national comparison. *European Sociological Review, 14*(2), 177–190.

Sethna, C. (2019). From Heathrow Airport to Harley Street: The ALRA and travel for nonresident women for abortion services in Britain. In C. Sethna & G. Davis (Eds.), *Abortion across borders: Transnational travel and access to abortion services* (pp. 46–73). Baltimore, MD: John Hopkins University Press.

Sheldon, S. (1997). *Beyond control: Medical power and abortion law*. London: Pluto Press.

Sheldon, S. (2016). The decriminalisation of abortion: An argument for modernisation. *Oxford Journal of Legal Studies, 36*(2), 334–365.

Sheldon, S., Davis, G., O'Neill, J., & Parker, C. (2019). The Abortion Act (1967): A biography. *Legal Studies, 39*(1), 18–35.

Sheldon, S., O'Neill, J., Parker, C., & Davis, G. (2020). 'Too much, too indigestible, too fast'? The decades of struggle for abortion law reform in Northern Ireland. *The Modern Law Review, 83*(4), 761–796.

Singer, E. O. (2018). Lawful sinners: Reproductive governance and moral agency around abortion in Mexico. *Culture, Medicine and Psychiatry, 42*(1), 11–31.

Sjørup, L. (1999). The Vatican and women's reproductive health and rights: A clash of civilizations? *Feminist Theology, 7*(21), 79–97.

Skeggs, B. (1999). Matter out of place: Visibility and sexualities in leisure spaces. *Leisure Studies, 18*(3), 213–232.

Skeggs, B. (2005). The making of class and gender through visualizing moral subject formation. *Sociology*, *39*(5), 965–982.

Smith, L. (1979). *The abortion controversy 1936–77: A case study in "emergence of law"*. PhD thesis, University of Edinburgh.

Smyth, L., & Mitchell, C. (2008). Researching conservative groups: Rapport and understanding across moral and political boundaries. *International Journal of Social Research Methodology*, *11*(5), 441–452.

Solomos, J. (2003). *Race and racism in Britain*. Basingstoke: Palgrave Macmillan.

South Wales Echo. (1977). New abortion facilities for Cardiff. *People's Collection Wales Safe and Legal Archive*.

Stein, A. (2001). Revenge of the shamed: The Christian right's emotional culture war. In J. Goodwin, J. M. Jasper, & F. Polletta (Eds.), *Passionate politics: Emotions and social movements* (pp. 115–131). London: University of Chicago Press.

Stone, N., & Ingham, R. (2011). Who presents more than once? Repeat abortion among women in Britain. *Journal of Family Planning and Reproductive Health Care*, *37*(4), 209–215.

Strhan, A. (2015). *Aliens and strangers? The struggle for coherence in the everyday lives of evangelicals*. Oxford: Oxford University Press.

Swales, K., & Taylor, E. A. (2017). *British Social Attitudes 34*. London: National Centre for Social Research.

Tauer, C. A. (1988). The tradition of probabilism and the moral status of the early embryo. In P. B. Jung & T. A. Shannon (Eds.), *Abortion and Catholicism: The American debate* (pp. 54–84). New York, NY: Crossroad.

Taylor, C. (2007). *A secular age*. Cambridge, MA: The Belknap Press of Harvard University Press.

The Independent. (1990, April 10). Priest 'led attack' on manageress of abortion clinic, 5.

Tomlins, S., & Bullivant, S. C. (2016). Introduction. In S. Tomlins & S. C. Bullivant (Eds.), *The atheist bus campaign: Global manifestations and responses* (pp. 1–23). Leiden: Brill.

Triseliotis, J., Shireman, J., & Hundleby, M. (1997). *Adoption, theory policy and practice*. London: Cassell & Co.

Turner, B. (2008). *The body in society*. London: Sage.

Turtle, K. (2021). Compassion and conscience: Understanding liberal faith discourse on abortion. Religious transformation and gender conference, Utrecht University (online), 10–12 March.

United Nations Human Rights Committee. (2018). General comment no. 36 on article 6 of the International Covenant on Civil and political Rights, on the right to life. Retrieved from https://tbinternet.ohchr.org/Treaties/CCPR/Shared%20Docume nts/1_Global/CCPR_C_GC_36_8785_E.pdf

Vaggione, J. M. (2016). Francis and 'gender ideology': Heritage, displacement and continuities. *Religion and Gender*, *6*(2), 302–307.

Vaggione, J. M. (2020). The conservative uses of law: The Catholic mobilization against gender ideology. *Social Compass*, *67*(2), 252–266.

van Luijk, R. (2017). A brief history of the Black Mass. In P. van Geest, M. Poorthuis, & E. Rose (Eds.), *Sanctifying texts, transforming rituals* (pp. 275–288). Leiden: Brill.

Walker, A. (2018). Rough music, community protest and the local press in nineteenth-century England. *International Journal of Regional and Local History*, *13*(1), 86–104.

Warner, M. (1978). *Alone of all her sex: The myth and the cult of the Virgin Mary*. London: Quartet Books.

Weeks, J. (1989). *Sex, politics and society*. London: Longman.

Weitz, T. A. (2010). Rethinking the mantra that abortion should be safe, legal, and rare. *Journal of Women's History*, *22*(3), 161–172.

White, H. R. (2009). Virgin pride: Born again faith and sexuality identity in the faith-based abstinence movement. In S. J. Hunt & A. K. T. Yip (Eds.), *The Ashgate research companion to contemporary religion and sexuality* (pp. 241–253). Farnham: Ashgate.

Williams, D. K. (2015). The partisan trajectory of the American pro-life movement: How a liberal Catholic campaign became a conservative evangelical cause. *Religions*, *6*(2), 451–475.

Wilson, C. (2020). Nostalgia, entitlement and victimhood: The synergy of white genocide and misogyny. *Terrorism and Political Violence*. doi:10.1080/09546553.2020.1839428

Wivel, A. (1998). Abortion policy and politics on the Lane Committee of enquiry, 1971–1974. *Social History of Medicine*, *11*(1), 109–135.

Woodhead, L. (2004). *Christianity: A very short introduction*. Oxford: Oxford University Press.

Woodhead, L. (2012). Introduction. In L. Woodhead & R. Catto (Eds.), *Religion and change in modern Britain* (pp. 1–33). London: Routledge.

Woodhead, L. (2013). *Religion and personal life*. London: Darton, Longman and Todd.

Youngman, N. (2003). When frame extension fails: Operation Rescue and the 'triple gates of hell' in Orlando. *Journal of Contemporary Ethnography*, *32*(5), 521–554.

Yuval-Davis, N. (1997). *Gender and nation*. London: Sage.

Index